Ballykilcline Rising

Ballykilcline Rising

FROM FAMINE IRELAND TO IMMIGRANT AMERICA

❧ Mary Lee Dunn

University of Massachusetts Press AMHERST

LC 2008014264
ISBN 978-1-55849-659-0 (paper); 658-3 (library cloth)

Designed by Dennis Anderson
Set in New Baskerville
Printed and bound by The Maple-Vail Book Manufacturing Group

Library of Congress Cataloging-in-Publication Data

Dunn, Mary Lee.
  Ballykilcline rising : from famine Ireland to immigrant America / Mary Lee Dunn.
     p. cm.
  Includes bibliographical references and index.
  ISBN 978-1-55849-659-0 (pbk. : alk. paper) — ISBN 978-1-55849-658-3 (library
cloth : alk. paper)
  1. Irish Americans—Vermont—Rutland—History—19th century. 2. Immigrants—
Vermont—Rutland—History—19th century. 3. Irish Americans—Vermont—
Rutland—Biography. 4. Rutland (Vt.)—History—19th century. 5. Quarries
and quarrying—Vermont—Rutland—History—19th century. 6. Ballykilcline
(Ireland)—History—19th century. 7. Rent strikes—Ireland—Ballykilcline—
History—19th century. 8. Famines—Ireland—Roscommon (County)—History—
19th century. 9. Ireland—Emigration and immigration—History—19th century.
10. United States—Emigration and immigration—History—19th century. I. Title.
  F59.R9D86   2008
  304.8'743704175—dc22

                                                                    2008014264

British Library Cataloguing in Publication data are available.

For My Sons

Daniel Dunn and Justin Allen Maguire

For My Parents

Walter Charles and Frances Allen Dunn

For My Immigrant Irish Ancestors

John and Catherine McNally Riley, from Roscommon
and Monahan respectively to Rhode Island and Hampton,
Connecticut

John and Bridget Kenny Burns, from Roscommon
to Hampton, Connecticut

Michael and Catherine Walsh Dunn, from Kildare
to Troy, New York

Patrick and Bridget Hanley Maloney, from Limerick
to Troy, New York

And in Memory of My Grandmother, Leah Burns Allen,
Who Gave Me Roscommon Roots

Sooner or later I would die, too—I understood that now, clearly. . . . And soon all the people who had accompanied me through life would be gone, too, and then even the people who had known us, and no one would remain on earth who had ever seen us, and those descended from us perhaps would know stories about us. . . . And then the stories would fade, and our graves would go untended, and no one would guess what it had been like to wake before dawn in our breath-warmed bedrooms as the radiators clanked and our wives and husbands and children slept. And we would move from the nearer regions of the dead who are remembered into the farther regions of the forgotten, and on past those, into a space as white and big as the sky replicated forever. And all that would remain would be the love bravely expressed, and the moment when you danced and your heart danced with you.

—Ian Frazier, *Family*

Contents

℞

Illustrations follow page 134

Acknowledgments

𝆕

Aᴛ ᴇᴠᴇʀʏ ᴛᴜʀɴ during this research, I encountered people who willingly shared their knowledge, time, work, and interest. This book is what it is because they did so.

I thank, first, my mother, Frances Allen Dunn, who started me down this road and helped at every step, and my father, Walter Charles Dunn, who died in 1991 but was very much interested to see it happen and would have been pleased, and probably surprised, when I found some of his family in County Kildare in 1992. I thank my sons, Daniel Dunn Maguire and Justin Allen Maguire, who gave me their sometimes rather bemused interest, their ear when I was bursting with surprise at some newfound twist in the story, and great tolerance through my many hours at the computer. My sisters—Jane Millett, Norma Slattery, and Patricia King—have followed my research enthusiastically, acquired books and records for me, and sometimes accompanied me on research trips.

I am grateful to Robert Scally for pulling the veil of time from the story of Ballykilcline with his book *The End of Hidden Ireland*. For descendants of the townland and the parish, it was a tremendous gift.

I thank Charles Levenstein of the University of Massachusetts Lowell, for his confidence, interest, and support. I am indebted to Robert Forrant for his sage advice; I learned much about the historian's task from him. John Wooding and Lawrence Gross introduced me to new ideas and to some of history's giants. Phil Moss and Chris Tilly directed me to Charles Tilly's work and gave timely and important help.

This investigation owes a great debt to Ruth-Ann Harris, historian and author in Boston College's Irish Studies Program; it germinated as a result of an email discussion with her, and she generously shared information. She also invited me to present my research at a Boston College Irish Colloquium, which opened some doors, and she spoke at the 2006 Ballykilcline reunion.

I also appreciated invitations to discuss my research at Quinnipiac University's 2000 conference on Ireland's Great Hunger as well as at an American Conference for Irish Studies section meeting, the Irish

xi

Ancestral Research Association, the Genealogical Society of Vermont, and to advise the New England Historic Genealogical Society for a seminar on Irish famine immigrant research.

My gratitude goes to Rev. Robert B. Whalen of St. Bridget's Church in West Rutland, who allowed me to transcribe the 1857 parish census, which provided crucial knowledge about the immigrants.

Members of the Ballykilcline Society shared their own family knowledge and research results. In particular, I thank Madeline (Lynne) Sisk, who produced many Internet research surprises and provided her own family story; Maureen McDermott Humphreys and Peter Hanley, who spearheaded the organization of the Ballykilcline Society and the communal approach to research; Ann Marie Bell, Rosemary Vandenburg, Kathleen Madden, Maureen Hanley Cole, Margaret Alberts, Cassie Kilroy Thompson, William and Doreen Padian, Roger Lamson, and William Vinehout, who supplied their own family stories; and Andrew Wood, who shares my interest in Irish social history and pointed me to Susan Hood's helpful research on Strokestown. I thank the Padian descendants who posted their family story on the Ballykilcline website. Nonmember researchers helped as well: I am grateful to William Powers, who turned over his notebook of Colligan research and records, and Julie Offutt, who shared Carlon family history. Member Rosemary Vandenburg provided pictures and accounts of the Winters's history; Margaret Alberts contributed records and photos of the Mulleras; Roger Lamson offered his research on the Kellys; Francis Kelly of Rutland provided Brislin information; and William Vinehout supplied photos of Terrance McGuire and the James McGuire family as well as an important Neary connection.

Recognition and thanks go to Thomas Burns, a cousin and fellow researcher who was present at the beginning of my Roscommon roots inquiry so many years ago, made some of the earliest breakthroughs, and offered much encouragement in a collegial spirit.

My special thanks go to The Friends of Ballykilcline in Kilglass Parish, County Roscommon, led by Patrick (Parks) and Marion Reynolds. They have been welcoming and helpful, sharing and fun, and what they have given is irreplaceable. I thank all of them warmly and salute our connections.

I am grateful to Helen and Michael Brennan and Sean O'Beirne, Roscommon researchers who have over the years shared their time, records, and insights; we share O'Beirne ancestry from Roscommon as well. I am grateful to Patrick Lavin for his comments on the manuscript; to Ed Finn and Laurie McDonough for their extraordinarily helpful Leitrim-Roscommon website and a data file; to Kathleen Healy for her willingness to share the poetry and story of her ancestor James Patrick Carney, whose voice captured important sentiments that city and federal records could not; and to Sister Joan McGinty and Joseph McGinty for help in piecing together their Minnesota family's history, even though they were not sure at first whether to believe a version that was new to them.

New York writer Peter Duffy, who also has written about famine-time Strokestown and Kilglass (*The Killing of Major Denis Mahon: A Mystery of Old Ireland*), has shared sources and insights. Michael Huggins, after he won the Beckett Prize from Four Courts Press for an essay on pre-famine Roscommon, e-mailed his prize-winning manuscript even as he was turning it into a book; I thank him for that kindness. Producer Josh Kessler of TerraNova Television asked me to serve as a history consultant for his Discovery Channel documentary about the famine and the Ballykilcline story, titled *Famine to Freedom: The Great Irish Journey*.

Prominent among particularly helpful Rutlanders were Michael L. Austin, who sent me a draft of his excellent work about Irish immigrants to the Marble Valley, and James and Helen Davidson of the Rutland Historical Society, who first told me about the Fenian archive that I later found at Catholic University, linked me to a Carlon descendant, helped me to access Rutland's early newspapers. For leads, photographs, and maps, I thank the Rutland Historical Society and the Davidsons. My hat is off, too, to the contributors to the Rutland Rootsweb Listserv, in particular, Patty Pickett, Cathy Habes, Peter Patten, and Andy Powers. Elsewhere on the Internet, Cathy Joint Labath gave me information about the Mulleras in Iowa, and David Bunzel supplied biographical material about his ancestor, Civil War soldier Patrick Hanley.

Walter Hickey, senior archivist at the National Archives and Records Administration in Waltham, guided me to seven boxes of Rutland naturalization records; Martha Mayo of the Center for Lowell History discussed Lowell's Irish and pointed the way in her archive; and historian Gray Fitzsimons of the Lowell National Historical Park introduced me to the work of economic historian Joseph P. Ferrie. Thanks to Timothy Meagher of Catholic University, who gave me access to the Fenian archive, and to his research associate, Patrick Cullom, who was preparing the data for the Internet site. Breeda Gilligan of the County Roscommon Public Library always responds helpfully both to me and to the Ballykilcline Society in our search for Roscommon records. My gratitude goes also to Beth Mullinax, a volunteer for the International Genealogical Society in St. Paul, Minnesota; to Laurie Burns of the Troy, New York, Public Library; and to an unnamed researcher at the Philadelphia Free Library.

Historian Kevin Whelan pointed me to Tyler Anbinder's Five Points study, for which I am especially grateful. I thank also James Callery, Luke Dodd, and John O'Driscoll of Ireland's Famine Museum at Strokestown for many kindnesses to the Ballykilcline Society and for access to records in the museum's custody. Des Norton of University College Dublin shared his work in the archive of land agents Stewart and Kincaid and graciously offered to the Ballykilcline Society's newsletter essays about famine-time Kilglass, derived from his *Landlords, Tenants, Famine: The Business of an Irish Land Agency in the 1840s*.

Many librarians gave aid and later copied records for me during visits to the National Library of Ireland and the National Archives of Ireland; I appreciate their help though I do not know their names. I thank Khanh Dinh of the University of Massachusetts, Lowell, for recommending the work of Ronald Takaki.

Among friends who helped me gain and maintain momentum, I thank Lenore Azaroff, Ann Bratton, Helen Butler, Carolyn Allen Fowler, Gail Deegan Huddleston, Marie McAuliffe Maguire, Judy Martineau, Callie Garguilo McDowell, Susan Shields McFarland, Susan Moir, Therese O'Donnell, Ann Helen Riley, Susan Scheible, Debby Thompson, and Clare Tidby. To them, my thanks and my respect.

I owe a great debt to Bruce Wilcox, director, and to Clark Dougan and Paul Wright, editors, of the University of Massachusetts Press, who chose to go with this narrative, and its board, staff, especially Carol Betsch, and two reviewers. I thank copy editor Patricia Sterling and indexer Martin L. White for their expertise. I thank Nancy Carter and Maryann Groves of Northwind Studio in Alfred, Maine, for preparing photos and maps. And I am grateful to Attorney James Keenan of Bernstein Schur in Portland, Maine. The faculty of the Department of Work Environment at the University of Massachusetts Lowell gave their support at an important time and I appreciate it, as well as the years we have worked together.

Finally, I thank all those institutions that have provided space for the Ballykilcline Society's annual reunions. A partial list includes Middlesex Community College in Lowell, Massachusetts; the College of St. Rose in Albany, New York, and its president, R. Mark Sullivan; the Percy French Hotel and the Famine Museum in Strokestown; the Shannon Key-West in Rooskey; and the Kilglass Community Center in Roscommon. The ability to gather with family researchers and friends to exchange information and advice has been crucial, because genealogy and local history are collaborative efforts.

Introduction and Methodology

THE IRISH have a long past, and yet it is paradoxical that so many Irish-Americans possess only a short history which stops at the Atlantic in the nineteenth century, a history abridged by the trauma of uprooting and relocation that was their forebears' exodus from their native land in famine time or earlier. Family Interrupted: they don't know where they came from.

For the descendants of the Famine Irish, the history may have been rather purposefully lost when the emigrants hugged to themselves in silence the sorrowful experiences of why and how they left Ireland, as if ignoring them would erase them but remembering would dishonor their native land. For Irish immigrants of the time, the daily grind, early deaths, and geographic dispersal eroded extended family relationships over generations. The consequence of these circumstances and of British policy and practices is that many people do not know where to call home.

But descendants, more than ever, are pursuing the answer. The resurgence of Irish culture and back-to-the-roots genealogical fervor are reestablishing the bonds of kin and place that were almost lost during the immigrant generation's difficult transplantation and adaptation or the British government's disruptions and dismissals in famine time.

This book is the story of one neighborhood, its people forced out of Ireland's ravaged County Roscommon during the Great Potato Famine. It looks at where the inhabitants came from and where they went, insofar as answers can be deduced from family knowledge and records, public documents, and local and national history. The search recognizes the mystery of how they got to America, and it honors and seeks to understand the decisions made and the individual choices involved. It nods to serendipity but also explores the visceral role of political, economic, and social factors.

It has been possible, with greater or lesser effort, to retrieve some knowledge of our past, of what was lost over generations, and at least find that home territory where we can walk in the footprints that our forebears left in the townlands (parts of a parish) of Ireland. Precisely how much can be regained will vary with the particulars of each family and will depend on the written and oral legacies handed down locally, as well as the ingenuity and creativity of those seeking to document the story. In some luckier cases—even though the repositories of public records in Ireland have imposed an enormous hurdle by drawing a veil over earlier times—it is possible to travel into the eighteenth century, or earlier, and actually make the link to particular families. And over the years, technology has given new muscle to the efforts, interest has grown, and governmental, civic, and commercial bodies have made, renewed, or expanded their commitments to helping, be it for altruism or for profit.

Even for those who can connect only with their ancestral home place, the search may still reward, since the stories of local events, the local history, may yield a profound understanding of the forces that over time created the Irish diaspora—made us and remade both our countries: the one we know and its ancestor, the one we came from.

I FIRST learned about Robert Scally's book *The End of Hidden Ireland* in conversation after a lecture in 1995 at the Famine Museum in Strokestown, County Roscommon. I had heard the name Ballykilcline previously but did not know then that it was part of Kilglass Parish, where my own Riley family came from, or that it might hold special meaning for my own family story. I had been researching the Rileys, a maternal line, for years. When I returned to the United States, I ordered Scally's book and was surprised to learn that my immigrants' parents' surnames—Riley and Colligan—were both present in Ballykilcline, and that the townland bordered others which by then I knew were associated with my family.

Several years later, one of my first Internet searches was on the name Ballykilcline. I was astonished when I found the weeks-old website created by Maureen McDermott Humphreys of Washington state and Peter Hanley of Virginia. Soon, we organized as the Ballykilcline Society to search for other descendants and to foster knowledge of the local history. The idea was that we could help each other, that numbers and commitment would empower such an undertaking. We persuaded the Associated Press to do a feature story about Ballykilcline just as the 150th anniversary of the Great Famine was ending.[1]

The Ballykilcline Society started to hold yearly meetings; the first, fittingly, was in Strokestown in 1999; the second was in Lowell, Massachusetts, a year later. After the Lowell session, two members who participated—Ann Marie Bell of New York and Maureen Hanley Cole of Illinois—went on to Montpelier, Vermont, to search the state archives for evidence about Ballykilcline people in and around the city of Rutland. Two families in Bell's background, the Hanleys and Brennans, she knew, came from both Rutland and Ballykilcline. In Montpelier, the researchers collected information about nearly thirty men from Kilglass, including a number from Ballykilcline, whose home places were recorded on their early naturalization records. The pair shared their new information.

Intrigued by the cluster, I decided to research the connection further, and this book is the result. It has been an amazing journey. We now know more about the people from Ballykilcline and the furies that visited them. The knowledge has rewarded the effort. May the search continue.

The hypothesis underlying this study of the immigrants is that the prehistory of an Irish-tenants' strike was one of class formation for the people of Ballykilcline, that those who left demonstrated agency during that strike, reconstituted their class identity and supports in Rutland, Vermont, and there, too, drawing on communal memory, employed agency in marble industry contests, in their decisions regarding the Civil War, and in their stance on Fenianism. I view literacy, acquisition of assets, nationalist activity, their stance on war, and community-building in Rutland as indicators, or telling factors, of agency.

My research began in Irish records to first establish the identities of the tenants of Ballykilcline in the pre-famine years. Among records naming the residents in the early 1800s were (1) new-found estate rent rolls dated 1800 to 1820; (2) the Tithe Applotment Books, which tell who was liable to pay support for the English church in Ireland in the 1820s and 1830s; (3) a survey map of Ballykilcline that recorded tenants' surnames on particular plots in 1836; (4) rent lists kept by Crown agents between 1834 and 1846; (5) a Quit Rent Office (QRO)—which managed Crown properties and collected their revenue—list of tenant families compiled about 1840; and (6) a government list that named the people who were evicted and who emigrated from the townland in 1847 and 1848 (reproduced in Coyle 1994, pp. 32, 33). These records covered a span of nearly fifty years.

For details about the social context in Ireland, I acquired numerous history books, researched the Outrage Papers (governmental reports of crime and disturbances) for Roscommon at the National Archives of Ireland (NAI) and read its posted database concerning the Irish who were transported to Australia, consulted multiple volumes of British Parliamentary Papers, read *The Making of the English Working Class* by E. P. Thompson, and did Internet research. I also accessed three manuscripts describing Roscommon then: Susan Hood, "The Landlord Planned Nexus at Strokestown, County Roscommon: A Case Study of an Irish

Estate Town, 1660–c1925"; Michael Huggins, "Social Conflict in Pre-Famine Roscommon"; and Padraig Vesey, "The Murder of Major Mahon." Ruth-Ann Harris's and Anne O'Dowd's books about Irish spalpeens also proved invaluable. Books about Irish labor history were useful, as were biographies of Daniel O'Connell and Archbishop John McHale, Donal Kerr's book about government and church relations, Charles Tilly's works on the development of social protest, Samuel Clark and James S. Donnelly Jr.'s *Irish Peasants: Violence and Political Unrest, 1780–1914*, and Gerard Moran's book about assisted emigration.

Ballykilcline was subleased to the Mahon estate at Strokestown from the 1790s until 1834. I obtained Mahon estate rent rolls for 1800–1820 on microfilm from the National Library of Ireland for the Ballykilcline Society and identified inhabitants of the townland between 1820 and 1846. I found the Quit Rent Office tenant list at the National Archives of Ireland and dated it to approximately 1840 (or a bit earlier, with some later notes written in), based on internal evidence and comparison with other tenant rosters. I found primary and secondary sources concerning the development of Irish combinations, collective actions, the famine in Kilglass, and the state of Roscommon.

In researching the U.S. portion of the story, I combed the indexes to nineteenth-century naturalizations at Rutland's town and county courts and at the National Archives and Records Administration (NARA) in Waltham, Massachusetts, to build a database of 227 Rutland-area men who had reported that they were born in County Roscommon—more specifically for some of them, in Kilglass Parish. Further, since the immigrants' gravestone inscriptions sometimes named birthplace, I visited cemeteries and made use of *Irish Famine Immigrants in the State of Vermont: Gravestone Inscriptions*, compiled by Ronald Chase Murphy and Janice Church Murphy. Their book provides records of about 15,000 famine immigrants in the state. I also sought vital and military records at the state records center in Middlesex and newspaper and other records at the Rutland Historical Society.

The painstaking process of identifying and classifying individuals in Rutland as evictees from Ballykilcline or as earlier inhabitants of the townland or of Kilglass Parish produced results with varying degrees of certitude: there is conclusive documentation for a number of potential subjects, less certain evidence for others. I counted as evictees only those people whose names appeared on the official list of evictees given in Coyle's book, meaning that they had been forced from their homes in 1847 or 1848 and that the Crown paid for their passage to New York City—or that they were members of one of those families. Readers must be sensitive to the designation of the people of Ballykilcline either as evictees or as residents (the two are not synonymous: evictees were all residents but not all early residents were evictees) as well as distinctions of place made between those from the home townland of Ballykilcline and others from the home parish of Kilglass (the larger unit), or from the Strokestown area. The period covered in this study extended to 1870, some twenty-two or twenty-three years after the evictees arrived in the United States.

To a great extent, my investigation relied on U.S. census information to develop a picture of the immigrants around Rutland. The Ballykilcline tenants arrived in America only two or three years before that 1850 turning point in demography when the federal census began to record *all* members of a household, not only the head of the family. This change in record keeping abetted searches for the townland's evictees, since the names and ages of all evicted family members were documented. Thus, even where the head of the household's name was a common one, if three, four, or five members of a family were listed in a census, they could be matched to the list of evictees with a high degree of certainty. In practice, however, the effort was constrained by family members' deaths and the early age at which Irish children left home for work (sometimes in neighbors' households), so that many family units are dispersed in the census records. In addition, some families' repeated usage of common first names—John and Patrick, Mary and Ann—complicated the work. Providing another written record, however, Irish immigrants to America placed ads in the *Boston Pilot* to trace family members lost to the chaos of famine and emigration; the practice continued for decades, and a number of the ads, extracted and compiled in the multivolume *The Search for Missing Friends,* provided information about former inhabitants of Kilglass, including several from Ballykilcline (Harris et al. 1989–, vols. 1–8).[2]

For the census searches, I used data recorded in the 1850, 1860, 1870, and a few 1880 censuses, as well as manufacturing censuses for Rutland in 1850 and 1860.[3] I started by focusing on the records for Rutland (of which West Rutland was a part before the 1880s), Dorset, and Poultney, since they were known places of settlement of the immigrants; I then searched in several other towns (see table 1 in the Appendix). For the literacy portion of the study, I conducted some searches in the 1880 federal census.

Surname, first name, age, birthplace, and other family members were the data points that warranted attention in the identification process; I tried to match the names in the evictees' list, which identified whole families, to those of individuals in the census, with various results. It should be noted that the imprecision of spelling (in the names) and ages in the record keeping of that time imposed an added burden on establishing correspondences. Thus, to identify individuals, I decided to accept individuals with a variant spelling of a name when it was similar in a phonetic rendering and to recognize that an individual's birth date might be recorded within ten years in either direction on different records. A further complication was Irish naming patterns, which produced multiple individuals of the same names in extended families. In such cases, other evidence had to be brought to bear on the issue.[4]

The government's questions at each census varied somewhat. Significantly for my purposes, the 1850 census, two to three years after the forced emigrations from Ballykilcline, asked questions about occupation, real estate value, and literacy. The 1860 census asked not only about "value of real estate" but also "value of personal estate." In 1870, new questions inquired whether parents were foreign-born, and separated the question about literacy for those of a designated minimum age into two parts: ability to read and ability to write.

I decided to incorporate the second generation of the immigrants in my primary database of former Ballykilcline residents in Rutland. I did this so as not to distinguish among those families who bore some children in Ireland and some in the United States, and because the children's family and cultural experience so closely replicated that of their parents. Once they were added (to the extent known), this database grew to approximately 260 people, most of whom may have lived in Ballykilcline but were not all evictees.

Beginning in 1860, the federal census data documented large numbers of Irish individuals working in Rutland's marble operations. I extracted the names of all Irish-born individuals who said they did quarry or stone work in the 1860 and 1870 censuses for Rutland and Dorset and created databases of them for each place and time period. In this way I identified 461 Irish quarry or stone-mill workers in the town of Rutland in 1860 and 275 in 1870; in Dorset, I found 37 Irish quarry workers in 1860 and 91 in 1870. This strategy helped to compensate for the fact that very few employment records existed for the early marble companies and that the censuses did not detail which men worked for which companies. An earlier record, however, did give that information for 1857: a census of approximately 1,300 people who lived in St. Bridget's Parish in West Rutland named family members in each household and gave ages, employers, and women's maiden names.[5] That parish census may be the earliest and only extant record linking particular men to particular quarry operations in the time before the Civil War.

To circumvent the lack of early records of the firms, I sought copies of the companies' legal actions to evict striking workers, since those records should have linked particular workers to particular firms as well as documented the names of the strikers. Unfortunately, the records could not be located in the repositories of the county, Supreme, or Chancery courts at the Rutland County Courthouse or in the municipal court records held at Castleton State College. Nor did a check at the National Archives in Waltham turn up records of this sort. (The Rutland courthouse records, however, did yield some paperwork stemming from a lawsuit about property claims that involved John Hanley, son Gilbert, and son-in-law Michael Hackett, although the court archive did not surrender the disposition of that case.) To flesh out the description of the local marble industry as it grew, then, and to address the motivation for owners' actions, I tapped the manufacturing supplements to the federal censuses.

One local historian examined the experience of the early immigrant Irish around Rutland in particular depth and intimacy: the book *Historical Sketches on West Rutland, Vermont* by Rev. Patrick Hannon, a pastor at St. Bridget's Church in West Rutland, detailed life in the quarries and presented a narrative of the quarry strikes based on local newspaper accounts. Father Hannon described the development of the parish as well. His book was a crucial source. I also had access to "Carving Out a Sense of Place: The Making of the Marble Valley and the Marble City of Vermont," the important doctoral dissertation of Michael L. Austin, whose subject was the development of the marble industry and related political and social conditions, particularly as they affected the Irish in Rutland.

Some portions of my portrait of Kilglass people in Rutland came from my reading of local newspapers in the middle 1800s; I consulted both the *Rutland Herald* and the *Rutland Courier* at the Rutland Historical Society. Much information stemmed from genealogists' family history knowledge, accessed to a large extent through the Ballykilcline Society, which includes descendants of the famine and pre-famine population of the townland, and the dedicated research community on the RootsWeb Rutland Listserv.

When I learned that according to local tradition, Fenian circles had existed in Rutland, I tried to find out whether Ballykilcline or Kilglass people had been involved. I figured that the disturbed state of Roscommon and the vigor of the Kilglass people's response to British rule might have inclined them to join such a cause in the United States. I therefore combed local newspapers and eventually found a news story that named the first officers of one local circle. When the Kilglass Parish surnames Carlon and McKeough appeared among the officers, I investigated the Fenians further by reading William D'Arcy's history of the organization and Henri Le Caron's autobiography, which recounted his years spying on the Fenians. Information about the quarry men's protests against the 1863 Conscription Act came from Rutland newspapers, as well as postings by and sources suggested by RootsWeb Listserv researchers, books about Vermont's history, my own Internet research.

At the same time, I acquired a library of scholarly books and journal articles concerning nineteenth-century popular protest, labor action, U.S. political history, immigrant experience, and the function of memory in such contexts. The immigrants' memory of their Irish past was crucial to the way they made their American futures.

Ballykilcline Rising

1

The Story of Ballykilcline

And what a people loves it will defend.
—John Hewitt, The Colony, in Pete Hamill's *Forever*

The struggle of man against power is the struggle of memory against forgetting.
—Milan Kundera, *The Book of Laughter and Forgetting*

The particular path of contention has an important impact . . . because each shared effort to press claims lays down a settlement among parties to the transaction, a memory of the interaction, new information about the likely outcomes of different sorts of interactions, and a changed web of relations within and among the participating sets of people.
—Charles Tilly, *Popular Contention in Great Britain, 1758–1834*

IN THE third year of the Great Famine and the thirteenth year of their contentious rent strike, the people of Ballykilcline were forced from their Kilglass Parish homes in Roscommon by British government agents, who evicted them from Ireland. In seven struggling groups during 1847 and '48, the several hundred tenants—couples, children, single and old people—trudged to Dublin, crossed the Irish Sea to Liverpool, and embarked uncertainly on the great rolling Atlantic to New York City. Their landlord, the Crown, paid for their passages to America to rid the countryside of such troublemakers.

Their exodus was a stunning end to a long chapter of extraordinary resistance to Crown authorities in a place that had witnessed withering famine distress and social chaos in the late 1840s and even earlier. The end of their remarkable rent strike was one event among several that happened around Strokestown in 1847 which forever altered Ireland, England, Scotland, Canada, and the United States. A second forced emigration from the area at virtually the same time involved nearly a thousand tenants evicted by Strokestown landlord Major Denis Mahon. More than half of

Mahon's evictees died before or upon reaching Quebec's quarantine station at Grosse Ile in the St. Lawrence River (Dunn 2002; Dunn 2001, p. 9); those who survived were in terrible condition. Only months later, Ireland and England were stunned by the assassination of landlord Mahon, who was ambushed in his carriage as he rode home from a meeting to his Strokestown manor house.

The three events—the Ballykilcline and the Mahon evictions and emigrations and the murder of Mahon—had significant repercussions for Ireland, even at the highest levels of government. The name Ballykilcline figured in parliamentary debate over government-subsidized emigration schemes in 1848 when Lord Monteagle argued about hypocrisy in the Crown's scheme for Ballykilcline in one session and later hailed the scheme's success (Gray 1999, pp. 193, 307). The illness and death of Mahon's emigrants aboard ship and in Quebec caused Canadian officials to protest vehemently to London about the deplorable state of the arriving Irish. The killing of Mahon turned British public opinion against the Irish people in the throes of Black '47, the harshest year of the Great Famine (Kinealy 1997, p. 132), thus stoking the enmity of the Irish into the far future and across the wide Atlantic. Mahon's death, and other murders, brought the harsh Coercion Act down on Ireland that December. Such measures—usually temporary—gave the government emergency powers to quell lawlessness and disturbances (Lalor 2003, p. 216). Moreover, it exacerbated local sectarian divisions, charged religious antagonisms, and generated a diplomatic controversy between England and the Vatican, which subsequently ordered a curtailment of priests' political activities in Ireland before Young Ireland's weak rising in 1848, when priests stepped in to steer the Irish people away from taking action. (Campbell 1990, p. 30). Young Ireland was a nationalist and cultural organization (Lalor 2003, p. 1161).

But what was it about their circumstances that put Kilglass's ten thousand or so natives in such a pivotal and conflicted position? What was the local situation that made what they did evoke such repercussions, like the ripples when a stone drops in the water? And what became of the poor people around whom the chaos and controversy swirled, the evicted tenants of Ballykilcline and their Kilglass relatives and friends?

The people of Ballykilcline had themselves been tenants on the Mahon estate for the forty years ending in 1834 when, through a middleman, the Mahons leased the townland from Crown authorities (Scally 1995, p. 5). One or more of the striking farmers were early suspects in Denis Mahon's murder in 1847 (Fox memo, Nov. 26, 1847). And among Mahon's dead on the shore at Quebec were the Ballykilcline farmers' relatives and friends. The strike, evictions, emigrations, and murder were links in a chain that connected Mahon, his tenants, the Ballykilcline strikers, and the people of Kilglass in what is now a famine story that is fairly well known, at least in outline, as a result of attention from historians and television producers in observance of the 150th anniversary of the famine in the late 1990s. But the only extensive, detailed account of the Ballykilcline story was told by Robert Scally in his 1995 book, *The End of Hidden Ireland: Rebellion, Famine, and Emigration,* and that narrative ended with their arrival in New York. This history goes deeper for context in their old homes and further in time, place, and experience in their new ones.

The Ballykilcline record is a story of collective action by a community of Irish farmers on the fringe of Connacht, the northwestern province that had long been assigned by the British to the oppressed native people: "To hell or Connacht," the English had ordered two centuries earlier as they seized and reassigned property all over the island to reward English settlers, punishing the Irish and pushing them toward the boglands along the western Atlantic coast. Within that long history, this account looks at where the Ballykilcline people came from and where they went, and it aims at some understanding of what happened to them and how they made their way in their strange and changing world. In particular, it focuses on their personal experiences, their collective consciousness and its expression, and their work and community history in an attempt to learn what happened in two very different nineteenth-century worlds: one around Strokestown in rural Roscommon, the other around Rutland on a marble ledge in Vermont, where some of them settled.

As Samuel Clark and James S. Donnelly Jr. have said, "The central role played by England in world capitalism has meant that the social upheaval which all peasantries have undergone or are now undergoing was experienced very early and acutely by the Irish. The great expansion and then brutal contraction of the Irish rural population in the eighteenth and nineteenth centuries, as well as the massive migration of Irish peasants to urban industrial centers in widely separated parts of the world, bear witness to the sensitive place that Irish country people came to occupy at a relatively early point in the evolution of world capitalism" (1983, p. 20).

That "sensitive place" can be seen through the lens of Ballykilcline. The focus here is on the experience of dozens of evictees and earlier emigrants from the townland who settled in Rutland, where some of them built railroads and others joined the workforce of the nascent marble industry in a place that through time, the marketplace, and their exertions became a world center for marble production. At least 17 percent of the 368 recorded evictee-emigrants from Ballykilcline had passed through or settled in Rutland by 1850, as did scores of other inhabitants of the townland and their neighbors from Kilglass civil parish, some of them likely evicted by Major Mahon before he was gunned down in a crisis-stricken season.[1]

"LIVES CRUELLY DESTROYED"?

Historian Scally's resurrection of the Ballykilcline story has been ac-claimed by, among others, Seamus Deane of the University of Notre Dame, who said of it, "Painstakingly researched, lucidly written, his work provides a sudden and intimate access to a world and a series of individual lives cruelly destroyed during the terrible forties of the [nineteenth] cen-tury" (qtd., Maynooth College website). The community of Ballykilcline certainly was destroyed in Scally's account; the townland was virtually emptied. But destruction of their townland and their life in Ireland is not the same as destruction of their lives. Many of the former tenant farmers settled into new lives in the United States, and the issue is what kind of life it was and how it was affected by their Irish past. Were the tenants' lives de-stroyed along with Ballykilcline, as Deane suggested and Scally wondered about? Or did they surmount their troubles in Ireland to make worthwhile new lives in America? What struggles confronted them in their new places, and what did they bring to them from their past experience?

My objective has been to identify the forces that led to the rent strike and assisted emigration, to trace the evictees who settled in Rutland, and some elsewhere, and to develop a picture of their American life and work experience, mostly in the area's marble quarries. My research moved both backward in search of the factors that inspired collective action in the form of the rent strike that began in 1835 and ended with the evictions and emigrations of 1847 and 1848, and forward to see how the immi-grants acted in Rutland and how they employed their mental and cultural legacies from Roscommon.

My investigation started with the prehistory of the Ballykilcline strike: the social and economic context in Ireland, the people's traditional cul-ture, and their particular economic and political predicaments. It in-cluded background on the "combinations"—that is, strikes—in Ireland; the Roscommoners' experience of life outside their own county as, for instance, seasonal migrant laborers elsewhere in Ireland and in Scotland and England; the external influences that came into Kilglass Parish and

County Roscommon from beyond their borders; and the secret societies that operated across the Irish rural landscape and were active around Strokestown. Since collective action was the primary method by which the people acted to protect themselves and defend their interests in both Ballykilcline and Rutland, how did they come to recognize that tactic as their best defense? In 1835 when the rent strike began, it seemed from Scally's history to be an unaccounted-for development, inasmuch as it occurred in a rural area where industry, which was a more usual strike setting, was so underdeveloped. Scally also depicted the townland's inhabitants as rural and isolated, cut off from much of the commercial and civilized Atlantic world. So why did the people turn to a strike in this purported backwater, and how unusual was it in that time and place?

The answers came out of the radical forces at play across the rural countryside of northern and eastern Roscommon, which converged around the land and its usage and set the social classes in opposition to each other. It also spilled out of the long experience of oppression imposed by the British and out of the public protest erupting in England from the distressed underclasses of the industrial and agricultural revolutions. In fact, that Kilglass was not as cut off as at first it might have appeared can be shown in a calculation of the number of seasonal migrant laborers who set off annually from the parish; consideration of communications, transportation, and economic infrastructure; a survey of the content of a county newspaper available to the people of Kilglass beginning in the 1820s; and an assessment of the size and influence of the police and military forces stationed throughout Ireland. Moreover, the Irish townspeople exchanged letters with earlier emigrants, including some who lived in Rutland. Indeed, the Irish had a widening world view.

On U.S. ground, the potential irony of the Ballykilcline tale as it played out in Rutland was intriguing: clues hinted that immigrants who had waged a strike in Ireland and thereby lost their homes and their homeland might have engaged in further strike activity in their new location and consequently lost their jobs and homes a second time. Did it happen again or, given their traumatic Irish experience, did they avoid altogether such collective action in their U.S. circumstances? Were they passive victims of circumstance and politics, or were they individuals attempting to control their own fate? Did they, in other words, exercise agency for their own benefit, or passively submit to the fate that larger forces decreed for them?

Of particular interest to my research was the issue of agency, which means to act so as to exert power over circumstance. What roles did the people from Ballykilcline play, if any, in collective activity in the United States, such as the three strikes that took place in Rutland's marble industry between 1859 and 1868, and what were the company owners' responses to the strikers' grievances? Further, protests against the Civil War Conscription Act which occurred in Rutland in 1863 and the Fenians' activities throughout the 1860s in pursuit of freedom for Ireland, for which Vermont and New York were theaters of action, warranted attention. Also relevant were any distinctions that could be demonstrated between the experience of the Ballykilcline and Kilglass people who went to Rutland before the Famine and those evicted because of the strike, since Rutland drew newcomers from both time periods. Of further interest were the literacy of the people from Ballykilcline as recorded in federal censuses after their arrival; their acquisition of assets, viewed as an index to their sense of agency and their conduct in the New World; and their family and community life. Did they maintain connections with their former neighbors from Ballykilcline; did they help each other and the Irish at home? Or did they just want to forget?

It seemed that tracing the Ballykilcline rent strikers in the United States potentially might enlarge Scally's view of them or contradict it; what they did and how and where they did it might shed light on the transplantation of Irish and other immigrants from rural, politically oppressed economies. It might provide insight into the development of political and labor organizations in nineteenth-century New England. Further, it should tell something about what happened to a consciousness incubated in a radical Old World setting after it was transplanted to a competitive New World economy. Clark and Donnelly have called for a "longitudinal analysis of how [Irish] collective action in a certain locality was transformed over time as a result of changes" in social structures (1983, p. 422). I asked how the mindset that produced collective action in Ballykilcline was transformed over time with the experience of moving to a new social setting in a capitalist economy. Clark and Donnelly also "stressed the need to link the Irish peasant experience to the larger process of the development of world capitalism" (1983, p. 432). Whereas their concern was its impact on Irish rural societies, I focused primarily on the effects on the immigrants themselves and the evolution of their actions in the new U.S. context while acknowledging that the forces in play helped to shape not only their new place in the world but also the community they left behind. In exploring these roots, I responded to historian Mary Blewett's observation that "the political legacies of all immigrant groups in industrial settings deserve evaluation" (2000, p. 263). Historian Tyler Anbinder

(2002) has called for additional studies of Irish immigrants' lives on both sides of the Atlantic. His own work on assisted immigrants from County Kerry to Five Points in New York City demonstrates that historians have sometimes underestimated the immigrants' capacity to survive, adapt, and even prosper—that is, to exercise agency in their own interest.

The multiple social and political convulsions that shocked Ireland and the world in the early and middle 1800s have been insufficiently studied as influences on and potential determinants of the important famine-time events that took place around Strokestown. The strained social and political relations there helped give the area a tough reputation. John O'Donovan, of the Ordinance Survey, a governmental mapping agency, visited Kilglass in 1837—not long after the Ballykilcline strike started and about the time that a priest named McDermott from a Ballykilcline family was inadvertently murdered during a local wedding party (Coyle 1994, pp. 36, 37)—and reported that the parish was "proverbial in this part of the county for its wickedness" (Sharkey 1927, p. 317). British officials would have agreed. During the rent dispute, they labeled the Ballykilcline tenants a "desperate set of characters" (Scally 1995, p. 98), a description of them that goes far beyond Scally's and seemingly is contradicted by the existing later evidence. Scally's account relied heavily on the British officials' records and correspondence in the Ballykilcline case, which by its nature was biased, since it represented the voice of only one side in the conflict. Irish events that involved the predominantly Catholic native people in that time were not well documented: the people left few written documents; even vital records, for instance, were not kept for Irish Catholics until 1864. Scally himself observed that because the record that does survive "was kept by outsiders whose main purpose was either to collect the rent or to enforce the law, the townland did not expose its mind to the record-keepers willingly. . . . [I]t was an axiom of survival to evade that surveillance by all means possible" (Scally 1995, p. 4).

Further, the record keepers for Ireland held a generally biased view of the Irish people, influenced by their own disdain for Irish Catholicism, their notions of Irish racial inferiority, and their colonial view of the Irish character as degraded, indolent, and incorrigible. Thus it seemed that locating the immigrants in their new American settlements, where official records were more widely and better kept, where the immigrants had less reason to remain invisible, and where they were freer to act, might compensate to some extent for the dearth of Irish records and provide a broader and deeper picture of their lives and their actions than the one drawn by Scally.

How Their Historian Viewed the Strikers

In Scally's portrait of them, the people of Ballykilcline were small farmers and agrarian laborers on an "obscure estate" near a "provincial market town" on "the very frontier of cosmopolitan Europe." In their world, these Irish people lived "half-apart—ragged, shoeless, and uncombed, speaking an exotic tongue, believing in miracles and charms, and surviving on a diet most thought fit only for beasts." Their holdings were small, their homes destitute, their lands overused. The land system in Ireland had forced the native people to "poverty and the potato," and "modern value systems [were] regarded as alien by the common people and associated with their oppressors." Accordingly, their moral economy "generally condemned private initiative and accumulation as something alien and inimical to the community." In consequence, Scally said, "The poverty of the townland population became its identity, both in their own eyes and in those of all others." (See Scally 1995, pp. 12, 41, 30, 33, 35)

Many of the tenants were literate, Scally conceded, yet they lived "outside the world of calculation" and were "insulated to a startling degree for Europeans from up-to-date knowledge of the outside world." Strokestown's commercial center was "one of the markets of last resort in Europe, where commodities of the lowest and most exhausted quality found their last buyer." Their world, as Scally saw it, revolved around scarcity: The townland's "characteristic features—its fatalism, its hatred of vanity, its faith in luck, its furtiveness and combustibility—were natural responses to the demands that scarcity imposed on both communities and individuals. All its traits had cultural roots in the deep past" (1995, pp. 32, 35). Those traits included consciousness of subjection, evident in the petitions emanating from Ballykilcline as the loss of their land loomed. When panic and rage set in, the leaders drew on communal discipline, which was imposed both by persuasion and coercion.

Scally pointed as well to the more general observations about the Irish people made by Alexis de Tocqueville, who traveled in Ireland about that time and wrote about his trip. The French author described the Celts' clear sense of identity, the powers of collective force that they could use protectively at least for a time, "a degree of mental contact with the European world," and "a stunningly vigorous and civil social cohesion amid the mud and rags" (cited in Scally 1995, p. 10). Communal memory formed their consciousness and sense of belonging. But Scally did not attempt to reconcile that view with his own, which is a dark, rather pessimistic view of the people of Ballykilcline, and one that seemed to afford them little chance in a new country where they would start out without means, with few occupational skills, and suffering all of the burdens of their stricken past. He apparently discounted that "cohesion," except as it led to their eviction and emigration.

Although Scally ended his tale with the arrival of the Ballykilcline people at the port of New York, he speculated that learning about them in their new life and new home might be revelatory: "It would be gratifying to know what became of the rump of Ballykilcline after their landing in New York, whether their bonds of family, kinship, and recent experience inclined them to resettle as a kind of remnant of the townland, reconstructing their defenses against a new 'outside.'" Scally posed a series of questions about how they might have acted in their new country and what they might have done. He questioned whether they might have remained a community; he worried that the fate of some would be played out in the wards of Bellevue Hospital, the asylum at Blackwell's Island, and the graves in potter's field. How did their consciousness persist? he asked. "Did their prolonged collective experience and their emigration as a community incline them . . . to settle together or work in occupations that gave them greater strength than working with strangers?" He wondered, too, whether they remained wary of Anglo-Saxons, how they interpreted antebellum New York, and what role, if any, they played in America's great Civil War. "With no experience of citizenship, did their idea of freedom consist simply of being left alone?" (Scally 1995, pp. 226, 227).

These are good questions; added to them, though, should be others about whether and how they might have perpetuated their links between America and the cherished homeland from which they had been forced out and how they perceived America's concepts of citizenship. Scally posed his questions as academic speculation, but he was correct that a study of the experience of these immigrants in America would be freighted with potential significance for knowledge generalizable to other immigrants and for new understandings of the ways in which Irish immigration affected the course of American affairs. I address some of his questions by training a wider lens on the Ballykilcline people's experience in both countries over a longer time period.

Descendants Find a Nontypical Story

The surprise following publication of Scally's story was that some descendants of the farmers of Ballykilcline read his account, came forward, and have taken up the tale, thus facilitating further investigation. The family historians among them who recognized their ancestors in his narrative have since organized as the Ballykilcline Society to press the search for other descendants, to learn the rest of the story, and to foster new knowledge about the history of that part of County Roscommon in Kilglass Parish and around Strokestown.[2] Significantly, in recent years they have identified former residents of Ballykilcline as having lived in a number of locations in the United States where evictees as well as earlier emigrants from the townland settled. In the mind's eye, no longer are the immigrants just a huddled mass on the docks of Manhattan where Scally left them. Knowing where some of them went makes possible further study of their experience and presses American records into the service of developing new knowledge about them.

Family members established that after a handful of Ballykilcline people had settled in Rutland, Vermont, several dozen other individuals from Kilglass had filed for citizenship there by the mid-1840s. Their findings suggested that a lively chain migration was operating between Roscommon and Rutland even before famine time. Census and naturalization records and gravestone information enlarged the group of known Ballykilcline and Kilglass immigrants to Rutland.

The techniques that Scally used in developing and telling his story, as historian Ruth-Ann Harris has suggested, may encourage the reader to think that this community and these farm people were typical of the rural Irish in their time (Harris 1996). In fact, though, much about their experience is unique.

First, the Ballykilcline strike and legal case were not typical events in the experience of the native Irish; there is no known similar case in which tenants challenged Crown forces and withheld rent for years before they were evicted because of their defiance and then "assisted" out of Ireland.

Second, the Ballykilcline people lived in one of those areas of Ireland most ravaged by famine, and the conditions created by the catastrophe contributed to ending their strike.

Third, historians until recently believed that only a select group of perhaps 50,000 Irish received "assistance" to leave their homeland during the famine period (Donnelly1997, pp. 155–73), but two researchers have upended that idea. Desmond Norton, for one, contends that scholars may have significantly underestimated the number of tenants assisted out of Ireland by their landlords. His case is based on his work analyzing an extensive archive of documents of the famine-time land agent firm of Stewart and Kincaid (Norton 2002 p. 26). And Gerard Moran, in a book issued in 2004, said, "Assisted emigration played an important, but as yet largely unacknowledged role, in the exodus from nineteenth-century

Ireland. A large number of emigrants owed their settlement in foreign lands to their passages being paid by the government, poor law unions, landlords and individual philanthropists. While it is impossible to calculate the exact figure, it would appear that the number assisted to North America was between two hundred and fifty thousand and three hundred thousand. This figure does not include the large numbers of friends and relations who paid the passage of these groups" (2004, p. 219). In many comparisons, the Crown's aid to the tenants of Ballykilcline appeared generous when matched with the small amounts expended by some landlords to clear their properties. Moran lamented the fact that neither the government nor the landlords could finance emigration on a broader scale as one solution to Ireland's chaos.

The Ballykilcline evictees may have been fortunate, since they were sent to the United States—often the destination of choice of Irish emigrants—rather than to Canada, where so many landlord-assisted emigrants from the west of Ireland, including hundreds of their own Kilglass brethren, died in passage or on the shore at Quebec in 1847 from famine-related causes. Famine diseases spread through southern Canada with the arriving immigrants during that season, bringing death to thousands more. Many of the survivors continued on to the United States.

THE SCHOLARLY CHORUS: ACCLAIM AND CRITICISM

Acclaim for Scally's book as social history has noted the extent of his research, the imagination he brought to the telling of the tale, his analytical range, and his subject of "hidden Ireland." William Fishman of the University of London said of it, "This work is based on painstaking research into an extraordinary range of primary and secondary sources. Overall it is an outstanding piece of original research . . . [a] genuine contribution to Irish, British, and U.S. social history" (qtd., Maynooth College website). Indeed, Scally's book *is* a significant achievement and one that has focused attention on the Kilglass story, which otherwise might have been buried in time. But his account is an unfinished one, raising those questions suggested above.

His Ballykilcline account also drew some serious criticism. Historian Ruth-Ann Harris commented about Scally's narrow range of sources, which relied too heavily on depictions of Irish famine emigrants as passive lonely exiles and victims: "The material available to Professor Scally had the potential for this to be an important case study that would fundamentally challenge the prevailing stereotypes of isolated communities, passive victims, and last resort immigrants. Unfortunately, he failed to draw fully on the available material, and when there was a choice the evidence was interpreted to reinforce the stereotypical view. . . . [T]he author has overlooked important evidence" (1996).

Peter Gray suggested as well that "there may be a dimension missing from his account"—that is, politics. Gray questioned why such tenants would be prone to "litigation as the primary means of protecting their rights to land and life." He posited that their choice might have stemmed from the influence of Daniel O'Connell, the great statesman of the Irish people who achieved Catholic Emancipation from the Penal Laws in 1829 and fought on for repeal of the 1800 Act of Union between Ireland and Great Britain. Gray astutely observed:

> O'Connellite popular politics must have had some impact on communities like Ballykilcline. "Catholic" political organization in Co. Roscommon dated from 1826, when the forty-shilling freeholders of that county were mobilized by priest and schoolmaster (two classes represented in Ballykilcline) in the cause of Catholic emancipation. . . . [T]he "monster meeting" of the summer of 1843 at Roscommon town (less than fifteen miles from the townland) apparently attracted over one hundred thousand people (more than a third of the county's population, if anyway accurate).
>
> It is possible that Ballykilcline was untouched by the popular political mobilization of the 1830s–'40s. Yet combine the presence of typical O'Connellite "agents" in the townland, the literacy of its more prominent tenants, the neglect of conspiratorial violence, and the resort to litigation (itself reflecting both O'Connell's political objective of "popularizing" the law and the widespread popular mythology surrounding "the Counsellor"), and there seems at least an *a priori* case to answer. (Gray 1998, p. 146)

This study examines the links to that "popular political mobilization."

From a different direction, Michael Huggins viewed Scally's *The End of Hidden Ireland* as an example of the "legacy of nationalist historiography," which he believed lacks explanatory power to describe the changes then under way. Huggins wrote about prefamine conflicts in Roscommon and demonstrated significant interrelationships between would-be reformers in Ireland and England, reciprocity of interests, and sharing of tactics: "The story of agrarian rebellion in county Roscommon was of the development of an underground culture of class antagonism, in the early nineteenth century appropriating Jacobin emblems and later influenced first by radicalism and then by trade unions and Chartism, all grafted on to Irish traditions. It would be difficult to ignore the social dimension of Chartism that must have mattered to the Irish poor." Huggins explored the terrain of the Whiteboys—a secret organization of the Irish—for motivations, forms, discourses, sources, and links with English radicals and argued that "a historiography of modernization is an inadequate explanatory model for agrarian conflict, which combined the traditional with the rebellious, the pre-modern with the modern and the parochial with the cosmopolitan. 'Molly Maguire' made some basic political generalizations, while taking specific actions over conacre rents" (pp. 53, 24, 22). The Mollies were another secret society of the rural Irish to protest the inequities of the land and political system.

Agrarian conflict was generated "outside the monolithic identities of confession and ethnicity" and was grounded more in class, customary obligations, and local economic conditions. Irish notions of patriotism and class were identical to those of the working people in England (Huggins 2000, p. 53).

Huggins pointed to the growth of fraternity and the inattention to religion as protest evolved before the famine and conflict became more regionalized, with particular events concurrently affecting Roscommon and nearby counties. His ideas grew within the "moral economy" framework of rights and responsibilities developed by E. P. Thompson (1996); he concluded that "conflict in the first half of the nineteenth century was accompanied by the incremental evolution of a customary consciousness into what may only be named a consciousness of class antagonism between the labouring poor on one hand and employers and landlords (whether farmers, agents, middlemen or owners) on the other" (Huggins 2000, pp. 24, 28, 29, 35).

What he saw in the rural Irish, though, was a "combined and uneven consciousness, like the one which can proclaim loyalty to Ireland and the Crown" (2000, p. 47). Huggins also disagreed with historians who regarded Catholicism as "a solidarity mechanism" that generated conflict in the 1820s and 1830s.

As a definition of class, I accept E. P. Thompson's classic description, developed in his study of the English: "Class happens when some men, as a result of common experiences (inherited or shared), feel and articulate the identity of their interests as between themselves, and as against other men whose interests are different from (and usually opposed to) theirs. The class experience is largely determined by the productive relations in which men are born–or enter voluntarily." Thompson made clear that in his view, class is developed over time as experience impresses consciousness. He also considered class a relationship that is worked out in a social role. This study will observe its development in the Irish smallholders generally and in the tenants of Ballykilcline in particular: "Class is defined by men as they live their own history" (1996, pp. 9–11).

The construction of class and its distinguishing characteristics have been studied by Ira Katznelson, who pointed to people's shared "understandings of the social system" and "values of justice and goodness." He called them dispositions, the "cultural configurations within which people act": "Groups of people sharing motivational constructs ('disposition to behave') may or may not act collectively to transform disposition to behavior. Even where workers have close contact at work and in their residential communities; even if this interaction promotes strong collective identities; and even if these workers share common systems of meaning that incline them to act in class ways, they may not necessarily act together to produce collective action" (1986, pp. 18–20).

On collective action, however, Katznelson quoted Charles Tilly (1995) that historians must learn "which sets of people, which resources, which common ends, and which forms of commitment were involved in different places and times." Variations warranted explanation: "New kinds of social relationships of production, new forms of exploitation, and new dimensions to the process of proletarianization ushered in vigorous defenses of the old order as well as new thoughts and deeds concerning the conditions of workers within the new order" (Katznelson 1986, p. 20).

If Huggins identified a symbiosis between Irish and English protesters who shared concerns person to person or group to group, Mary Blewett found "carryover effects" among immigrant workers in the United States from their lives in their home country, a movement of action and idea from place to place. In *Constant Turmoil*, her history of the textile workers and mills in southeastern Massachusetts, Blewett demonstrated that immigrants from Lancashire imported and made use of workplace organizing tactics and traditions in the fractious economy of Fall River. "Based on their legacies of organization and protest, many Yorkshire and Lancashire immigrant operatives in New England were neither invisible nor conservative. . . . The legacies of class consciousness . . . among Lancashire workers would become important to New England labor politics" (2000, pp. 78, 80). She demonstrated a carryover of world view for English millworkers that may well apply to Irish workers, caught as they were between farm and wage work. Numbers of Roscommon emigrants went first to the teeming cities of Lancashire (Bolton, for instance) and lived there for a time before moving on to the United States. The radicalizing thought patterns of the Ballykilcline rent strike may have become so ingrained over the thirteen years of the strike that those habits of mind came with the immigrants to their new settings to be applied in new circumstances.

What they were "carrying over" was the recently evolved form of politics, and the mental attitudes associated with it, that had emerged in England, a development described by Charles Tilly: between 1750 and 1840, "groups of ordinary people came to participate directly in national struggles for power, and to do so on their own account. On the way, the British people spread the use of the deliberately organized special-purpose association as a political instrument. The idea and the fact of mass mobilization around a national program took shape. . . . [M]ass assemblies and marches [were used] to demonstrate popular determination, and doctrines of popular sovereignty. . . . [N]ational and autonomous popular politics had become Britain's regular style" (1995, pp. 142, 143).

In his study of contentious popular action in Great Britain, Tilly asserted that between 1758 and 1834, the period that most threatened a "revolutionary situation" was from 1830 to 1832, which saw mass efforts for reform by Parliament. It was also the period just before the rent strike started in Ballykilcline—the farmers' own "deliberately organized special-purpose . . . political instrument" (1995, p. 50). The unhappy underclasses had found new ways of expressing their discontent, pressing their causes, and achieving change; contentious actions taken in England were apprehended and comprehended and adopted or adapted in Ireland, which had its own new approaches as well in O'Connellite politics.

In considering the causes of conflict in Ireland, a concept from Ted Robert Gurr seems to fit the case well. Gurr's theme was that "positive perspectives on politics make men good subjects—willing to support and obey, unwilling to attack the political system," and he developed notions around the idea of governmental legitimacy: "The intensity of regime legitimacy is the extent to which the political unit, its governing institutions, and the incumbents are thought proper and worthy of support" (1970, pp. 185—86). The underlying concept was singled out by David M. Potter in his history of 1850s America: "The attitudes of various groups in a society toward upholding the law is [sic] in direct proportion to their approval or disapproval of the law which is to be upheld" (D. Potter 1976, p. 296).

Clark and Donnelly have focused attention on organizing by the Irish people: "Catholic aspirations to overthrow Protestant domination could facilitate the organization of peasants in an effective agrarian challenge to the established order." They point to the anti-tithe war (which started about 1830) and the land wars as examples of movements that capitalized on a shared Catholic identity: "The magnitude of pre-famine agrarian rebellion—an impressive succession of regional movements punctuating every decade between 1760 and 1840—indicates the capacity of Irish peasants for effective action without external assistance" (1983, p. 15). If one views the Ballykilcline strike and the events that surrounded it as part of that network of rural protest (and how can one place them outside it?), then how could the Ballykilcline farmers be seen as merely victims of unfortunate circumstance and inactive in their own cause? Just as the Ballykilcline strike ended, two leaders of the Young Ireland movement in Dublin were calling for the withholding of rents nationally (Hachey, Hernon, and McCaffrey 1989, p. 90), and decades later the tactic used by the antitithe forces and the Ballykilcline farmers was employed again in the land war that led to concessions from the British (Inglis 1956, p. 150).

Tyler Anbinder has lamented the dearth of studies of Irish immigrants in both their Old World and New World settings: that is, studies that follow them on both sides of the Atlantic. He traced one group of "assisted" tenants from Lord Lansdowne's estate in Kerry to the Five Points neighborhood of New York City.[3] Using New York's Emigrant Savings Bank records, Anbinder showed that the wretched, transplanted famine tenants of Ireland's mountainous western seaboard were able to save surprising amounts of money in their first decade in the United States and that they remained clannish in their new home:

> A few things are certain. First, the degree of financial success achieved by the Lansdowne immigrants despite their decrepit surroundings suggests that the famine immigrants adapted to their surroundings far better and more quickly than we have previously imagined. . . . In addition, the Lansdowne immigrants' story demonstrates the value of tracing the lives of famine-era immigrants back to Ireland, adding a transatlantic perspective that has generally been lacking in the field of immigration history. That Five Pointers from the Lansdowne estate achieved their modicum of financial security . . . after their arrival in New York makes those monetary accomplishments all the more remarkable. Their saga demonstrates that we still have a lot to learn about how nineteenth-century immigrants adjusted to—and were transformed by—life in modern America. (Anbinder 2002, par. 68)

Both Tilly and Kevin O'Neill have addressed the legacies of past experience. Tilly pointed to how knowledge builds and events alter what comes later, changing the terms for the future through the accretion of experience, relationship, results, and so on: "Collective claim-making constrains its subsequent forms, influencing the very issues, actors, settings, and outcomes of popular struggle. The particular path of contention has an important impact . . . because each shared effort to press claims lays down a settlement among parties to the transaction, a memory of the interaction, new information about the likely outcomes of different sorts of interactions, and a changed web of relations within and among the participating sets of people" (Tilly 1995, p. 37). Certainly, for the former Ballykilcline strikers who participated in Rutland's labor battles, much, obviously, had changed. One wonders who the strikers perceived as their heroes then and for whom they afterward held new grudges, how they reckoned their strike's success or failure, how the Rutland quarry men used the knowledge derived from their past strike as they walked out of the marble quarries for higher wages, and who were the new leaders among them then.

Kevin O'Neill's locus is memory itself, individual and group. He cites James Fentress and Chris Wickham's argument (1992) that "all systems of memory are functional and suited to the present environments in which social groups find themselves." Whereas social memory changes gradually over time for most groups, it functions differently in immigrants: "For most social groups, at most moments, social memory, while in flux, seems to remain constant, allowing us to mistake it for 'tradition.' But for groups such as immigrant communities this process can be far more rapid, and produce a painful sense of dislocation in both temporal and social identity. This was especially true for immigrant groups who moved from rural and agricultural cultures in which place and landscape formed important structural elements of social memory to communities that were urban and industrial" (O'Neill 2001, p. 121).

In immigrant communities there was a lack of elders to help renegotiate past events, and for the famine Irish there was the great difficulty that "accessing their memories of Ireland posed. They fled from Ireland with images of failure, devastation, and pain etched deeply into their personal memories. Their arrival in a new social and political environment posed a serious challenge to the capacity of their social memory system to provide useful and coherent bridges to membership in the American community." O'Neill termed it a kind of "cultural dysphasia." It took the Union's Civil War victory to win acceptance for the Irish as Americans, enabling them to leave the famine behind; the war "helped to fuse Irish and American nationalisms" (O'Neill 2001, pp. 121, 122, 135).

The theory of popular protest developed by George Rude integrated two types of apprehension: what he called inherent knowledge and derived knowledge. The first is what a person is born with; the second comprises the intellectual ideas he or she acquires through life. Inherent knowledge encompasses, for instance, tradition, culture, and communal memory; derived knowledge covers what individuals learn from other people, including religion and politics. But it is circumstance and experience that determine the final mixture or content, the way the individual integrates what he or she encounters (1995, pp. 22–29). This research shows great individual variability in that integration process governed, nevertheless, by inherent knowledge.

The development of class contributed to the growth of nationalism, a significant relationship. American historian David Potter looked insightfully at how nationalism springs from cohesive forces: "Cohesion can scarcely exist among an aggregate of people unless they share some objective characteristics. Classic criteria are common descent (or ethnic affinities), common language, common religion, and most important and most intangible of all, common customs and beliefs. But these features alone will not produce cohesion unless those who share them also share a self-consciousness of what they have in common, unless they attach distinctive value to what is shared, and unless they feel identified with one another by the sharing" (D. Potter 1976, p. 450). Although the criteria he described obviously were present in the people of Ballykilcline, de Toqueville's description of them, cited by Scally, suggests that they also shared the self-consciousness, sense of value, and identification that Potter thought so necessary to move a group to action.

My work pursues the pre- and posthistory of the Ballykilcline people's rent strike. It follows the tenant farmers for two decades of their lives in the United States—as far as 1870. Not only did the Irish occupy a "sensitive place" in the development of world capitalism, but capitalism in its evolution came to represent a "sensitive place" in their lives as well as in the development of American society.

Here then is another picture of the lives of the rebel farmers of Ballykilcline.

RENT STRIKE, EVICTIONS, AND ASSASSINATION

Ballykilcline first represented a special interest to England's ruler, James II, it is assumed, about 1688, when the land was confiscated by royal troops and became part of the Crown Estate. That meant that it was amalgamated in the collection of hereditary properties belonging to the monarch, who was supported from their income but barred from selling the lands; they could thus be passed from one ruler to another. In 1760 the new king, George III, chose to exchange the income generated by the Crown Estate to support the monarchy for a fixed annual payment from the government; revenue from the Crown Estate was then assigned to the public funds (Answers website). Thereafter, the special commission that managed Crown properties rented out the farmlands to generate public income.

In 1749, about thirty families lived on Ballykilcline's six hundred or so acres, according to a census of the sprawling diocese of Elphin taken by the local Protestant bishop (Synge Census).[4] The inhabitants farmed small plots, and worked the land cooperatively under multiple joint tenancies, or *rundale*, with their neighbors in an arrangement called a *clachan*, where farmers grew potatoes on small plots of ground assigned from community lands. The bishop's head count opened a window on Ballykilcline in the middle of the eighteenth century and showed that the townland was home to 121 people, while Kilglass civil parish had some two thousand residents. The largest family groups in Ballykilcline were O'Beirnes, a sept whose ancient territory was at Jamestown, a few miles to the north, and McGuires, who had removed from County Fermanagh, to the northeast. There were twenty-six people named O'Beirne (or variants of that name) in six households, and twenty-two McGuires (Maguires) in four homes, constituting altogether 40 percent of the townland's population.[5] Most of the Ballykilcline men were listed as tenant or cottier, which meant that they were either farmers of record with small leaseholds or laborers whose pay came in the form of a patch of land instead of wages, for which they worked a specified time period. The residents included a tailor and a smith, a herder and a cart man. The census of the parish showed at least seventeen Kilglass men whose occupation was beggar, but none of these individuals lived in Ballykilcline. An equal number of weavers lived in the parish but, again, none resided in the townland. Nor did any widows live there, though there were at least fifty in the parish; however, several men with children at home apparently had no wife and mother present in their households. Over the next century a number of the surnames in the townland disappeared, attesting to some churning of the population (Synge Census).

From the 1600s, the Mahons of nearby Strokestown had been among the most important local property owners. In 1845, when Denis Mahon inherited the 11,000-acre property in fertile mid-Roscommon, the estate was one of the county's largest. The Mahons, like so many others over the years, had received their land in return for aid to England's king. The Mahons came from princes of Munster, by family accounts. Nicholas Mahon, who was a sheriff in Roscommon in the middle 1600s, after Cromwell, settled at Strokestown (P. Duffy 2007, pp. 5, 52). He was rewarded after Cromwell's victories with property that formerly had belonged to

O'Connor Roe, a descendant of an Irish high king, and over time the Mahons expanded their estate. In 1750 they rebuilt the Big House (Vesey 2002, p. 2). Maurice Mahon was given a peerage about 1800 as Lord Hartland (Lavin 2003, pp. 147, 149), a title that ended when his grand-son Maurice died childless in the 1840s (O'Flanagan 1931, p. 69). The first Lord Hartland borrowed money after 1800 to enlarge his estate, and when he died, the property had debts of 15,000 pounds, which grew 50 percent under his successor (Vesey 2002, p. 2). In politics, the family ex-pressed concern about Catholic interests. Stephen Mahon, for instance, who was elected to Parliament in 1806, voted repeatedly over the years for Catholic relief bills, in opposition to high officials. The first Lord Hart-land ran his own property. Until about 1820, the estate was managed lo-cally; after that date, the Mahons brought in overseers from elsewhere to supervise the property (Hood 1994, pp. 198, 170).

Denis Mahon, born in 1787, was the son of Rev. Thomas Mahon, who for a time was Church of Ireland rector at Annaduff in County Leitrim, which is adjacent to Roscommon on the northeast. Denis's brother was the rector and vicar at Newport in County Mayo for sixteen years before his death in 1825 (Newport Historical Society website). But Denis took a different path as a military man, gaining the title of major with the Lanc-ers. He married Henrietta Bathhurst and his only child, a daughter, was named Grace Catherine. Her marriage in 1847 to Henry Sandford Pak-enham, the dean of St. Patrick's Cathedral in Dublin, linked the Mahons to the prominent Duke of Wellington. But until 1845 when he inherited the Mahon estate, Denis Mahon was a tenant in Farnbeg who, like so many others, carried an arrearage (Scally 1995, pp. 44, 45).

In the 1790s, the Mahons leased Ballykilcline for forty years from a middleman who leased it from the Crown. In 1834, Maurice Mahon sur-rendered the lapsing lease, owing to his financial burdens. After Denis brought an action which led in 1836 to an official declaration that his Un-cle Maurice was a "lunatic," Denis contended for the estate with a cousin in Galway. The Chancery Courts and the Commissioners of Woods and For-ests supervised the property between the time Maurice lost it and Denis gained it; Denis had been named executor in the interim and the guard-ian of Maurice (Vesey 2002, p. 22). Nevertheless, the estate's affairs were thoroughly confused for the inheriting major in 1845, when its debts had risen to 30,000 pounds, largely in support of other Mahon family mem-bers and earlier generations' decisions (Scally 1995, p. 45; Vesey 2002, p. 11). The transfer of Ballykilcline from the Mahons back to Crown con-trol in 1834 seemingly had obscured the leaseholds of the approximately five hundred farmers who then worked the land and opened the possibility, or provided a rationale, for the rent strike (Scally 1995, pp. 24, 25). By 1845, that strike had its imitators, including some of Mahon's nearby tenants, whose withholding of rents was taking its toll on the estate's revenues and operation.

As Vesey pointed out, Denis Mahon had no other income and thus focused on increasing his rent revenue in a policy recommended by his land agent, which gradually hardened as he turned to evictions and forced emigration as his course. "We are not doing any tyrannical or cruel act," Mahon declared. "If we allow those persons to escape paying their rent now, we shall find it impossible to get hereafter." Observed Vesey, "His estate was everything to him. Its possession conferred on him a leading position in the society of his day" (Vesey 2002, pp. 14, 18, 19, 82).

Beginning of the Rent Strike

As Ballykilcline changed hands from the Mahons to the Crown, the inhabitants' rent strike against the Crown and its agents began slowly when, in 1835, eight farmers did not pay their rents, which ranged for all tenants of record from one to twenty-two pounds annually.[6] In starting their strike, it is possible that the tenants were taking a cue from other disaffected tenants who, during the previous spring at nearby Gillstown and Ashbrook, had created disturbances and called for group action against landlords (Lombard and Mullaney 1999, April 19, 1834). Or perhaps they adopted the action from the antitithe battles waged during the 1830s, when numbers of the Irish withheld their rents rather than pay to support the Church of England.

Refusal to pay rent was one tactic used in western Roscommon during the 1830s antitithe war, but certainly there had been earlier strikes—called combinations then—in Roscommon, when people protested work conditions and price increases for the needs of daily life. In June 1823, for instance, at a road construction site near Strokestown, workers objected to a fixed-fee payment schedule for their job. In protest, they destroyed a ditch at the building site, and a local observer remarked, "A combination exists amongst the workmen . . . that employment might be afforded the longer to the laboring classes." The workers apparently wanted to be paid for their *time* on the job, not merely for completion of the job itself. In Roscommon town and Athlone there had been industrial actions at several mills. When disturbances broke out in England in 1830—the so-called Captain Swing riots—over the transformation of social and economic relationships between the social classes across the rural countryside to ones based on market factors, the *Roscommon Journal* gave those actions substantial coverage in its pages. The newspaper also expended ink on the Birmingham trials of Chartist radicals in 1839. Chartism, founded in 1838, was a workers' movement for various reforms, including universal suffrage and a secret ballot (Connolly 1998, p. 85). Irish seasonal migrants, or spalpeens, who returned from British harvests, according to testimony given to a government committee in 1831, had seen the English "swear to be true to each other, and join to keep the people upon their ground" (Huggins 2000, pp. 32, 34).

"Keeping people upon their ground" by securing lower rent charges was the motivation for action in Ballykilcline (Coleman 1999, p. 33). However slowly the Ballykilcline strike took shape, by 1836 it had spread: seventeen farmers paid no rent that season (Commissioners of Woods and Forests, pp. 10–13). Years followed in which virtually the entire population of the townland withheld their rent payments; numbers of householders and their families were evicted but then quietly reclaimed their homes; a government survey of the land market tended to substantiate the tenants' complaints about high rents (Commissioners of Woods and Forests, p. 60); and the Crown appointed an unsympathetic agent named George Knox, who was familiar with local people and practices, to handle relations with the farmers of Ballykilcline—the Crown's middleman (Scally 1995, p. 60).

Evictions

A group of fourteen farmers became the visible front of the strikers, and they were dubbed the Defendants (at least by Scally).[7] Official actions against the strike most often targeted this group of leaders, and they were evicted repeatedly. The tenants eventually pooled their resources, each paying five shillings per acre per year, and hired lawyer Hugh O'Ferrall of nearby Ashbrook, who also had a Dublin office, to represent them. James Donnellan, the son of a Ballykilcline family, was a steward for O'Ferrall (O'Ferrall letter, Sept. 28, 1842; Scally 1995, p. 79). Early on, each time the townspeople were evicted, they simply retook their holdings, which inexplicably had been left standing, thereby interrupting the legal process of eviction. A county newspaper reported about one of these "most unheard of and novel proceedings" in July 1844 after authorities in midwinter sent a corps of military and police into the townland and dragged "the unfortunate inmates out of their wretched cabins . . . sending them wandering on the world." Several weeks later, when the tenants were found to have returned to their former homes, the officials conferred again and, using an "almost obsolete act," sought the empanelment of a jury to retake the properties and raze the tenants' cabins. They took the necessary legal steps, and the sheriff swore in "the first twenty-four gentlemen who answered" the call for jurors, but not before the tenants secured the services of counsel, Messrs. Blakeney and Harkan, and their agent, O'Ferrall. In lengthy remarks in court, Blakeney told the jurors that "unless the entry was violent that they could not find for the crown" or a dangerous precedent would be set. The Crown, he said, must proceed through the usual channels of the law. In the end, only three jurors sided with the Crown, and the people of Ballykilcline rejoiced at regaining rights to homes that had been "for generations occupied by them and their ancestors." The newspaper's headlines called the events "Extraordinary Proceedings" (*Roscommon Journal*, July 6, 1844). Meanwhile, the tenants paid no rent and acquired a reputation locally.

The authorities drew up a list of tenants in the late 1830s, or by 1840, which along with the list of evictees in 1847 and '48 allows a comparison of the town's population early in the rent strike and in the year that it ended—over nearly a decade. That it was a crucial decade of change becomes obvious in an analysis of the documents. Scally put the population of Ballykilcline at approximately five hundred people during the strike, including some unrecorded inhabitants who had no leases and fringe members of some households. The two tenant lists, though, identify more than six hundred individuals who made Ballykilcline their home at some time during those troubled years between 1835 and 1848. The overall number at any one time apparently remained fairly constant, but it appears that there was substantial mobility into and out of the townland: perhaps a dozen families moved in, and others moved away from Ballykilcline during the 1840s, since approximately two hundred people on the earlier list of tenants do not appear on the list of evictees.

Some who did not arrive in Ballykilcline until the 1840s were evicted in 1847 and 1848 along with earlier residents. They are easier to document than the people who were present in 1840 but who are not on the list of evictees. Voluntary emigration and famine deaths, of course, account for some significant but unknown number. Scally found little emigration by the residents before the evictions, but it is now established that some did leave Ballykilcline for America as early as 1834. John and Sabina Brennan Hanley and family and Daniel and Nancy Winters McGuire went to Vermont, some Nearys to Illinois, and Arthur Mullera to New York, all in the middle or late 1830s; John Downey was in Massachusetts by the mid-1840s. The famine deaths of nearly thirty residents have been documented: for example, those of Thomas McGann, Dominick and James Coyle, Margaret Mulligan, and five children of Patrick McGuire. And since at least thirty-eight people on the earlier list were described as at least sixty years of age, presumably a number of them had died by 1847 from famine, disease, or natural causes.

Some of the younger women in Ballykilcline must be camouflaged in the record through marriage name changes. And both males and females likely married out of Ballykilcline; the record identifies several who did so: John Fallon and Winifred and Mary Connor, for instance. Surely though, the opposite also was true and others from nearby townlands such as Knockhall and Legan married *into* Ballykilcline. It also is likely—though not clear—that the earlier list included many landless residents who were not given the emigration option in 1847 and '48 and must have moved elsewhere locally. Thomas Geelan was one resident having no legal claim in 1847, according to Scally (1995, p. 120), who said that at least fourteen others also fell in this distressed category. If by "others" Scally meant heads of households, then this group with their families might actually account for dozens of residents. Geelan and the ten members of his household, however, were not named on either list, although the earlier record identified two other families (Eleanor Fallon's and Patrick McCormick's) as mere "cabbiners" who presumably did not receive money to go to America. But how many others were, like Geelan, officially "invisible" in the government record?

Dozens of inhabitants may simply have moved elsewhere locally as a matter of choice, either after the evictions or earlier. Where, for instance, did the families of John Clements, Thomas Fitzmaurice, Ann Flower, and Michael Mulligan go? If they moved by choice, perhaps it was a personal response to the contentiousness of the rent strike or their perspective on how it would end. Were some families intimidated enough to leave by the collective action of their neighbors in the townland or the authorities' response to it? Clearly though, not everyone was so fearful about the strike's repercussions, since many people apparently moved to Ballykilcline in the 1840s. They included Michael Hoare's family of seven and Francis Fox's family of five, who joined Francis's brother Thomas. And though Owen Carolan apparently went elsewhere before 1847, John Carolan moved his wife and three daughters to Ballykilcline. Also notable was the number of young children who were not listed in their families' households about 1840 but were recorded as emigrating in 1847 and '48. Patrick and Eliza Cline Kelly had three children by 1840, but none documented on the earlier list. The opposite also was true: John Winters, then between nine and fifteen years old, lived with his family about 1840 but did not emigrate with them to Vermont, though he did show up there later. Perhaps the authorities were either sloppy or inefficient in compiling records; the officials' notes on the earlier list showed that they struggled to determine who lived in Ballykilcline—"made a mistake of eighteen in the whole tab" says a note at the end of the list. The two lists together attest to surprising mobility in the townland around a core group of long-term tenants of record who were named on both lists, bringing the total number of people identified as living in Ballykilcline at some time during the contentious strike years to approximately six hundred.

The turnover in population must surely have had implications for the conduct of the strike. It seems likely that those who objected to it may have left the townland as the strike progressed and that those who chose to move into a known situation in Ballykilcline more likely would have favored the strike. Such a realignment within the townland likely produced greater cohesion among the tenants there rather than less; it would have presaged a more united front against the authorities—at least until the famine hit with force.

After 1840 the Crown's agents got more serious about dealing with the recalcitrant strikers. The Defendants were evicted again, took back their homes once more, were charged with trespassing, and endured a trial. In a stunning verdict they prevailed against England's Crown: a jury found for the Defendants. Afterward, a Crown agent castigated the jurors in the case as "a Set of the lowest and most ignorant Men that would be impannelled [sic], and a Disgrace to any Court of Justice" (qtd. in Scally 1995, p. 98). But that jury's decision was short-lived: the Crown overturned it in 1846, as the famine worsened. By then, Lord Clarendon had succeeded Bessborough as Lord Lieutenant (the top British official) of Ireland; tenants elsewhere in Roscommon—including many who lived on Denis Mahon's property—had begun withholding rents in imitation of the strikers in Ballykilcline; and the government's worries about the exasperating situation mounted. Clarendon pressed for a resolution, and new negotiations with the tenants followed but failed when the Ballykilcline farmers, now thoroughly demoralized by the two-year-old famine and its accompanying fever and death as well as their plight on the land, and probably paralyzed with indecision, did not respond by the imposed deadline. The British prepared to evict them.

Ever mindful of its image with the local people, however, the government postponed any action throughout the winter. Finally, on May 26, 1847, dozens of police—some mounted—trooped into Ballykilcline, routed the

Defendants, and razed their homes. To rid the land of the troublemakers once and for all, officials had decided to evict all the tenants and send any to America who would go. Since evicted people died in great number on open ground (the previous winter had been notably severe), and local people frequently were barred from aiding them, most took the bounty to leave, even a number of them who petitioned unsuccessfully to stay. In September 1847 the first of seven batches of people from Ballykilcline was dispatched from Strokestown; they trekked to Dublin and crossed the Irish Sea to Liverpool, where they embarked for New York City. The evictions and emigrations continued through April 1848 and, in the official if imprecise count, sent about 368 people out of Ireland.[8]

The emigrants were counted at three places during their passage: when they left Strokestown, when they boarded ship in Liverpool, and when they landed in New York. The numbers in the official counts do not always match, reflecting much confusion in arrangements for the travel and the authorities' reliance on underlings for its planning and implementation. The imprecise numbers also may indicate, as Scally suggested, that the confusion was an advantage for the Irish: that is, it permitted an underground "conspiracy" by the people, a hidden "market" for paid tickets (Scally 1995, pp. 224, 225), which would allow those who wanted to stay to remain around Strokestown and those who wished to leave to go with family and friends under the names, initially at least, of tenants who had legitimately received the Crown's bounty for transportation. In other words, some of those who left may have assumed the identities of certain Ballykilcline tenants until they were safely at sea on the vast Atlantic, beyond the reach of British agents.

Such a scheme had operated among the Irish who went to Canada as part of Peter Robinson's government-assisted plan in the early 1820s: "Some of the chosen were selling their tickets. . . . Among those who changed their names and ages to match those on forged or purchased tickets, Thomas Shenick of Churchtown called himself John Regan, the name of the man from whom he had bought his ticket, and since Regan had no teenaged boy, Shenick's son William had to masquerade as a girl named Abigail. John and Catherine Grady of Mallow, who had seven children, sold their ticket to a family with the same name and same number of children." Robinson had made extra efforts to ensure that the people who boarded ship matched the ones he had selected. But the ship slots had become valuable commodities. Indeed, Robinson chose only 2,000 to leave Ireland out of about 50,000 who applied for his passages (D. Mackay 2002, pp. 86–88).

The idea that the government or landlords should assist the Irish to emigrate had been discussed since the 1820s, but it gained increasing attention as the famine worsened. "In January 1846, six hundred people, many of them landlords, attended a meeting in the Rotunda in Dublin to demand that assisted emigration schemes be implemented. . . . Tenants, too, demanded that emigration be provided and were prepared to try any source that would help them leave" (Moran 2004, p. 35). When England changed its Poor Law to make Irish owners pay the workhouse costs of their destitute tenants, landlords increasingly turned to eviction and emigration to escape the mounting expense.

Farewells were soon common in Strokestown. In May 1847, Denis Mahon's even larger assisted emigration started off from the town. Mahon, convinced by his estate agent that he needed to rid his lands of much of his tenantry in order to make a profit from the property, forced more than 3,000 people from their homes and "assisted" 981 of them to Quebec in places chartered aboard four ships: the *Naomi*, the *Virginius*, the *Erin's Queen*, and the *John Munn*. But theirs were cursed trips, which many of them did not survive; in fact, more than half of the Strokestown emigrants died in passage or on landing at the Canadian quarantine station at Grosse Ile in the dreadful summer of cholera there (Dunn 2002, pp. 116, 117; Charbonneau and Drolet-Dube 1997).[9] The Canadian government was appalled at the condition of Mahon's arriving former tenants. Grosse Ile Superintendent Dr. George Douglas reported:

> Fear and dysentery cases came on board this vessel [the *Virginius*, fully chartered by Denis Mahon for his evicted tenants] in Liverpool, and deaths occurred before leaving the Mersey. On mustering the passengers for inspection yesterday it was found that 106 were ill of fever, including nine of the crew, and the large number of 158 had died on the passage. . . . [T]he few that were able to come on deck were ghastly yellow looking specters, unshaven and hollow cheeked, and, without exception the worst looking passengers I have ever seen; not more than six or eight were really healthy and able to exert themselves. (Laxton 1996, p. 45)

Six or eight of 476 passengers: 268 of Mahon's former tenants on that ship died crossing the waters or at the quarantine station (Charbonneau and Drolet-Dube 1997, p. 108). Mahon's ships became notorious during that tragic season, and the Canadians protested angrily to the British. An inquiry targeting conditions on the ships from Ireland was held later, though not of those carrying the Strokestown tenants. And when Colonial Secretary Earl Gray joined a debate over a coercion bill for Ireland after Mahon's murder, he spoke up in the House of Lords for "Mahon's liberality" and never mentioned the deplorable condition of Mahon's tenants when they arrived in Quebec (Campbell 1990, p. 22).

Assassinations

It was in early November 1847 that landlord Denis Mahon was ambushed and shot dead as he rode home from Roscommon town with a local doctor named Shanley, after attending a meeting of the Poor Law guardians. Upon learning the news, the local people lit fires on the hills. Although no motive for Mahon's murder has ever been certainly established, many reasons are possible. One credible theory was that he was punished for the deaths of so many of his tenant-passengers to Quebec. Whatever the cause, his murder and the killing of Rev. John Lloyd of Aughrim, another Protestant landlord, only three weeks later and ten miles away, undermined the famine-frayed social order across the Roscommon countryside. Protestants fled or armed themselves. They sought stronger police protections and accused local Catholics of conspiracies against them. In the aftermath, Rev. Michael McDermott, the parish priest in Strokestown, became the target of the British aristocracy's and press's ire in the effort to assign blame for Mahon's assassination. The controversy escalated into an international furor that reached the pope at a time when Britain was making vigorous efforts to restore diplomatic relations with the Vatican so as to secure papal support for its governance of Ireland (Kerr 1994, p. 91).

Mahon was the first landowner gunned down, and his death shocked other property owners in a social landscape where crime had escalated and tenants, pressed hard by searing famine losses, had both openly and secretly fought the harsh conditions imposed on them. In November and December 1847, with owners receiving threatening letters, some landlords took their families and fled from the chaos in Roscommon. In the House of Commons, Henry Grattan linked the murder to the "disastrous [sic] condition of the people and the indifference of the landlords and maintained it was the catastrophic outcome of the Strokestown emigration which had caused the people to turn against Denis Mahon" (Campbell 1990, p. 25).

When Lord Clarendon then warned Prime Minister John Russell that he would resign his post in Ireland because of constraints on his ability to move against agitation, Parliament passed a Crime and Outrage Bill only weeks after Mahon's death. Russell initially had opposed coercive measures, telling Parliament, "It is quite true that landlords in England would not like to be shot like hares and partridges. But neither does any landlord in England turn out fifty persons at once, and burn their houses over their heads, giving them no provision for the future. The murders are atrocious, so are the ejectments" (Kerr 1994, p. 93). Russell also had newsman Alexander Somerville "state the case against Mahon to the cabinet." Yet although Russell resisted the crimes bill, it nonetheless passed easily (Gray 1999, pp. 183–187). Police and military troops flooded into Roscommon as authorities pursued the investigations of Mahon's and Lloyd's murders.

Such was the state of society in parts of Roscommon. In December, Lord Farnham, of the Orange Order, defended the reputation of the late Mahon in Parliament.[10] He accused Rev. Michael McDermott of having assailed the landlord during a mass, saying, "Major Mahon is worse than [Oliver] Cromwell and yet he lives" (Kerr 1994, pp. 92, 97).[11] The British press took up Farnham's charge, which fanned the sectarian conflict and turned British public opinion against the Irish, who were derided as having repaid England's famine generosity with murder (Andrews 2001, p. 145). Lord Palmerston, who had "expressed sympathy for the exemplary transportation [to the penal colony in Australia] or hanging of agitating priests" (Gray 1999, p. 182), instructed a British envoy in Rome to tell the pope that his priest had denounced Mahon, making "all the people in the neighborhood think the [assassination] deed a holy one" (Kerr 1994, p. 93). Said the *Times* (London) on November 14: "It is now the time to meet an evil more serious than famine or pestilence. A murderous organisation is to be broken and suppressed" (qtd. in Campbell 1990, p. 24). Some aristocrats alleged a Catholic conspiracy against property owners, and the *Times* described an angry pact among Protestants, who declared that any time a Protestant was killed, they would take the local parish priest's life (Kerr 1994, p. 93).

A British Catholic lord wrote to Archbishop John McHale of Tuam in the west of Ireland to ask whether priests commonly issued invectives that led to murder. In response to allegations that priests were inciting the people against landowners, McHale wrote to Russell in defense of the clergy, promising to suspend priests who were guilty of such an action. He declared that the "calumnies [were] a justification for their [England's] lack of help for the starving." He also castigated the English press (Andrews 2001, pp. 145, 146; Kerr 1994, p. 95). The powerful McHale had previously warned Clarendon that government relief for the Irish was inadequate and that the destitution of the people endangered "the peace and order of society" (Andrews, p. 144).

For his part, in a letter to the *Evening Freeman*, Father McDermott called the charges against him false, "a monstrous calumny." He described the awful scenes of eviction he had witnessed and said they "had more to do with the murder of Major Mahon than all the thundering denunciations the Vatican could effect" (qtd. in Campbell 1990, p. 28). No such aspersions against Mahon had occurred at Sunday mass, the priest declared in self-defense. McDermott was supported by his bishop and twenty-eight parishioners who stood ready to give sworn testimony. Thereafter, an anonymous letter appeared in the *Times*, signed only "an Irish Peer," which alleged that McDermott had lied and had spoken against Mahon instead at the All Saints' Day mass on the following Monday. Thus, the suggestion spread that Catholics were untruthful and deceitful (Kerr 1994, p. 94).

Catholic gentry in England angered their Irish counterparts by accepting the accusations and joining in the fray. Lord Shrewsbury, for one, vented his ire in a newspaper letter, where he catalogued the sins of the Irish, including famine deaths and "one great conspiracy against property." He demanded "some better reason than has yet been given . . . why Father McDermott should still be permitted to exercise his ministry" (qtd. in Kerr 1994, p. 96).

Historian Donal Kerr, who has written the most extensively on this incident, noted that although Mahon, two months before his death, had accused McDermott of misusing Relief Committee funds, "no ground existed for Palmerston's claim that his [the priest's] guilt was well established" in the alleged denunciation of Mahon. When trials were held for the men arrested in the landlord's death, McDermott's name was never even mentioned; moreover, trial evidence showed that the assassination had been "planned before the Sunday in question." Kerr argued that the anonymous letter to *The Times* by "an Irish Peer" may actually have been written by Lord Clarendon himself, since he had a "propensity to use the press anonymously." Kerr's argument rested in part on Clarendon's disclosure to Russell that his aide, Thomas Redington, had investigated the matter and "did not feel sure that the priest had denounced Major Mahon at all!" Although the charges against the priest and their repercussions shocked the Catholic hierarchy in Ireland, they stemmed in part from political maneuvering between clergy and aristocracy in the English Catholic church (Kerr 1994, pp. 97, 98, 101).

In Rome, meanwhile, a flurry of letters and visitors sought to win the ear of the pope on Irish matters as the bishops defended their own actions and explained their fear that the British were trying to gain control of the Irish church. One new Irish bishop believed that restoring British relations with the pope "would lead to a veto over Church appointments [and] . . . 'it will utterly derange all the existing affectionate relations of

Priests and People.'" Some of the bishops' letters revealed their deep distrust of government (Kerr 1994, p. 103). At one point, a cardinal's missive to Ireland's archbishops, which was leaked to the newspapers, quoted the pope as demanding answers to the reports that the clergy "approved of murders." Public reaction to the leak in Ireland was heated. Archbishop Michael Slattery responded to the cardinal at length; he "traced the source of all the trouble to one cause: the treacherous English government, being Protestant, wanted to gain control of the Catholic Church." His statement was followed within two months by a bitter one signed by seventeen Catholic bishops, a number of them moderates. Kerr called it the "clearest indication yet of the serious damage that the smear of connivance at assassination had done to relations between the bishops and the government. . . . [I]t was difficult to see how trust could be restored" (Kerr 1994, pp. 103, 107).

In February 1848, word came from the Sacred College of Propaganda in Rome that the Irish clergy should "abstain from political agitation." In effect, the order prohibited Irish priests from activities in the Young Ireland movement (Campbell 1990, p. 30), almost on the eve of the organization's ill-fated insurrection that year. Archbishop John McHale received a letter from Archbishop Paul Cullen about the same time: "I explained matters to the Pope and showed him how the priests were calumniated, and that oppression was the only source of the murders" (qtd. in Andrews 2001, p. 153).

The furor sparked by Mahon's actions and his murder, playing out in five countries (Ireland, England, Canada, the United States, and Italy), was testament to the desperation of British officials to gain and maintain control of the Irish situation and the tactics that they used to do so. It also reflected the raw situation on the ground across midlands Roscommon, and the vortex that whirled around the affairs of the small landholders in Kilglass and Strokestown.

Police tactics in the investigation of the Protestant Lloyd's death paralleled those in the Mahon case: the authorities employed informers, evictions, reward money, and support funds for witnesses in order to apprehend their suspects and ensure prosecution of them. Two "villains"—Patrick Hasty and Owen O'Beirne, one in each murder case—were hanged alongside each other in Roscommon town in August 1848 in a public display of British justice. Afterward, a relative of Mahon's suggested in a letter to the Strokestown landlord's son-in-law that authorities might not have prosecuted the real villains: "The *on dit* is (I know not how true) that . . . the jailor admitted a strange priest to [name illegible, presumably one of the chief witnesses] when dying from whom he wrung a declaration of the innocence of the parties he had charged" (Campbell 1990, p. 44). Some of the Irish who were arrested in the murder cases died of fever in jail, and others were transported to the colonies. The British had been sending "criminals" to Australia then for more than fifty years.

One other man who was involved also made it out of Ireland, according to Patrick Vesey, who traced his steps in police records: Andrew Connor, whose name was recorded as a conspirator in July 1848 when three other men were charged in the killing; trial testimony described his role in the conspiracy. Connor had a history: he lived with his brothers Martin and John in Mahon's Yard and led a gang of highway robbers; his name appeared frequently in the records of the Mahon estate. Vesey called him perhaps the top conspirator in Mahon's murder. According to police, Connor was "a wild and strong person in appearance, speaks mild and easy, is very shrewd and cunning, can read and write and [is] rather intelligent." In Vesey's account, Connor made good two escapes from pursuing authorities: first from Ireland and then from Canada. In the summer of 1849, after convictions of several other men and a year after Hasty's execution for Mahon's murder, the Lord Lieutenant of Ireland received a letter from a John Kearney, who claimed to have met Connor in Port Robinson, Montreal, Canada, where he was passing as a soldier who had deserted; Connor lived there with his brothers who were said to be laborers on the construction of the Welland Canal. But police did not act quickly enough, and Andy Connor left some six weeks before the authorities were ready to apprehend him, though his brothers remained longer in Canada. The Canadian police chief wrote that Connor was "supposed to be somewhere in the neighbourhood of New York" (Wheeler letter, Aug. 10, 1849). British authorities never caught up with him (Vesey 2002, pp. 48–50).

An echo of that version of the crime has turned up in Australian records in the case of transported prisoner John Murray, formerly of Graffogue in Kilglass Parish. Murray and several others had been sent to New South Wales after standing trial in Longford on February 23, 1847, for assaulting John Connor at a country fair. Denis Mahon had submitted a character reference to the court for Murray. And in November 1848, John Ross Mahon, Denis's land agent and probably his cousin, intervened seeking clemency and a reversal of Murray's transportation order: "I have enquired particularly as to the character John Murry for which I find was very good—his father Peter Murry I know, he is a very proper man & was useful in assisting the bailiffs of the late Major Mahon when engaged during ejectments in the neighbourhood where he lives, which was an exceedingly disturbed one principally owing to the Connors one of whom was, I am informed, the chief witness against John Murry—the Connors fled from this country to America in consequence of being concerned in the murder of Major Mahon as appeared on the trial of Hasty, who was convicted for the murder" (Zada communication; Convict Reference File, NAI).

As the police investigation and trials in Roscommon played out, another Mahon relative advised the late landlord's daughter and son-in-law to forget about their property in Roscommon for years, since it would take that long for the district to recover from the social chaos and upheaval (Campbell 1994, p. 51). Yet convulsive as they were, those were not the only furies visited on Kilglass Parish and Strokestown at that time.

THE FAMINE IN KILGLASS

The forced exodus of so many local people in such a short time and the murders of the two landlords took place against the awful backdrop of the famine, which ravaged Kilglass and much of Roscommon. From September 1845 the people faced the loss year after desperate year of their primary foodstuff, the potato, which was the victim of an intractable and unfamiliar fungus—the blight. Government aid for the catastrophe was irregular, ineffectual, and chaotic; many official policies actually caused greater harm; and local authorities' actions were inadequate to the catastrophe. Work was scarce; food was hard to find, high-priced, or rationed; clothing was insufficient or unavailable; animals dined on the bodies of the dead. The workhouses bulged with inmates. Families were broken up; members were lost, separated, or sometimes abandoned. And disease claimed whole households. Some townlands in Kilglass Parish lost more than 60 percent of their people to death and emigration between 1841 and 1851. Indeed, land agent Joseph Kincaid reckoned the population of Kilglass in mid-1847 at 5,753 people, a little more than half what it had been in 1841 (Kincaid testimony, June 21, 1847). County Roscommon lost 80,000 people in that decade.

Witnesses told about the famine's horrors in Kilglass. In July 1847, two months after the evictions began in Ballykilcline, Rev. Henry Brennan, the parish priest, wrote to the *Freeman's Journal* in search of help for the people, eight hundred of whom were stricken then with fever: "Fever has made its way into almost every house. The poor creatures are wasting away and dying of want. In very many instances the dead bodies are thrown in waste cabins and dykes and are devoured by dogs. In some parts the fields are bleached with the bones of the dead that were previously picked by dogs. There is not in Ireland any parish where fever and destitution prevail to so fearful an extent as here" (qtd. in Killen 1995, p. 148).

In a letter to a local newspaper, Father Brennan lamented,

> Oh! It is not easy to behold the scenes of misery and woe it is our fate to witness during our visits to the sick. Many of them are mere skeletons—half alive, half dead. Turn where we will, we are certain to meet the fruits of the ravages made by the destroying angel—misery—destitution—famine—fever—dysentery—yellow jaundice—dropsy—pestilence—the deaths increasing every week to an alarming amount !! —the dead very frequently buried without coffins!!! . . . The two thousand three hundred employed by the Board of Works are not able to support the tenth part of the population. (*Roscommon & Leitrim Gazette*, Feb. 27, 1847)

The priest's view of the state of Kilglass was echoed by Kincaid, who as land agent managed property in many counties and knew the state of the countryside generally. He testified before a Parliamentary committee that "the People [of Kilglass] were extremely distressed; Numbers were dying. There have been more Deaths in this Parish than in any other with which I am acquainted, from actual Want I believe, and from Disease consequent upon it. The People were in that State of Destitution that they entreated to have a few Pounds to take them away anywhere" Kincaid said that he had visited Ballykilcline only weeks before giving his testimony in June 1847.

A Dr. Shanley, who had accompanied Denis Mahon on the trip to Roscommon the evening he was shot and who was the doctor at Strokestown's temporary fever hospital, gave the Central Board of Health a picture of Strokestown several weeks after Mahon's murder:

> I beg leave to state, for your information, that disease and mortality consequent on privation and neglect are frightfully on the increase in this district, and if funds are not forthwith available even for the decent burial of the dead the consequence to the surviving portion of the population must be truly alarming. As many as five in and within half a mile of this town have fallen victims to disease within the last few days, without any covering to protect their remains from public observation, save a few boards widely nailed together. A charitable donation of ten [pounds] was some time since given by the chairman of the Board of Guardians of the Union, drawn in favour of Major Mahon, but in consequence of his sudden and barbarous assassination was forthwith returned. Almost all of the resident gentry have left this neighbourhood, and the remaining few, from the number of [Molly] Maguireite notices they are in the daily habit of receiving, are afraid to leave their own homes, or take a part

in public business. All aid from English and other charitable societies is withdrawn, on the plea that they would "no longer continue support to murderers."

This doctrine, if universally acted on, I make no doubt will have the effect of quartering at least the well disposed of the lower orders, while the assassins can walk abroad with the most perfect impunity, shooting and getting rid of the wealth and intelligence of the land, that they may have the country to themselves, which is avowedly their object. (Shanley letter, Dec. 8, 1847)

Oral tradition as well preserved accounts of the devastation. Mrs. Peter Reynolds, born in 1871 in Kilglass, recalled being told that "there was one whole family died of hunger in Ballykilcline and they were dead a whole week before they were found. The men that entered the house got weak and sick and had to be given whiskey" (qtd. in Porteir 1995, p. 86).[12]

In January 1848 the Vice Guardians reported to the Poor Law Commissioners about how matters stood in the Roscommon poorhouse when they took responsibility for it:

We found 1072 paupers in the house and temporary fever hospital, of whom 188 were in fever, forty-two in dysentery, and eighty-one labouring under other diseases. . . . Upwards of a hundred were in the convalescent wards, confined to their beds for want of wearing apparel; thus retarding their own recovery, and interfering with the order and cleanliness of the establishment. . . . The new fever hospital had not been occupied, and was very deficient in accommodation, having no supply of water, no sewers, no water-closets or necessaries, no beds, bedding or other requisites, and no boundary wall enclosing it or the poorhouse. (Vice Guardians' letter, Jan. 12, 1848)

In that season of despair when the Ballykilcline people left home 720,000 people in Ireland labored on the public works for their daily bread; three million received daily rations in the soup kitchens alone, and more were fed by private charities (Ó Tuathaigh 1972, pp. 214, 215). The famine broke the Ballykilcline strikers' unity. Facing such overwhelming and straitening circumstances, it is not difficult to understand why the tenants there may have altered their position and left their cherished land for paid passage out of Ireland and life itself.

2

Shifting Ground in Roscommon

❦

> The conflicts and changes of 1828 to 1834 marked British politics for
> generations. . . . [They] cemented in place a claim-making repertoire
> of meetings, marches, petition drives, electoral campaigns, social move-
> ments, associations, firm-by-firm strikes, and related forms of action.
>
> —Charles Tilly, *Popular Contention*

> The following amendment is to be proposed by Mr. O'Connell, on the next
> stage of the Irish Coercion bill:—"That a select committee be appointed to
> inquire into the causes which have produced outrage and murders in cer-
> tain districts in Ireland; and especially to ascertain to what extent agrar-
> ian disturbances may be traced to the practice of depopulating estates,
> and to 'other circumstances connected with the existing relations between
> landlord and tenant in that country'; in order that such crimes may be
> prevented by the removal of their causes, and specially by the enactment of
> just and salutary laws relative to the tenure and occupation of land."
>
> —*Roscommon and Leitrim Gazette*, May 2, 1846

No UNDERSTANDING of the rent strike in Ballykilcline is possible without knowing the ground on which it happened: the history preceding
the strike of both the Irish people generally and the residents of Kilglass
Parish in particular.

By the 1830s, when the rent strike began, the Irish had opposed the
British in Ireland for centuries. A major battle in the Williamite War took
place at the River Boyne in 1690 when the Protestant William of Orange
defeated the Catholic King James II for the Crown of England, an outcome with enormous repercussions for Ireland. Soon after, the English
seized Ballykilcline, which was only a mile or two west of the Shannon
River. A bridge over the Shannon waterway at Ruskey in Kilglass Parish
links Roscommon with Counties Leitrim and Longford. Roscommon has
been called the heart of Ireland, and geographically it is that—a land-
locked county in the middle of the country, in the province of Connacht,
which nevertheless has miles of shoreline on the rivers and lakes that lace

its countryside. Central Roscommon is a broad fertile plain, but a ridge of low mountains, Slieve Bawn ("white mountain"), cuts through the barony of Ballintobber North and the parish of Kilglass. In antiquity, this territory was peopled by the Firbolgians, a dark-haired tribe short in stature. Robert Kee called them the true Irish race (Kee 1972, p. 9).

Ballykilcline was and is part of Kilglass civil parish, which hugs the Shannon River several miles northeast of the market center at Strokestown. After taking Ballykilcline, the Crown then leased out the property. A century later, in 1793, the townland was sublet to the Mahons for forty-one years, which ended in 1834 (Scally 1995, p. 25).

The name Ballykilcline means, loosely, the place of the church of Cline, and indeed Clines lived there even in famine time; they too—the family of Patrick and Eliza Cline Kelly—were evicted from the land by Crown authorities. Kilglass means "green church" in Gaelic, and the local Catholic history dates to St. Patrick's travels in the vicinity about 400 A.D., when he Catholicized the Irish people. References to a Catholic church in Kilglass can be found in twelfth-century church records (Coyle 1994, p. 17). The tenants' embrace of Catholicism is an important factor in their story, since it separated them in Ireland from their rulers and later in Rutland, Vermont, from the Yankee elite; in consequence, it forged a powerful sense of social, political, and cultural identity among the Irish.

After the Boyne battle, in 1703, the English imposed the Penal Laws to keep Irish Catholics in economic and political bondage. Informers who told on lawbreaking Catholics were rewarded. The laws forbade Catholics to buy land or to lease it for longer than thirty-one years. When a Catholic died, his land had to be divided equally among all his heirs, guaranteeing that their holdings grew steadily smaller. Catholics could not vote or hold office. They could neither enter the professions nor serve in the military. They were barred from education (a restriction that produced the clandestine "hedge" schools). Catholics could not carry a sword or own a gun or a horse of any value. They could not engage in some kinds of commerce and had to pay special fees to trade in towns. Their bishops were banished; priests had to register and were barred from keeping church registers (Connolly 1998, pp. 438, 439; Gilder Lehrman website).[1] In 1703, Catholics owned less than a quarter of Roscommon. A year later, only one Catholic in the county had a license to bear arms, and only forty-nine Catholic clergy had registered with authorities (Duffy et al. 1997, p. 77).

Britain's laws weighed onerously on traditional Catholic society, grinding the native people down and binding them to the poorest boggy lands in Ireland. In the early 1700s the people of Kilglass practiced their religion in secret, flocking to the hills of Legan, which was adjacent to Ballykilcline, to hear Mass offered by an outlawed priest using a rock as an altar and with sentries posted nearby. The repressive laws remained in place for generations, though enforcement of them lessened in the later 1700s.

British law in other areas as well followed British rule to Ireland, subverting the traditional ways of life. Into the 1600s, Peter Ellis pointed out, "the soil had been collective property of the . . . clans," and the Irish followed "common rules" for farming. "Property that has only rights and no duties is absolutely beyond the ken of the Irishman. . . . [A] society consistently seeking personal property in order to raise their status [was] a social system totally alien to the Celtic one, and totally contrary to Celtic law of land ownership." Officials were elected, and the traditional Brehon law of the Irish did not support primogeniture, by which the oldest child inherited the family's estate. A female could be chosen as chief, lead in battle, retain what she brought to a marriage, and pass down a chieftainship. The clan cared for the ill, the weak, and the disabled (P. B. Ellis 1972, pp. 11–22). Many such traditions were abolished under the English. In the 1500s, for instance, justices of the peace were given the task of regulating wages. It is uncertain exactly when journeymen began to form combinations against their masters, but their existence was officially acknowledged in 1729 by an act, the first of many, that punished with imprisonment workmen guilty of combining (i.e., striking) to secure higher wages or fewer work hours (Boyle 1988, p. 1).

The Irish Parliament restricted laboring people who organized to alter the conditions of work and in 1743 forbade even their efforts to relieve unemployment. An act in 1757 ordered hard labor and a whipping for those who gave or took oaths or for interfering with those who had agreed to work for a given price. "Proof of combination could be of the slenderest nature; a 1780 act provided that a workman leaving his master before the end of the agreed term, being absent for three days or returning work unfinished without his master's consent, constituted evidence sufficient to convict. Certain acts of violence attracted the death penalty" (Boyle 1988, p. 9).

Such terms of life and work oppressed the restive Irish to such a degree that by the middle 1700s their opposition surfaced in visible ways when they adopted offensive tactics to protest and press for change, capitalizing on their numbers and, at times, secrecy. Despite the laws governing work, they continued to form unions and initiate combinations.

The Irish organized socially as Freemasons; a lodge was established in 1759 in Strokestown, and about two hundred men joined over the next ninety years, some of them, their names suggested, from Ballykilcline (Freemasons lodge). Kevin Whelan has contended that the lodges became "cover" for the political dissent that burst on the public scene in the 1790s (1996, pp. 85–88). Beginning in the 1760s, the secret societies that were to gain influence across the Irish landscape for generations were organized and acting out a primitive form of guerilla warfare that sought improvements in living and economic conditions and the "people's justice" in land and other situations deemed unfair. Soon, in various guises, Catholic groups pressed increasingly for political power.

By the later 1700s, combinations were not infrequent in Ireland, and they increased in the 1790s. In 1792 alone, strikes occurred in a half-dozen trades (Boyle 1988, p. 10). Unionists often were accused of undue violence, and it was said that combinations harmed Irish industry. To that charge, John Boyle said, "The evidence shows that they [the workers] were engaged in a defensive situation, vainly trying to protect their standard of living" in a harsh economy (1988, pp. 15, 16). Most combinations occurred in the few urban centers where unionized jobs existed; unionists found it hard to organize elsewhere because of the wide geographic dispersal of workers across the mostly rural countryside. By 1824, though, the carpenters' society had "extended its influence over the whole island," and about that time a society of saddlers in Dublin, facing questions, turned the tables and accused their employers of combination after a lockout over wages (Boyle 1988, pp. 12, 13). That year and the next, in landmark legislation, British authorities repealed the Combination Acts of 1799 and 1800: "Trade unionism and strikes were no longer offences as such" (Thompson 1966, p. 517). By the mid-1830s, four unions in Ireland had regional scope, and a "shoemakers' representative . . . declared that Irish journeymen were in communication with no fewer than thirty-nine different trades extending throughout Great Britain, France, and Germany" (Boyle 1988, pp. 30, 31).

THE RISE OF SECRET SOCIETIES

The secret societies arose in rural areas initially to threaten evicting landlords. A pamphlet in 1760 rebuked landlords who enclosed common lands (P. B. Ellis 1972, p. 59), as had happened earlier in England, which had witnessed massive assaults in many forms on the common rights on which poor people relied for a living (Neeson 1993). The secret societies were perhaps the earliest and crudest form of modern organization of the native Irish people, the predecessor of more formalized and structured groups that aimed at social, economic, and political goals. The societies existed for decades in a number of forms, under many names, and with various targets, motives, and characteristics; they employed secrecy, oaths, passwords, anonymous threats posted in public places, and various rituals of action such as dressing in costume and moving at night. In general, their goal was to preserve and uphold traditional Gaelic order and custom, protect access to land and a subsistence living, and mete out justice on behalf of the native Irish—their actions focused "on all aspects of economic life in order to ensure the satisfaction of subsistence needs"—though their efforts involved intimidation, threats, and violence. Even before the 1840s famine, in trying to curb the costs of land, provisions, and tithes to the Church of England, the societies showed "a consciousness that was able to make general conclusions about the need for working people to pursue collectively held interests, and it identified the enemies of those working people precisely as the landlord and employers" (Huggins 2000, pp. 7, 28).

Multiple examples point to their purpose as the preservation of basic needs. In May 1758, for instance, at Jamestown in County Leitrim, just north of Roscommon's Kilglass Parish, a mob "had been in motion all the day; but their business was only with the forestallers of the market, who had bought up all the corn far and wide, to starve the poor, and load a Dutch ship, which lay at the quay; but the mob brought it all out into the market, and sold it *for the owners for the common price*. And thus they did with all the calmness and composure imaginable, and *without striking or hurting anyone* [emphases added]." Looters sometimes aimed solely at "enforcing a just price" (Boyle 1988, p. 18).

In some places, the societies were called Whiteboys, Carders, Rockites, and Threshers; in Roscommon, by the 1840s, they mostly were called Molly Maguires (or Mollies) and Ribbonmen. Elsewhere, at least two societies in the 1770s, the Hearts of Steel and Oakboys, were counterpart organizations of Protestants, "remarkable proof," Ellis said, "that the struggle . . . was rapidly changing to a class war between landlord and tenant" (P. B. Ellis 1972, p. 62).

Scholars generally have agreed that the societies were linked somehow with the faction fighters of the late 1700s and early 1800s. From 1790 on, class conflicts multiplied between the peasants and the graziers and large farmers, and the secret societies "all displayed a substantial degree of cohesion across social-class lines within the agrarian population." Historians point out that such movements gathered strength from and capitalized on other simultaneous threats to Protestant interests; that the societies were effective even without external assistance; that conflict frequently flared when land values rose as they did between 1750 and 1813; and that the 1793 antimilitia riots, which protested tax increases imposed to support the police force, were a turning point after which the peasantry and officialdom increasingly used greater violence against each other in such confrontations. The societies operated despite the opprobrium of the Catholic Church, which often threatened to excommunicate the midnight riders so as both to preserve social order and to build favor with the government (Clark and Donnelly 1983, pp. 421, 15–16, 31–35).

The Mollies and Ribbonmen were not the only people in Roscommon who took matters into their own hands. Roderick O'Connor, of a family of ancient kings, did so as well with an attention-getting action aimed at restoring the lands of his dispossessed family. The O'Connors had lost their property through confiscation. In January 1786, Roderick sought to retake a 20,000-acre estate in Ballintobber from a family named Burke; in doing so, he had the help of some 2,000 local followers. His assertion of the O'Connor claim so startled British authorities and the local elites that O'Connor's brother and other Catholic gentlemen of Roscommon felt compelled to repudiate his action in order to placate the presiding powers and calm the political crisis he had engendered: "We also look upon all claims or pretenses of claims to any lands or estates, on account of their having been in former ages in the possession of our ancestors, if unsupported by the laws and statutes now in being of this realm, as unjust, and highly subversive of that good order and government which it is not only our duty but our intent to support" (qtd. in Whelan 1996, p. 36).

Roderick's action had touched off a furor that aroused even the Parliament and the Vatican, and Kevin Whelan pointed to the incident and the Catholics' response to it to illustrate the "insecurity" of the well-to-do Catholic middle class (1996, p. 36). Clearly though, the incident also demonstrated that land issues remained a flashpoint in Catholic Ireland, where so many displaced native people lived in poverty on estates that once had been owned by their ancestors.

Collective movements of the Irish grew and developed. At Strokestown in 1759 the Freemasons established a fraternal lodge, one of the earliest in the county, and welcomed Catholics and Protestants alike until the 1830s, when the Church began to frown on Masonry. The lodge met even before the easing of the Penal Laws, and its establishment nearly coincided with the formation of secret societies of many types. Whelan has linked the two, suggesting that the Freemasons were a cover for the political activities that eventually led to the Rising of 1798. "The United Irishmen also utilized pre-existing groupings as a necessary cover for political mobilization. . . . Freemasonry provided the substrate for much of this organized activity. . . . Freemasonry . . . became a precursor of the concept of citizenship, while also indicating proleptically the possibilities of constructing a new social order" (Whelan 1996, pp. 85, 86).

The decade of the 1790s was a time of portentous change in Ireland. Various Catholic groups extracted some concessions, such as the vote, from the political powers in Dublin. An organization seeking political change, the United Irishmen, sought to fuse in one powerful organization both Catholic and Protestant yearnings for change. The French Revolution and pamphleteering in northeastern Ireland and in Dublin stirred the souls of Catholics and others with Thomas Paine's revolutionary ideas about the rights of man. John Boyle argued that after 1794 "a growing proportion of the rank-and-file membership and sympathizers [of the United Irishmen] belonged to the 'lower orders'—urban workers and peasantry" (1988, p. 21).

A secret society called the Defenders, "politicized by the United Irishmen," were active in Roscommon about 1795, according to Anne Coleman. The government's agent, Lord Carhampton, illegally transported without trial as many as a thousand men for service in the Queen's navy. Responding to protests over his actions, the Queen's men pointed to the presence of United Irishmen in Roscommon and the fear of an invasion from France. Then a prominent United Irishman and Defender was arrested during a Roscommon jail visit with friends, and a Strokestown man labeled Catholic country schoolmasters locally as "Defendermakers in this county" (Coleman, 1999, pp. 14, 15). Disturbances occurred in 1795 when a band of 3,600 Defenders encountered a government militia force on Drumsna bridge in Leitrim, near Kilglass, and men from the parish participated. Several Defenders who were captured on the bridge were later tried and executed in Roscommon (Jones 2003, p. 2). In the battle, some Defenders were killed, and more were injured, as were several militiamen (Michael McTeirnan's website). The series of antimilitia disturbances took two hundred lives. Afterward, clashes turned ever more violent as "the legacy of that decade was weighty indeed" (Clark and Donnelly 1983, p. 35). For years, the government was successful at quelling Defender unrest, but it later re-formed as Ribbonism (Coleman 1999, pp. 14, 15).

When Wolfe Tone and Edward Fitzgerald ignited the Rising of '98, some Kilglass people were involved at least peripherally; although details of their roles are not well documented, "in Kilglass, a rebellion also took place, and many set out in arms to defend their country. In Kilglass Graveyard . . . is an old headstone to the McGuires of Ballyfeeney, which

records brothers' deaths in 1798 at the Battle of Ballinamuck. Roger Farrell returning from the Battle . . . came cross country using the hills as a
guide. He swam the Shannon at Tarmonbarry, and cut across to Cuilbeg.
He was weak with exhaustion and wounded from battle and . . . he lay
down and died." Coyle also pointed to the 1889 obituary of Thomas Colligan, age 102, which gave his "memories of viewing the incidents of the
1798 Rising in Kilglass, when he was just a boy of twelve years" (Coyle
1994, pp. 34, 74).

An estimated 30,000 people died in the 1798 Rising, and after the British put it down and reasserted their authority, officials adopted punitive
measures and transported many Irish participants to Australia. Others
escaped to America. By the Act of Union in 1800, the British eliminated
the Parliament in Dublin, and Irish affairs from then on were handled
as part of England's. The loss of their own parliament rankled the Irish
both symbolically and economically, and its restoration became a battle
cry for decades to come, a cause pushed vigorously by Daniel O'Connell,
the political giant of the new century.

The increasing commercialization of the late 1700s and Britain's re-
laxation of the Penal Laws meant that some native Catholics were able to
move toward greater economic security. Around Strokestown, economic
well-being was facilitated by the extension of the Royal Canal from Dublin to the River Shannon at Tarmonbarry. Further progress came after
1793, when the Irish who held a forty-shilling freehold were allowed to
vote, though not hold office. A freeholders' list for Kilglass in 1796 shows
thirty-nine local men whose holdings were sufficient to enfranchise them,
but none of them held property in Ballykilcline (Kilglass Parish Freeholders List). In 1793 the Mahons stepped between the Crown and the Ballykilcline farmers by becoming the middleman holders of the Ballykilcline
estate, with a lease lasting for forty-one years. Thereafter, the tenants
worked their lands under the Mahons and trudged to the Strokestown
manor house on rent day.

Local farmers who needed to augment their resources also took advantage of a government scheme to reward those who sowed flax for the
linen industry of the northeast and thereby helped lessen the need to
import the material. By doing so, a farmer could obtain a spinning wheel
or other utensils (Irish Ancestors website); a number of Kilglass people
grew flax for the bounty. But that option disappeared a generation or so
later. Joel Mokyr argued that the collapse of the cottage textile industry,
in "rapid decay after 1825," was the most serious prefamine blow to the
small farmers' income (1983, p. 281).

STROKESTOWN IN THE EARLY 1800S

While commercialized Ulster and the southeastern farming areas of Wicklow and Wexford did well in the early 1800s, one eyewitness account of the landscape around Strokestown in 1809 indicated that prosperity kept its distance from that part of Roscommon. An English traveler named Edward Wakefield wrote about what he saw on the Mahon estate:

> I crossed it from Strokestown going towards Longford, and found everywhere cabins of the most wretched aspect, infamous stone roads, very minute divisions of land, and what usually follows it, a superabundant but miserable population. . . . I could not help calling to mind an expression of a writer whose opinion on agricultural subjects ought to have great weight, "Go to districts where the properties are minutely divided, and you will find . . . universally great distress, and even misery and probably very bad agriculture."
>
> . . . I don't recollect to have travelled so many miles through any estate in Ireland which presented such a scene of desolation. . . . This is another [instance] of great mismanagement under a resident landlord. (Wakefield 1999).

Wakefield wrote with an English eye during harsh times around Strokestown when a vigilante group called the Threshers was active. Wage, tithe, and tax issues were singled out by Lord Hartland of the Mahon estate as the causes riling the people. The Threshers became "an organizational and social base for the poorest landless labourers, desperate to survive in the light of increasing prices and shortage of land." Hartland moved against the protests with his force of yeomanry (based in the town after 1796), and later the yeomanry who lived in the countryside were ordered for security's sake to store arms in Strokestown (Hood 1994, pp. 199, 196). In 1813 the bishop of nearby Elphin wrote to Dublin Castle, "Notices have been posted up in Strokestown desiring that no person should deal with any shopkeeper who is an Orangeman [i.e., a member of a Protestant organization] and the [T]hreshers have sworn all the people in this neighborhood not to work for Orangemen. . . . Three men (one of whom has nearly been put to death) were cruelly carded [i.e., their flesh was raked], for having bought some articles in Strokestown from Protestant merchants." Susan Hood found the people's anger directed at "the urban middle classes, including shopkeepers, publicans and merchants, some of whom were also Protestant" (1994, p. 197). Conceding that such protest aimed to protect natives' access to land and reasonably priced goods, she also observed a sectarian aspect to the hostilities which was fueled by failed relief efforts for Catholics and stalled moves for Catholic emancipation. Hood said that Strokestown was the site of meetings of the national Catholic Committee, which was first established in 1759 to pursue relief measures but which at this time was seeking Catholic emancipation under the leadership of O'Connell, who dominated the organization by 1808 and made emancipation his cause for years thereafter (Ranelagh 1983, pp. 87, 96, 97). "At the local level, tentative evidence suggests that Strokestown was a regular venue for meetings of the Catholic Committee outside Dublin between 1806 and the early 1820s. Miscellaneous items of correspondence from one Luke Taffe to Owen O'Connor at Belangare [in Roscommon], one of the primary forces behind the movement, reveal that several important resolutions concerning the committee were made either at Strokestown or Roscommon during this period" (Hood 1994, p. 198).

Although the Protestant Mahons had supported Catholic relief bills "against the wishes of government" and other Anglos, the demographics of the local population produced friction and unrest, not only between groups but within them. "The suspected presence of members of the Orange Order in the estate town on the Mahon estate is interesting, demonstrating the polarization of local society along political lines, and, undoubtedly, the town became the focus of local divisions and tension. Strokestown was on the fringe of landlord-induced settlement; indeed west of it this form of settlement seemed to peter out, to be replaced by the more homogeneous and indigenous population beyond it. This explains perhaps why the town, occupied as it was by a number of Protestant families, became the focus of antagonisms from outside." On one especially fear-ridden night, all the Protestant women and girls were brought to the barracks in Strokestown for protection (Hood 1994, pp. 198, 201, 202).

The boycotts against Protestant merchants in Strokestown succeeded to some degree: several of the town's businessmen had moved elsewhere by 1818. A Dublin attorney and two Dublin merchants moved into the properties of two of the Protestants who left. Hood's account of the tensions around Strokestown during this period is valuable not only because it illuminates a period about which little is known but because she demonstrated that at least two properties of targeted merchants were re-let to businessmen from outside the local area, bringing more cosmopolitan forces into the town. Meetings of the Catholic Committee in Strokestown must have brought in sophisticated outsiders as well. Hood thus showed the organized nature of the campaign by Irish Catholics, both locally and nationally, to protect their own interests more than twenty years before the rent strike began in Ballykilcline. The local people were linked to national networks.

A turning point in the group relations around Strokestown, according to Hood, occurred in 1819 when the first Lord Hartland died. "The old paternal relationship which had existed between the [Mahon] family and the tenants, including the town tenants, was gradually replaced by a series of estate managers and receivers, brought in to run the estate against a background of worsening economic conditions and changing family circumstances" (Hood 1994, p. 170). The outside "managers and receivers" assuredly acted far more frequently for commercial reasons than out of any concern for the local people whose lives their decisions affected. Deference and reciprocal obligations disappeared in the social, economic, and sectarian competitions that strained the social fabric of town and townland. Into the breach came notions of disaffection from England: Michael Huggins reported that "in 1820 Wills wrote that English men and Scots had been among the people in Roscommon and 'talked a good deal about the distresses and grievances of the people,'" and "a Mayo magistrate reported 'that communication exists between the disturbers in England and those in this country . . . swearing in Ribbon Men at the Chapels after the Priest goes away'" (2000, pp. 16, 17).

Another turning point happened in 1815 when the end of Napoleon's European wars brought an economic depression; the widespread havoc it caused reached into rural Ireland. Rent arrearages grew in the early 1800s, and landlords began to give shorter leases, more responsive to current markets, or none at all—making many small farmers tenants-at-will who had to renew their leases yearly. Mokyr pointed out that short leases gave the landlord more frequent opportunities to adjust rents to account for market changes. Landlords also sought to "change the direction and the organization of Irish agriculture" from tillage to grazing (1983, pp. 83, 84). Irish exports (linen and agricultural products) declined in both volume and value between 1810 and 1820 (Duffy et al. 1997, p. 88). In 1821–22 a famine struck, and food shortages were widespread.

Compounding these troubles, the population multiplied rapidly: from 1750 to the middle 1840s, the population of Ireland quadrupled. This demographic pattern can be traced locally from 1749, when the Bishop of Elphin conducted the Synge Census, which counted 2,105 people in Kilglass. The parish's numbers rose more than fivefold during the next century— faster than those of the country as a whole—so that just before the Great Famine, in the early 1840s, the population numbered 11,391 (Coyle 1994, pp. 23, 36). By 1820 the country had nearly seven million people (Duffy et al. 1997, pp. 88, 89). Such numbers had consequences, especially in conjunction with the land conditions that prevailed in Roscommon.

THE LIBERATOR

If the times were hard, the Irish recognized one hope for the nation: Daniel O'Connell, nicknamed the Liberator. In a stunning move, he delivered Catholics from the last of the Penal Laws. His opening campaign tactic was the founding of the Catholic Association in 1823, which built a network across the country and enlisted the help of Catholic priests. "Although the removal of the catholic disabilities was a goal but imperfectly understood by the Irish peasant, emancipation was accepted as a kind of embodiment of victory over an ascendancy responsible in some way for all the grievances of the Irish countryside. . . . [H]ad O'Connell called upon [the Irish] to take arms at any time between 1826 and 1829 the majority would have done so" (Broeker 1970, p. 160).

The government watched O'Connell and the Catholic Association with foreboding during these years and strengthened its police forces and magistracy. But crime and disorder instead declined; even the "banditti"—the secret societies—ceased activity at a crucial point in deference to O'Connell's work. In an astounding victory in 1828, O'Connell won a seat in Parliament. Even though the law barred Catholics from serving there, authorities feared that blocking him from his seat would lead to revolution. In the end, the government blinked, and early in 1829 the king revised the laws on Catholics. "Lower-class Ireland under 'leadership of a higher order' had won" (Broeker 1970, pp. 160–188).

O'Connell became the first Irish Catholic Member of Parliament in a long time.

> In the face of vast movements pro and con in Ireland and Great Britain, Wellington and Peel finally (and quite reluctantly) engineered its [Emancipation's] passage. They attempted to limit political damage by dissolving O'Connell's Catholic Association, increasing the property requirements for suffrage in Ireland, and restricting activities of any future political associations on the island. Mobilization on behalf of religious rights subsided immediately. But the precedent stood: *government had made major concessions in response to a deliberately organized, associationally based social movement.* Almost immediately, reformers seized the precedent [emphasis added]. (Tilly 1995, p. 312)

It was O'Connell—the shrewd attorney, the orator who eschewed violence, the cunning strategist, the shaper of a democratic process for change—who worked tirelessly though unsuccessfully to repeal the Act of Union of 1800 in order to restore a Parliament in Dublin. He spearheaded collective action: he organized and controlled massive coalitions that very publicly supported native interests and served notice on the British, who eyed them warily. O'Connell created the "penny rent" by which Catholics supported him with their pittances, multiplied by hundreds of thousands. Each time his organization was outlawed, O'Connell formed another one under a new name and carried on only slightly differently but in conformance with the law.

In his last big campaign for repeal, O'Connell set off after Easter 1843 on a series of "monster meetings." There were forty of them; thirty-five drew more than 100,000 people each, and the largest saw a million eager Irishmen at the Hill of Tara. Nearest to Kilglass, a huge meeting was held in Roscommon town (Gray 1998)—O'Connell had a personal connection: in 1840 his son had married Kate Balfe, the daughter of a Roscommon landlord (Trench 1984, p. 258). Another took place at Longford. As Charles Trench described O'Connell then: "European liberals revered him as the man of the people who was challenging and looked like defeating the immensely powerful British aristocracy; nationalists saw him as the man who had taught the Irish to be a nation; Catholics saw him as the man who had wrung Catholic emancipation from a government of Protestant bigots; liberal Catholics saw him as the man who had wedded Catholicism and liberalism, who had 'baptized liberalism and made it Christian' and 'sprinkled the first drops of baptismal water upon that savage power which we call Democracy'" (1984, p. 278).

And then it ended stunningly when the British, fearing rebellion, barred the great meeting at Clontarf in October 1843 and arrested the Liberator. After months in prison, the aging O'Connell emerged worn and debilitated and never recaptured his previous fire.

Despite his political goals for the Irish, O'Connell, who was a Catholic landlord himself and a defender of the rights of property and public order, did not advocate certain significant changes—such as withholding rents—and repeatedly gave allegiance to Queen Victoria. He devised political strategies but frequently compromised to achieve lesser—yet nevertheless some—progress, which brought criticism on his head. One breakthrough was his achievement of municipal reform in 1840, which opened local offices to Catholics. A major legacy was his demonstration of how to win by organizing democratic politics. Said his biographer Fergus O'Ferrall, "Perhaps only the United States had a more advanced party organization than O'Connell had in Ireland during the 1820s" (1981, pp. 40, 61). It meant that the Irish were exposed to sophisticated, goal-oriented politics, and they learned about tactics and participation in the polity.

O'Connell's record on labor is mixed. In 1837 he opposed combinations for "their pernicious influence on trade and their addiction to intimidation and violence." A year later he assailed trade unions. John Boyle argued that O'Connell and the Chartist leader Fergus O'Connor could have welded the interests of the Irish with those of the industrial underclass in England, but O'Connell viewed the Chartists as "subversive," and it never happened (Boyle 1988, pp. 43, 44). Similarly, on the land question, O'Connell opposed the "no-rent campaign of passive resistance" proposed by William Connor because it would have jeopardized the security of property (on those grounds, he likely would have opposed the Ballykilcline strike) and Connor was expelled from his Repeal Association (O'Ferrall 1981, p. 113).

For these kinds of policies, O'Connell earned the enmity of some Young Irelanders. In his post-Ireland writings, rebel John Mitchell, for one, castigated him for preaching submission to the government. He called O'Connell "the magician" who "bewitched [the people of Ireland] to their destruction." And, alluding to the famine, he said, "Because the Irish have been taught peaceful agitation in their slavery, therefore they have been swept by a plague of hunger worse than many years of bloody fighting." Agrarian protest leader Michael Davitt also was accusatory (qtd. in Donnelly 1996, pp. 55, 56). Labor leader James Connolly viewed O'Connell as "the most bitter and unscrupulous enemy of trade unionism Ireland has yet produced," but O'Ferrall depicted him as the working man's friend, one who "supported peaceful and legal activities by trade unions. In the Commons in 1838, he defended the freedom of workers to combine for the purpose of raising wages or to prevent them being lowered." O'Ferrall cited O'Connell's social concern, support for artisans to organize, and development of strategies of agitation (1981, pp. 99–101).

For decades, O'Connell remained popular and capable of galvanizing the people. As the constabulary force went into Ballykilcline in May 1847 to evict the rent strike's Defendants, however, word came from Italy of the death on May 15 of the ailing O'Connell as he traveled to Rome on a personal pilgrimage. Within days in that month of upheaval and shock, the people of Ballykilcline lost not only their homes, their lands, and the neighbors who were forced to Quebec by Denis Mahon but also their legendary Liberator. One can imagine their despair.

THE ANTITITHE WARS

One of the greatest burrs and burdens for pre-famine Irish landholders was the tithe they were required to pay to support the Church of England, which was already seen as "grossly overendowed" (Trench 1984, p. 204). As Gearóid Ó Tuathaigh observed, "Opposition to the payment of tithes had been a feature of every outbreak of agrarian disorder from the eighteenth century onwards." Tithes had become a kind of property by the 1830s, when about 20 percent of them were collected by laymen. Starting in 1830, the people's complaint broke into major disturbances, instigated in the province of Leinster by the clergy (Broeker 1970, p. 205; McDonnell-Garvey 1995, p. 59; Ó Tuathaigh 1972, pp. 173–174, 176); the conflict ended eight years later in a law mediated by O'Connell.

The right to collect tithes could be leased out to reviled "proctors," who pressed the farmers hard for payment. Certain lands were exempted for a time, meaning that small farmers who tilled the land had a heavier tithe burden than large farmers until an 1823 law closed that loophole. In doing so, it also extended the conflict to graziers. "The principal objectors to tithes were the sort of farmers who would not engage in terrorism, so the anti-tithe agitation spread the area of protest, often violent protest, wider than Whiteboy terrorism," observed Trench. Magnifying the people's complaints even further, "tithes had priority over rent, so a farmer who had paid his tithes might find himself faced with eviction because he had no money for his rent. This, and the recouping by tithe-payers through increased rents, inflated an antitithe campaign into a campaign against the payment of rents as well, and brought the Whiteboys into association with it" (1984, p. 205).

The refusal to pay rents occurred especially in the west: "From parts of the country, particularly the west, there were reports of peasants demanding rent-reductions, or, in extreme cases, total abolition of all rents, rates and taxes. . . . [M]any peasants turned again to the familiar agents of 'instant remedy'—the secret societies" (Ó Tuathaigh 1972, p. 166).

The stock and goods of a defaulter could be seized, or distrained (but only between sunrise and sunset when the animals or crops were in the field) and subsequently sold to pay his debt. It was taboo among the Irish, however, under penalty of retribution from the secret societies, to purchase distrained goods; if the goods got as far as the auction block, the people boycotted the sale. "The resistance campaign soon spread throughout the entire country. By 1833 more than half the tithe arrears of the previous two years were still outstanding. In 1834 only a third of the composition was paid, in the following year less than one-eighth. . . . [Resistance] enjoyed overwhelming support from all sections of the agricultural community—landlords, comfortable farmers, small farmers, and labourers. . . . The methods of the poorer classes were often direct, desperate, and violent—arson, intimidation and assault" (Ó Tuathaigh 1972, pp. 176, 177). Richard Trench, Archbishop of Dublin in the 1860s, recalled the tithe war from personal experience: "He always shivered when he remembered the open graves the peasants dug for him and his family on the lawns of his father's estate at Stradbally, in County Laois. 'Did I possess any property in this country I would sell it at any loss,' he wrote in July 1831" (qtd. in Tanner, p. 221).

Roscommon was not spared these problems. Maire McDonnell-Garvey, historian of Roscommon lands to the west a few miles from Strokestown, wrote of "several bloody encounters" when troops rode out to collect tithe payments, and, in 1830 and the following year, "secret societies again made their appearance. They were opposed to rent increases as well as tithes" (1995, p. 68). As much as two decades earlier, Lord Hartland at Strokestown had blamed the tithe issue for roiling local relations, and the surrounding countryside remained greatly disturbed through the 1830s.

The British government, concerned to maintain order, responded to the protests and adopted new measures: in 1832, an act was passed which, among other points, based the calculation of tithes on corn prices between 1823 and 1830; notably, "tenants-at-will and tenants from year to year were to be exempt"; and a rebate was offered to those who paid. The government set money aside to relieve tithe owers whose debts remained uncollected, and authorities brought the police and military into the collection process, evidence of the power of the tactics employed by the insurgents and the worries they gave British officials: "[Troops commander Sir Richard Hussey] Vivian had expressed strong reservations to [the Lord Lieutenant, Lord] Anglesey, about using troops to enforce the payment of tithes, given that 'the feelings of the whole people' were opposed to them. In Vivian's opinion, the situation presented the government with two alternatives: 'concession or rebellion. . . . Ireland has never been in such a state as it is in consequence of the collection of tithes under the late law, nor were the Government or the troops ever placed in so difficult a situation'" (qtd. in Crossman 1996, pp. 372, 373).

The period, as a result, saw several reforms in the police and military forces. Eventually, in the 1838 settlement of the issue, tithe became a charge payable by the landlord, who could recoup it in the tenants' leases (Ó Tuathaigh 1972, pp. 178–181). The government finally passed a bill that "exempted the poorest, spread the burden among the less poor and made tithe collection administratively easy," although it still held non-Protestants liable for the Anglican church's bills (Trench 1984, p. 254).

It is not hard to see how the antitithe protest may have had a major influence on the rent strike in Ballykilcline, since they roughly coincided, stemmed from similar roots, adopted the same tactics. And at issue in both protests were payments required under what the Irish regarded as an unfair system.

LAND AND THE POTATO

The Irish people relied almost exclusively on potatoes for their foodstuff. Their dependence on a single crop, which had begun in the late 1700s, developed because the potato yielded large quantities for each acre sown, grew on poor land, and was difficult to transport. Its major disadvantage was that it would not keep as long as a year; thus, each summer, food shortages occurred. The potato crop also facilitated the seasonal migrant labor that supplemented family incomes during planting and harvesting. The potato achieved its popularity despite incentives offered by the government after 1750 to grow grains (Gacquin 1996, p. 21). Another official policy, however, pushed people to the potato: because of the Penal Laws that shaped life for Irish Catholics throughout the 1700s, Catholics were required to divide their land among all their children; in each generation, therefore, individual holdings got smaller—and only the potato grew in sufficient quantities on such small plots to feed a family. Fortunately for the people, it was nutritious as well.

The potato also supported landless laborers and cottiers who depended on the conacre system for their family's food, which meant that each spring they negotiated to rent just enough land to grow that season's supply for their own tables. Laborers, though, because they were at the bottom of the land market and had to negotiate new terms each year, often paid the highest rents. Conacre land in Roscommon was comparatively expensive at seven to nine pounds an acre, sometimes quite a bit higher. In a case near Boyle, the charge was thirteen pounds an acre, paid to a subtenant of Lord Lorton; the subtenant likely rented the land himself for about twenty-six shillings an acre (Coleman 1999, p. 20). Nevertheless, for the poor, the conacre system was the only way to get food, especially since little other employment was available in rural Roscommon. "To be denied conacre was to be denied leave to live," wrote journalist Alexander Somerville from Strokestown in February 1847 (1994, p. 87).

Somerville's work exposed many faults of the land system that Britain imposed on Ireland. In northern Roscommon, in pursuit of profits, agriculture had started moving in a significant way in the 1820s from tillage to dry-stock grazing of cattle and sheep, which required extensive fields but needed little labor. Soon, a man looking for conacre land had a hard time finding any available; the big landowners, with an eye on their commercial interests, wanted to graze cattle and sheep on their land rather than rent it out to potato growers. At one point, an angry Denis Mahon threatened to make a sheepwalk of Strokestown (Campbell 1990, p. 4). And a tillage farmer with fifty acres in nearby County Meath offered more jobs than a Roscommon grazier who had 2,000 acres (Coleman 1999, p. 20).

Policy only exacerbated these conditions: the land situation worsened when local officials decided that leasing land in conacre did not have the legal status of a tenancy. The decision meant that landholders could no longer seize the crop in lieu of rent if the conacre man defaulted. "[The landholders] now had a further reason to refuse to set land [for conacre], and when they did set it [the owners] demanded security in the form of joint notes, so that the occupier had to get a 'better farmer' than himself to accept joint liability" (Coleman 1999, p. 21).

Further, the landowners eschewed the farmers' conacre practice of burning the land to increase crop yields, maintaining that it ruined the fields for grazing animals. Burning was a widespread practice in Kilglass (Kincaid testimony, June 21, 1847), but around Strokestown, where tillage farming was practiced more frequently than elsewhere, "cattle rearing was better understood than cropping" (Coleman 1999, pp. 19, 20).

A London newspaper described the situation succinctly: "When more food, more cultivation, more employment, were the requisites for maintaining the Irish in existence, the Legislature and the landlords went about introducing a species of cultivation that could only be successful by requiring fewer hands, and turning potato gardens, that nourished the maximum of human beings, into pasture grounds for bullocks, that nourished only the minimum" (*Illustrated London News*, Dec. 15, 1849).

After seeing the natives excluded from lessons in good farming practices, journalist Somerville, writing from Roscommon, summed up their dilemma:

> So Catholic tenants are turned out of small farms, and small farms are turned into large ones, and given to political Protestants who vote right; and when the public voice proclaims the illiberal act to be persecution, or something very like it, the best excuse that can be offered, that ever has been offered, is, that the Protestants, being men from the north, are the best farmers. Yet here is Catholicism studiously made a disqualification for learning the science of manuring, green-cropping, subsoiling, and draining. The Catholics, forming the great majority of the population,

are denied land, denied the information how to make it profitable if they have land, are denied conacre if they have not farm land; are denied work if they have not conacre; are denied poor-law relief if they have not work; and, having no work, have only the choice of facing death by slow degrees with no food in their stomachs, or death by quick degrees with bayonets and bullets, from Athlone [a market center south of Strokestown], in their stomachs. They were shot dead when digging up land to plant potatoes in 1845. (Somerville 1994, p. 103)

In March 1845 in Lissonuffy Parish, near Strokestown, a hundred native Irish had tried to force the landlord to rent conacre land by digging up his ground. Six policemen who showed up were allegedly attacked and "forced to fire." John Gavagan was killed and others were injured (Lombard and Mullaney 1999).

The Irish were squeezed mercilessly, which gave the secret societies cause to strike back in forms of self-defense that sought to change a system careening toward chaos. They acted on it. One can see the extent of protest and disturbance at that time by paying attention to the laws passed by the British Parliament to deal with them: "In Ireland major acts and proclamations included the Banning of Popular Meetings (1828), the Suppression of Dangerous Societies (1829), the Irish County Franchise Act (raising the property qualification for parliamentary elections from forty [shillings] to 10 pounds in 1829, as part of the price for Catholic Emancipation), the Coercion Act (1832), the Local Disturbances Act (1833)" and so on (Tilly 1995, p. 295).

Boyle singled out 1834—that year when Ballykilcline tottered on the edge of its rent strike—as a "year of intense trade union activity and of sustained counterattacks by employers. Prosecutions for illegal combination involving attempts to limit apprentices, intimidation, conspiracy, strikes in violation of contracts, and even membership of a benefit society took place in Londonderry, Lisburn, County Antrim, Dublin, and Cork" (1988, p. 38).

How Poor These Poor?

Though the people of Ballykilcline were poor, as Scally said, not all the residents were at the bottom of the scale. But clues to clarify this issue are few and often circumstantial. Scally inventoried the farmers' assets in 1841:

The 42 recorded tenants of October 1841 had raised 174 stacks of oats, thirty-three cocks of hay, and 103 acres of potatoes, and possessed sixty-

six cows, seven horses, and twenty-six sheep. . . . If added to the approximately 100 to 150 acres of potatoes cultivated by the remaining cottier
subtenants, who possessed little else, the total cash value of their resources
might have amounted to half the rents they owed, at best, perhaps as much
as fourteen hundred pounds. Even after five years of living rent free, the
nearly five hundred occupants of the townland had thus accumulated an
average capital of less than three pounds per head (just ten shillings short
of the current transatlantic fare for one adult). (Scally 1995, p. 86)

Scally pointed out that some residents of other townlands were involved
in joint tenancies in Ballykilcline; for example, he said that John Clem-
ons and Luke Henry, who lived elsewhere, had a holding in Ballykilcline
along with three McCormicks and John Hanley. But Scally's reckoning did
not consider the opposite possibility—that Ballykilcline tenants may have
held land in nearby townlands, and if so, those holdings and what they
produced would have augmented their assets. Elsewhere, however, he did
acknowledge in a footnote a rent ledger reporting joint tenancies by John
Connor and Luke Narry in Farish Bottoms in the 1820s (Scally 1995, pp.
57, 245 n. 27). It also appears that Scally did not figure in income from the
farmers' wage or seasonal labor. Nor did his estimate appear to count the
tenants' cash assets or the value of the domestic or farm goods and imple-
ments that some of them owned, as he again acknowledged elsewhere.

Before he emigrated, Patrick Kelly, for one, had goods to sell. In March
1848 he wrote officials to say that his wife, Eliza Cline, who had been ill
when they were scheduled to leave, was now "fit to go," and he requested
that officials respond in timely fashion "as I have several articles to dis-
pose of" (Kelly letter, March 18, 1848). What the articles were Kelly did
not specify, but he must have thought the potential remuneration important, since he mentioned it in such a letter.

Recent physical evidence illustrates the tenants' connections to commercial markets for domestic goods. During the five years following publication of Scally's book, Charles Orser supervised archaeological excavations
at several sites in Ballykilcline in an effort to learn about the material
culture of the prefamine Irish tenant farmer. At Nary [Neary] cabin sites
in Ballykilcline, Orser's team unearthed hundreds of artifacts, including
shards of fine English earthenwares that had apparently belonged to two
generations of the family and showed that "each household owned two sets
of tableware." Items from the younger couple's home hinted that "they were
attempting to establish their position within society through somewhat
contemporary, but distinctive decorative teaware." But their purchases of
it seemed to be occasional ones, dishes bought "piece-meal and over time

rather than as a complete set." The analysis supported a larger interpretation as well: "The fine earthenware finds indicate, for instance, that at least some of the people who lived there were participating in the global economy. The Narys clearly had the desire to use wares and vessels that were considered 'modern' and forward looking. . . . The social action of striving may have applicability to Ballykilcline. The townland's inhabitants appear to have had an ample supply of Irish redware, yet they still chose to purchase refined English earthenwares" (Brighton and White 2005).

These clues suggest that "many men and women in early nineteenth-century rural Ireland were forward thinking and more sophisticated than is often accorded them by contemporary travellers and modern-day historians." Orser has observed that one implication of the archaeology work is that "instead of paying their annual rents to the Crown, the tenants used their meagre funds to improve their material condition" (Irish Excavations Reports website). A hint of Orser's findings can be found in Isaac Weld's 1832 survey of Roscommon, in which he delighted in watching the scene at a market day in Strokestown, which he called the "most picturesque in Ireland": "He noted the colours of the dresses and the scarlet cloak or mantle still worn by the older women. Younger women wore vivid scarlet shawls and 'the fondness for finery amongst the female peasantry and the eagerness with which they survey it in shops and windows almost surpasses belief" (Coleman 1999, p. 11).

Some of the townland's residents did have means. In the 1820s and '30s, dozens of the tenants were liable to pay the tithe to support the Church of England because they had the wherewithal to lease agricultural lands—that is, they had some means. Later, with their rent strike in full sway, they pooled their funds to hire a lawyer, each tenant paying five shillings per acre per year (Scally 1995, p. 73). In 1842, when a house invasion occurred in Ballykilcline, thieves took thirty-five pounds and four shillings "in bank notes[,] gold[,] silver and copper" from Patrick Reilly. That amount, which Reilly apparently kept at hand, was about five times his annual rent payment; officials recorded the arrearage he owed in January 1842 at just over thirty-eight pounds. In the same invasion fracas, Patrick Reynolds surrendered "three pounds in gold and five or six shillings in silver"; in comparison, his rent was slightly more than five pounds a year (Lands of Ballykilcline, Feb. 16 and 19, 1847; Commissioners of Woods and Forests, pp. 10–13). The raiding party did not find money with James Kelly or Thomas Hanley, though that fact did not prove that they lacked means. Afterward, government officials, probably to facilitate prosecution, recommended that Reilly receive fifteen pounds in government compensation for his loss, and Reynolds was to be awarded ten pounds (Outrage Papers, Aug. 10, 1842, and Outrage Papers, x 25/16609).

In 1846, the agent George Knox estimated that the leaders of the strike were each worth between twenty and one hundred pounds. Scally took a skeptical view of those sums and warned that Knox's totals should not be taken too seriously. The highest total rent paid by any tenant in the town-land was the nearly twenty-two pounds due each year jointly from Hugh McDermott, who supported a large family and also ran a shebeen—a drinking house—in Ballykilcline, and his brother John (Scally 1995, pp. 73, 75; Lands of Ballykilcline, Feb. 16 and 19, 1847; Commissioners of Woods and Forests, pp. 10–13). At the other end of the spectrum, John McGann had a job as a timekeeper on the public works during the famine years (Fox memo); such jobs paid very little.

During the months when the emigrations took place, the Crown re-ceived offers from several tenants which showed that they, at least, were not destitute. When the strike began, Godfrey Hogg wrote in 1836 on behalf of tenant Thomas Fallon: "I at all times found him honest and industriously inclined," and Hogg vouched for Fallon's punctual payment of rent (Hogg letter, Sept. 24, 1836). In April 1848, Rev. Henry Bren-nan, the priest in Kilglass, wrote on behalf of three tenants who did not want to leave and who tried to lease land again in Ballykilcline: John and Pat Connor and John Stuart: "I can vouch for their good conduct and industrious habits. They are considered by the people to have some money. They have means to live at home and in consequence won't go to America" (Brennan letter, April 12, 1848). The authorities refused to admit the former occupiers on new leases, however: a few years later, im-migrants named Pat Connor and two John Stuarts, at least one of them from Ballykilcline, according to U.S. naturalization records, lived in or near Rutland. Other evidence of means comes out of nearby eviction pro-cesses pursued by Denis Mahon in which, as Vesey described it, "tenants who had failed to pay rent for upwards of three years often did so when the sheriff appeared in the townland to take possession of the farms of defaulters" (2002, p. 17).

In trying to rent lands for himself in Ballykilcline after the emigrations, Father Brennan reminded officials that by evicting the townspeople, they had significantly reduced his own income: "I trust you won't forget that as Parish Priest here I ought to have some claim on you as by removing the late tenants from the Crown lands you have considerably reduced my revenues to which they liberally contributed" (Brennan letter, Aug. 18, 1848). Apparently the people of Ballykilcline had given generously to the church, or at least their pastor was willing to say so. His statement, however, may have been primarily self-serving.

Evidence from County Kerry about country ways may be meaningful. Cormac O'Grada, in studying Irish banking, examined the failures in May 1848 of two Kerry banks, which were investigated by a man named Pratt, who reported: "As numerous Tralee account-holders handed in their pass books to the clerk, it emerged that 'some of the farming class, apparently poor, had sums to a surprising amount lodged—even over a thousand pounds each.' Similarly in the wake of the collapse of the Killarney savings bank, 'tenants, who pleaded extreme poverty to their landlords, paupers from the workhouses, and men whose outward appearance would lead you to look on them as objects of charity, were soon at the office door'" (O'Grada 2002, p. 23). Although Pratt later was forced to withdraw some of his claims for lack of evidence, the suggestion that some tenants concealed their own business affairs resonates likewise in Scally's account.[2] Nothing suggested that any Ballykilcline tenants amassed sums comparable to the amounts purportedly held by the Tralee farmers; nevertheless, the Kerry finding is a caution about accepting matters at face value.

Some of the farmers of Ballykilcline borrowed funds during the famine years from a program begun in 1824 to help the "industrious poor." Called the Irish Reproductive Loan Fund (IRLF), it operated primarily in rural areas of the island, including Counties Roscommon, Galway, Mayo, Sligo, Cork, and Tipperary (UK Moving Here website).[3] Significant fund records have survived for the famine period and plainly show that a number of Kilglass and Strokestown people borrowed from the IRLF (which was administered locally), among them at least ten men who lived in Ballykilcline.

The IRLF archive is invaluable for its detail about its borrowers' circumstances, residence, and death or emigration. In addition to evictees who were borrowers, the records also supply the names of several previously unknown residents of Ballykilcline, perhaps landless people whose names were unrecorded elsewhere. Among the evictees were Edward McCormick, Thomas Fallon, and Thomas Hanley Sr., as well as Thomas McGann, the father of evictee John McGann and his siblings. John Quinn, a listed tenant in the 1830s, apparently never left Ireland, since the IRLF record indicates that he died there in 1848. Another name raised questions: John Mullera of "Mullough" (probably Mullaghmacormick, which adjoined Ballykilcline to the northwest), who was using the fund in 1846 but left for America in 1847, almost certainly is the John Mullera evicted from Ballykilcline; the IRLF record also disclosed the death of the senior

John Mullera in Ballykilcline in 1847. New to the Ballykilcline record from the IRLF ledgers were Pat Farrell, Terance [*sic*] McDonald, and Thomas Shannahan. There was a Pat Farrell, wife, and three children among the evictees, so presumably this man was another Pat Farrell. If not, then this record is evidence that Farrell conspired to remain in Kilglass after taking the Crown's bounty to leave. Farrell of the IRLF and McDonald died in Roscommon in 1848 and 1849 respectively; Shannahan emigrated in 1847, though not as an evictee. The record shows that 50 percent of the recorded borrowers from Ballykilcline died in Ireland between 1847 and 1849 (UK Moving Here website).

Clues suggest that at least some of the Ballykilcline tenants had means, if small, even during the famine and as their strike ended—no surprise, perhaps, since they had not paid rent for years. Unfortunately, the U.S. census in 1850, conducted only about two years after the people from Ballykilcline arrived in Rutland, recorded only real estate values and not personal assets, so it offers little help in determining what the tenants brought with them. The fact that very few famine immigrants acquired property soon after their arrival, however, suggests that whatever assets the evictees had had in Ireland likely were small and had been expended in surviving the famine and traveling to and settling in Rutland. That this was the case is buttressed by the numbers of them who immediately flocked to railroad and quarry wage labor in Rutland rather than buying farmland. It is also supported by the limited personal savings and real estate holdings they reported in the 1860 U.S. census. During the following war decade, some of them did start to build assets, but others never did at all during the time period of my study. Of course, it is possible that the promise of jobs in the United States prompted some emigrants as they headed out of Roscommon to leave funds that they may have viewed as their extra margin with famine-stricken family members at home, to help them survive.

POROUS BORDERS

After generations of experience with the repression of the hated Penal Laws, which reached into and detracted from every facet of Irish Catholics' life, the Irish raised their heads in the middle 1700s and began to organize to protect and preserve their way of life and their identity. During the second half of that century, their activities took the form of secret societies, workers' unions, and fraternal associations which in the 1790s, as the French underclasses toppled an aristocracy, built on a growing Painite sense of the world. Their own bid to overturn British rule in 1798 failed at Vinegar Hill and elsewhere, and in 1800 a punitive England imposed the Act of Union. In the early 1800s, O'Connellite politics developed, arising in part from O'Connell's work with the Catholic Association and culminating in Catholic Emancipation (which he achieved in the later 1820s) and battles to repeal the Act of Union. Organizing also grew out of an understanding of their foe that they shared with angry English underclasses as public expression and contentious action developed more modern forms. After emancipation, the dominant protests on Irish ground came during the antitithe war. These developments, though, borrowed from actions in other parts of the Atlantic world as ideas seeped across and leapfrogged over physical boundaries; the Irish Sea, the Atlantic Ocean, and the River Shannon could not bar entry. But more than new political ideas and social contacts brought change to their environment; physical infrastructure in the communications, mail, transportation, and financial systems were modernizing, and people were traveling more.

The Ballykilcline strike was produced not only by administrative fumbling and a set of land ownership and transfer circumstances unique to the townland but also by a confluence of factors, many of them entering from outside, which crossed the Shannon in numerous ways; the river was a border but not a barrier. External influences came with seasonal migrant laborers, some of whom lived in Ballykilcline; they were swept in from commercial channels, such as the newspapers then developing in Roscommon, travelers on the Royal Canal, the Shannon, and the Bianconi coach (named for Charles Bianconi, who established horse-and-carriage routes), and the mail networks; they arrived with British police and military forces sent to and through Roscommon and with returning Roscommoners who had served in British forces; and they were introduced by mercantile Protestants moving into Strokestown, as happened before 1820, which Hood (1994) demonstrated. Further, family members who had emigrated from home townlands—and there were a number of them—wrote to parents, sisters, and brothers about new jobs, new places, new difficulties, as well as opportunities. All these factors amplified the political protests in both Ireland and England in the years before and during the rent strike. And Ballykilcline was embedded in this larger economic and political context.

By the 1840s, 64 percent of the farms in Connacht were less than five acres in size, and 93 percent were smaller than fifteen acres (Mokyr 1983, p. 19). County Roscommon was one of the two most rural counties in all of Ireland: just over 6 percent of the population was urbanized (Hood 1994, p. 151).

The economic difficulties of the people were underscored by the laborers' seasonal migration to take in the harvests of Scotland and England, and even the crops in other parts of Ireland, to earn the money it took to hold and work Roscommon's small farms. In the mid-1830s the income of laborers' families in Connacht each year averaged less than 60 percent of the income of similar families in the eastern province of Leinster (Donnelly 2001, p. 3). Given the prevailing land usage and arrangements, western laborers had to go elsewhere for wage work, and there were seasonal hiring centers near Kilglass (O'Dowd 1991, pp. 105–108).

The migrant laborers, called spalpeens, brought back new ideas, political notions, and social experience when they recrossed the Irish Sea each fall after harvesting the fields of Scotland and England. Sometimes, they brought back firearms (Coleman 1999, p. 40; Dillon letter, March 25, 1842). By migrating yearly, they made connections with modern life, the market system, current politics and protest, and the world outside their parish and county. They witnessed the social conditions and political and economic conflicts then prevailing in Britain, and saw how England's radicals responded. In England and Scotland they not only worked within a different sociocultural context but took in the crops alongside and exchanged information and viewpoints with laborers from other parts of their own island.

Many spalpeens, returning year after year to the same locales for harvest work, became students of British protest. "Such interfaces with the cosmopolitan world encouraged the growth of organic leadership of the rural poor," Michael Huggins observed. Citing Scally's portrayal of Irish townland inhabitants as isolated and insulated from "the outside world," Huggins argued that, instead, "the world of the Irish peasant was, from the late eighteenth century onward, not so parochial and enclosed as often supposed," nor did it depend on elites for information from other places (2000, pp. 33, 30–31). The new knowledge carried by the Irish was direct and personal rather than secondhand.

The spalpeens' migration began each spring: after they had planted their own potato beds, the men trudged the rutted roads to east coast ports to board boats to Liverpool or elsewhere on the sister island. There they found work as common laborers for English and Scottish farmers until after the harvest, when they headed home again to take in their own potato crop. This practice became a way of life for thousands of Connacht men and their families, including some who lived in Kilglass and across north and central Roscommon. By the 1840s, many of the seasonal Irish laborers had branched out to work on England's construction projects as well (Harris 1994, p. 31). The strategy of external summer employment for subsistence support began early; the need was long-standing. One study turned up evidence of a Roscommon spalpeen whose estimated birthdate was 1645. More evidence came from the diary of Charles O'Connor, who wrote in the early 1700s that "the bad harvest of the year had resulted in the loss of employment for the seasonal workers who had traveled from north Roscommon to Leinster [the southeastern province around Dublin]" (qtd. in O'Dowd 1991, p. 13). In the 1830s, migrant laborers were most numerous in "Kilkeevin and Castlerea, Co. Roscommon from which 'great numbers' went primarily to England and also to Leinster and Munster; Estersnow [only a few miles from Kilglass] and Kilcolagh, Co. Roscommon which sent 'considerable numbers' to England. . . . The second area of high concentration extends from east Roscommon. . . . [T]here were two migratory workers between every nine families from the parish of Kilglass" (O'Dowd 1991, pp. 59–60). Most of the migrants from eastern and central Roscommon worked in England.

The area around Strokestown was one of three locales in Roscommon where significant numbers in the early 1830s regularly took seasonal work (O'Dowd 1991, p. 75). This evidence points to the weakness of the local economy in supplying the needs of the people, since the cause of seasonal migration was local economic insufficiency. With Anne O'Dowd's information, it is possible to calculate the approximate number of Kilglass spalpeens. By the 1841 census, the population of Kilglass was 11,391 (Coyle 1994, p. 36); the average size of a household on the Mahon estate was 5.6 people (Orser n.d.). Working with these figures indicates 425 spalpeens in the parish in 1838.[4] That was a sizable portion of the adult male population, men who undoubtedly shared what they learned across the Irish Sea with family and friends. The number of the migratory population demonstrated that many people in the parish had experience in and knowledge about the wider world, either firsthand or from a relative or friend.

There is evidence too that some young people in Ballykilcline were part of the movement for wage labor. An 1848 police report pointed out that John McGann had traveled in Munster for a time (Fox report, Nov. 26, 1847, Outrage Papers). Bridget Wynne was working in England when her family was evicted from Ballykilcline, probably doing domestic work; a special petition requested that the Crown pay her way to America, since her family was being sent off, and the government consented (Burke letter, Feb. 17, 1848). A rent roll of the townland described Michael Connor, twenty-one, as "married, now in England, harvesting" (List of Tenants).[5]

By 1841, the number of migrant workers from all of County Roscommon totaled 16,386, including men and women who migrated for jobs both in Ireland and to Britain. Internal migration was primarily within an individual's own province. Few women worked seasonally abroad; only 477 were recorded that year (Harris 1994, pp. 94, 95, 99). Unless those numbers increased dramatically over the next few years, Bridget Wynne's job in England at the time of the evictions was unusual.

As the 1840s progressed, and attacks, arrests, and judicial proceedings increased dramatically, one of the landholders' greatest fears as matters escalated was the people's access to firearms, which were thought to have been procured frequently by spalpeens; in England, the Staffordshire police acknowledged that "many Irishmen who come here to reap the harvest purchased arms during their stay." When officials compiled a list of men in the Strokestown area who owned illegal firearms, about half the men identified lived in Kilglass (Dillon letter, March 25, 1842). That fact tends to support the belief that Kilglass had a significant core group of seasonal migrants. After the two landlord murders in Roscommon in 1847, county magistrates complained to Dublin about arms in the hands of the Irish underclasses. The record books for 1845 alone show fifty-five raids exclusively for arms, and police recorded that in Boyle, northwest of Kilglass, one night in December 1846 ten raids for arms were conducted by groups of fifty or a hundred men at a time.

At least one tenant in Ballykilcline kept a gun. The government was informed in 1842 that "there are quantities of unregistered arms at present in the hands of the peasantry" in Ballintobber and Roscommon baronies. Thomas Dillon told officials that, "persons who visit England for the purpose of making up the harvest are in the habit of bringing over gun barrels and locks and getting them stocked in different parts of the country." He volunteered to help the government "take up" the weapons by supplying the names of persons and their home townlands who were known to have arms. The government accepted Dillon's offer, and a list of forty-eight men, nearly half of them from Kilglass Parish, was turned in a few months later. Among the gun owners listed, who were expected to surrender their arms, was Patrick Colligan of Ballykilcline. Colligan's designation also raised the question of whether he too was a spalpeen, but it is not clear which of the two Ballykilcline men of this name was referenced. Also listed was Bernard Calegan (Colligan) of adjacent Knockhall, perhaps of the same family line (Dillon letter, March 25, 1842).

Some weapons certainly were used in the commission of crimes; some were merely instruments of intimidation—a tactic by itself of the secret societies, reinforced now and then with evidence that indeed, if pressed, they would resort to personal and property damage (Coleman 1999, pp. 40, 41).

Ruth-Ann Harris discovered an Irish Folklore Commission account from Longford, near Kilglass, which testified to organization among the spalpeens: "The first thing a harvest worker did in England was to join a society like the Molly McGuires or the Fenians. 'If he didn't he wouldn't be let work.'" Harris remarked, though, on the sparseness of the record before 1850 concerning such organizations (1994, pp. 22, 23).

New ideas came to eastern Roscommon from newspapers, travelers, and in-migration as well as from migrant labor. Nearly 7,000 men and women in Ballintobber North—the barony of which Kilglass was part—could read in 1841, according to the census that year (Scally 1995, p. 249), and in an era of change that was politically charged, when O'Connell held "monster meetings" of the Irish (1843) and mass gatherings made a political statement, the newspapers certainly found their audiences. The *Freeman's Journal* was available as early as 1763 (University College Dublin website), and in the 1840s the Kilglass parish priest and the Bishop of Elphin both made use of its letters columns (Killen 1995). The county's earliest newspaper began in 1822 when the *Roscommon and Leitrim Gazette* was founded; the *Roscommon Journal and Western Reporter* started publishing in 1828.

The interests the two papers covered were wide ranging. Not only did the *Gazette* publish a range of local news, but it also ran numerous stories from outside the county's borders. On December 21, 1822, for instance, "national and international news covered copy from papers in Derry, Limerick, Mayo, Galway, Cork, London and other English cities for unusual events. Much historical coverage [was] of wars in Greece, Spain and France" (Lombard and Mullaney 1999). As well, the *Gazette* paid attention to politics, economics, and commerce; crime and the courts; illness, death, and disease (one of its earliest issues reported that 60,000 people had died of famine and related diseases in 1818); society, religion, and emigration.

In the spring of 1831, according to the *Gazette,* there were thirteen ships in port at Sligo that were "crowded with people intending to emigrate," and a month later the newspaper reported that three hundred people had left "this year so far from within three miles of this town." In November 1834, readers learned about an explosion at a quarry in Boyle that killed two men named Reed and McHugh. Its columns reported in March 1825 that Michael Tiernan was sentenced to seven years' transportation for stealing two sheep from General Mahon; that there were 8,685 forty-shilling freeholders in the county in June 1825 (before emancipation changed the terms for voting); and that Lord Lorton, who had extensive Roscommon holdings, had voted against a Catholic Emancipation bill in 1827 "from knowing that it would give powers to the most bitter enemies of the most free and tolerant constitution in the world." The following year, Lorton delivered a speech in the House of Lords about Catholic Emancipation in which he denounced popery and priests (Lombard and Mullaney 1999). News that crossed the Shannon to appear in these publications enabled the poorest person who could read, or whose friends could read and share the news, to follow what was happening in distant Dublin and London.

Two great waterways, the River Shannon and the Royal Canal at nearby Tarmonbarry, brought traffic, goods, and visitors into the region from other parts of the country, though the canals of Ireland were not as extensive as England's.[6] Nor was the canal system used for public travel as much as had been expected (Connolly 1998, pp. 67, 68); nevertheless, before there were railroads, these water highways did bring traffic. And Roscommon, given its geographic location between the country's populous eastern shore and the Connacht coast, often hosted travelers from the northeast and the Dublin area.

Both transportation and postal systems in Ireland experienced significant development from the late 1700s to the famine, Desmond Norton has pointed out. Norton spent several years analyzing 30,000 documents of Stewart and Kincaid, a land agent firm that operated widely across Ireland in the 1840s and down to modern time. Ireland's mail coach system was improved from 1789; the country had four mail coaches by 1801, and by the 1830s forty cars left Dublin daily. When Bianconi's coaches began to carry the mail in 1815, cross-routes were developed so that mail headed to the provinces no longer had to pass first through Dublin, an improvement that simultaneously increased efficiency and decreased costs. "Under the new scheme, a single sheet cost nine pence for sixty-five to ninety-five miles, rising to fifteen pence for over three hundred miles within Ireland. A letter of three sheets traveling over three hundred miles within Ireland cost forty-five pence." Postal reforms in 1839 and '40 introduced the "uniform penny post [whereby] half an ounce prepaid to anywhere within the United Kingdom now cost a penny." Norton also noted that no letter in the land agent's archive complained about "inability to get from A to B due to deficiencies in transport." The firm's representatives sometimes traveled by canal but more frequently by coach; they also confidently used the mail system to forward the collected rents (Norton 2002, p. 14).

Agent Kincaid detailed a trip he made through Strokestown on November 26, 1843:

> I left Clonteem [the lodge of the Marquess of Westmeath on the western (Roscommon) side of the River Shannon] yesterday morn'g for Strokestown & there met Ja's Nolan [Stewart and Kincaid's agent in Co Roscommon] who . . . assisted me in the Collection of Lord Westmeaths Rents. We were busy till half past six. We then dined & at seven I started by Bianconi for Longford. . . . During the two hours I was on the Road. . . . the Car was so Comfortable & the air so mild that I did not feel it. . . . I will go tomorrow Morn'g by Bianconi to Drumsna [on the eastern bank of the Shannon, opposite Clonteem] & remain with his Lordship at Clonteem tomorrow (Monday) Night after which I go over to the Kilglass property [south of Clonteem]. (Qtd. in Norton 2002, pp. 11–12).

One further point from Norton's work may cast light on the utility of Irish economic experience for emigrants who moved to the U.S. system, and at the same time it seems to challenge Scally's characterization of the people of Ballykilcline as "outside the world of calculation." Norton found that "contrary to the views of some modern historians, it seems that it was not the case, outside the few large urban concentrations, that Ireland in the 1840s was basically a barter economy without money (in which goods were usually exchanged directly for goods, and in which labour services were usually provided in lieu of rent). In fact, the financial system in regard to payment of rents from the estates managed by [Stewart and Kincaid], and in the context of other transactions on those estates, was surprisingly sophisticated" (2002, p. 24).

In researching the economic system, Cormac O'Grada investigated the network of Irish savings banks and found that the country had seventy-four of them in late 1846—far fewer than in Britain; still, the system had been established, with greater concentration in urban areas, by the 1820s. By famine time, the savings banks held three million pounds entrusted by approximately 100,000 people, who earned interest of about 3 percent. Although the banks were opened ostensibly to encourage the poorer classes to save, evidence before the 1830s Poor Law inquiry attests that, in fact, "farmers, shopkeepers, and tradesmen were much more likely to be account-holders than labourers, though servants also feature prominently in the categories listed." Nevertheless, "laborers, servants, and journeymen," as a category, had 4.8 percent of all funds in Irish accounts in 1852, and their account assets averaged eighteen pounds each—an average lower than that of all other groups in O'Grada's analysis except for "dressmakers, shopwomen, and female artisans." Women *were* depositors, though not in proportion to their numbers: married women, spinsters, and widows had 18.2 percent of nearly 52,000 accounts. Twenty-eight pounds was the average for all Irish savings bank accounts, O'Grada found. But 36 percent of accounts at Boyle savings banks in north-central Roscommon held twenty pounds or less, likely a reflection of local economic conditions and demographics (O'Grada 2002, pp. 1, 5, 8, 9).

This developing social and commercial infrastructure was augmented by military and police forces. In Ireland, the British police and military, which maintained a visible presence through the early nineteenth century, were significant channels of outside influence. Some of the units were primarily British; others comprised both British and Irish. The police forces included the Peace Preservation Force, the County Constabulary, the Irish Constabulary, the army, the militia, and various yeomanry groups, under the direction of either the county magistracy or the central government in Ireland (the Lord Lieutenant or his designee). Over time, their numbers were significant. The troops assigned to Ireland at any point in time in the early 1800s have been estimated as ranging from 15,000 to 30,000, a sign of "the weak hold of civil government" (Crossman 1996, p. 358). A substantial portion of the British army was Irish—42.2 percent and 37.2 percent in 1830 and 1840 respectively (Spiers 1996, p. 337).

After 1811, the law permitted a quarter of the English militia to be stationed in Ireland. "Apparently it was hoped that the exchange would 'civilize' the Irish units and at the same time provide Ireland with troops not closely connected with the people and therefore more reliable in quelling disturbances or possible revolution" (Broeker 1970, p. 33). Importantly, the law also allowed a third of the Irish to serve in Britain for two years each. As with the spalpeens, these policies facilitated the Irish people's exposure to intergroup dynamics and British influences.

After the Napoleonic wars in Europe ended in 1815, authorities decided to base a peacetime force of no more than 30,000 in Ireland, 10,000 fewer than the number that officials closest to the problem felt was required. In seeking to quell agrarian disturbances, authorities often strengthened numbers in troubled districts in an islandwide movement that rotated police personnel like pawns as local circumstances warranted: in Connacht in 1820 the number of troops rose from about 2,500 to 5,900. There were approximately 7,400 men in the Peace Preservation Force and the Constabulary in 1833; by 1840, the number was 8,600 and by 1850 it had risen to 12,758. The army, which was frequently used for police purposes rather than military defense, had 16,700 to 20,400 men stationed in Ireland in the distressed time between 1830 and

1832 (Broeker 1970, pp. 225, 176, 207). At times, the government also called on retired pensioners of the yeomanry to support the police establishment. Roscommon, which suffered extensive outrages periodically during the early 1800s, was ripe ground for this continuous shuffling of manpower. It meant a churning in the population on the ground, which led to constant interaction between the groups, introducing the rural populace to experience with Anglos and exposure to British culture.

A final source of expanded cultural awareness came from emigrants who left Roscommon and wrote home about their new lives in the United States. Occasionally a letter was published in the Roscommon newspapers; frequently, families shared letters with neighbors. Among dozens of people who moved from Kilglass Parish to Vermont even before the famine, there is evidence that at least one family wrote home to Ballykilcline about their new property in Rutland, and that others in Rutland carried on correspondence and received "foreign" letters in return, facilitated by the improved mail and transportation systems that Norton described. Such communications gave the families at home a picture of life "outside" and kept emigrants informed about the conditions of life "on the ground" in their home parish.

POLICY AND PROTEST: ACTION, REACTION

The Irish people, in responding to oppression by the British, relied on their numbers and covert activity, and they developed their own sense of social class to oppose the ruling Anglo gentry. In the eighteenth and early nineteenth centuries they banded together in secret agrarian organizations to oppose the officialdom they viewed as a usurper of their property and their rights. Many of these contests revolved around land issues, since land was the key to their livelihood. But they also took collective action for social, political, and economic advantage. By the 1830s, protest had become more open, yet the secret societies continued to operate well into midcentury. Galen Broeker learned that the tithe protests were the last actions in which the secret societies "were able to control sizable areas of rural Ireland for considerable periods of time" (1970, p. 237).

As the government's Devon Commission, which studied Ireland's agrarian system from 1843 to 1845, saw it, "There can be little doubt . . . that the real original source of agrarian outrage, as well as most other national disorders that exist in Ireland is the disproportion between the demand for and the supply of labor. . . . The possession of land, however small its extent, has become the only security for a supply of food; and to lose that security is, in fact, to risk the very existence of the family from which it was taken" (qtd. in Mokyr 1983, p. 128). In his powerful study, Joel Mokyr found that the secret societies' actions worked successfully to curb landlords' efforts to clear out tenants by eviction so as to consolidate their properties: "The evidence in the Devon Commission strongly supports the hypothesis that consolidation was slowed down considerably and in some places stopped altogether by violence, the landlords' fear of violence, or the landlords' compassion for the tenants who would be dispossessed" (1983, p. 132).

Evidence about crime and prosecution underscores the conclusion that violence was effective and not always punished. Anne Coleman found that convictions in Roscommon for seven consecutive years in the 1840s were just over one-third of those arrested: "Taken in conjunction with the level of crime indicated by the Outrage Papers, the capacity of the Molly Maguires to intimidate persons from prosecuting, or from coming forward with information to enable convictions to be had, was massive. If the creation and maintenance of a climate of fear to enforce their rules was a prerequisite to their survival, the evading of punishment as demonstrated by the low levels of conviction was a good index of their success" (1999, p. 39).

So, violence worked. And the power of the group worked in Kilglass, too, to stymie prosecutorial efforts. In documents concerning the house invasion in Ballykilcline in the 1840s, for example, Godfrey Hogg commented that even rewards did not induce the local Irish to give information against their neighbors: "For the last four years large rewards were offered in this district without producing any beneficial effect, and in no instance did a single person come forward to give information" (Hogg letter, Aug. 16, 1842). A few years later, under the pressure of the famine and evictions, that must have changed, since the police assigned to the Mahon and Lloyd murder cases did deal with informants in their investigations.

Parliamentary sources "emphasize[d] the success of agrarian movements in achieving reductions in prices and especially in lowering rates for conacre" (Huggins 2000, p. 13). On the other hand, agrarian violence also was an important deterrent to outside investment in Ireland in that time (Mokyr 1983, p. 284), thus reinforcing the depressed economic conditions that generated the people's protests. That consequence, however, would have been an invisible one to the Irish farmer on a small parcel in the countryside.

The people's communal efforts were not only offensive, and aimed at the authorities, but also defensive in that they sought to share the burden of sustenance and protection and to preserve a cultural legacy. From at least the 1790s forward, the Irish were politically conscious and active, as seen in the advances that Catholics had made by then; the buildup to the Rising of '98; Daniel O'Connell's Catholic Emancipation victory in 1829 (at some cost); his gaining of a seat in Parliament and his campaign for Repeal of the Act of Union of 1800. O'Connell is best known for his shaping of a powerful, islandwide democratic movement for change. The Irish learned at his feet. They saw the power of their own numbers at his Monster Meetings, and they remained committed to activism. They also watched what British authorities would tolerate as public protest evolved across the Irish Sea in response to industrialization, economic squeeze, and more commercialized agriculture.

The Irish in the rural Roscommon countryside were linked to and participated in the massive movements of their time through their seasonal trips to England and Scotland, and to other home provinces, for labor; through local geography and demographics; through the developing infrastructure in Ireland, which saw improvements in transportation, banking, and postal systems, and the spread of newspapers; through proximity to the British police and military; through Daniel O'Connell's various tactics and campaigns, which raised their political consciousness and kindled hope; and, not least, through continuing contact with earlier emigrants from their parish, including those who had gone to the United States.

The emigrants, in turn, tucked the memories and experiences of what they had seen and heard, what they had learned on Irish ground, into the mental baggage that crossed the Atlantic with them.

3

Resettling in Rutland

> Nothing struck me more, in Burlington, than the great number of Irish emigrants. They have filled the British provinces to the brim, and still continue to ascend the St. Lawrence, in infinite tribes, overflowing by every outlet into the States. . . . Such is their multitude, in comparison with any possible demand for their services, that it is difficult to conceive how a third part of them should earn even a daily glass of whiskey.
>
> —Nathaniel Hawthorne, "The Inland Port," 1835

> I bought so much land for $250 that you couldn't cross it on horseback in a day.
>
> —Immigrant John Hanley, writing home to Ballykilcline in 1844

NATHANIEL HAWTHORNE described the bustling port of Burlington just as John and Sabina Brennan Hanley arrived in Vermont from Ballykilcline and as their relatives and neighbors at home began their rent strike. The couple may have been part of the "infinite tribe" that mesmerized Hawthorne, though no information on the Hanleys' route has survived. Hawthorne might have been surprised to find them as landowners and farmers only nine years later when Hanley boasted about their new property in a letter home (Hannon 1986, pp. 50, 51). No information has come down that tells why the Hanleys left home when they did, though undoubtedly the views expressed in another Roscommon emigrant's letter captured at least some of their reasons for leaving: "Guernsey, July 12, 1847. I have purchased a neat cottage and excellent garden loaded with fruit of all kinds, for three hundred pounds; and I am more independent than ever I was, having no rent to pay—no juries to attend—nor no master to control me, and am in the midst of plenty; and what is better still—among a rational people, when my life at least is not in danger, and that's a great matter you will allow" (*Roscommon and Leitrim Gazette*, July 17, 1847). The Hanleys likely followed or traveled with friends to Rutland. McGuires and Colligans arrived there about the same time (Vandenburg communication,

71

2002; Butler letter, March 12, 1969). As early as 1830, a John Carrington lived in Rutland, and that was the name as well of a farmer in Ballykilcline whose son and namesake went to Rutland in 1847 as an evictee (U.S. census, Vermont, 1830), but their connection is not known.

In 1850, just after dozens of evictees from Ballykilcline arrived in Rutland, the town was a busy community where friends and relatives could help them find homes and jobs and introduce them to life in America. Rutland's landscape must have looked familiar to the Roscommoners, something like Kilglass except that they saw Otter Creek instead of the Shannon, Bomoseen Lake instead of Kilglass Lake, the Green Mountains instead of familiar Slieve Bawn. And if sheep had become a threat to their way of life in Kilglass, one can only wonder at their reaction to the extensive Merino herds grazing on the hills of Vermont, which by 1840 was feeding 1.7 million of the animals. The industry declined a few years later because of competition from western farmers after the Irish built a network of railroads. That effort changed the market and cut prices, which greatly distressed Vermont's sheep farmers (Vermont History website). On the other hand, it must have heartened the Irish immigrants to learn that the biggest crop in the state, at nearly five million bushels, was the familiar potato. Vermont land was valued then at $19.09 an acre (*Vermont Business Magazine* website).

Central Vermont had an advantage of place for the Irish because its new rail lines linked it to the leading Atlantic port of arrival in New York. If relatives followed the emigrants out of Ireland and landed in the Northeast, they could easily get to Vermont, a comparatively short trip from New York or Boston. In addition, some of the nearly five hundred Mahon evictees who had survived the coffin ships to Grosse Ile in 1847 must have scattered across southern Canada and northern New York and Vermont. If they wanted to reunite with family and friends who had settled in Rutland, they would not have had to travel far to do so.

The evictees' Rutland location too would have given them exposure to an event then playing out around Albany and Troy, New York, which were closely bound to Rutland by rail, commerce, and markets: they would have learned about the anti-rent wars in New York by newspaper or word of mouth from family and friends. One can only wonder what the rent strikers of Ballykilcline thought when they heard about the tenant battle and rent boycott underway by tens of thousands of farmers who were seeking to break up the vast land-grant estates of the Van Rensselaers and other elite families who were their landlords in the Catskills and the Hudson River Valley. Around Albany and Rensselaer County, tenants' resistance in that battle continued after 1860, though elsewhere much of it was waning just as the Ballykilcline evictees arrived. The struggling New York farmers employed some of the same tactics that the strikers of Ballykilcline and secret societies had used at home. The historian of the New York rent wars, Reeve Huston (2000), has chronicled the social issues involved in that dispute: land distribution, laboring relationships, American social structure, and the development of democratic movements, popular protest, and political parties.

One can only wonder whether observing and discussing New York's land war gave the Ballykilcline immigrants any great insights into their own past battle or helped them to any crucial understanding of their U.S. home and their place in the world. Certainly, at least, it must have astonished them to see their own home battle writ so large in a U.S. setting. Did it mean that the new place felt more familiar, and did they believe that their experience had equipped them for such threats? Or did it cause them to cower at finding in the United States battles so similar to the ones they had just lost at home? Or, in their view of it, having come out of their Irish rent strike with paid passage to America, had they *won* that battle at home?

The Evictees Who Went to Rutland

By 1850 some 760, or 20 percent, of Rutland's 3,715 people, had been born in Ireland. At least sixty-three of them were evictees from Ballykilcline, about 17 percent of the townland's 368 former inhabitants whose eviction and emigration in 1847 and 1848 were documented. They included the seven Brennans (Sabina Brennan Hanley's father and siblings); the four in James Hanley's family; five or more of the Winters; at least seven Mulleras; two Kelly families totaling seventeen people; at least four or five in Edward McCormick's family;[1] four to seven of the family of Michael McDermott;[2] a rent strike Defendant, Bartholomew (Bartley) Neary, his son Michael, and brothers William and Patrick, also a Defendant, with his wife Mary and daughter Bridget; William Cline, the father-in-law of Patrick Kelly; Ann Colligan, Patrick Winn (Wynne), and John Stewart and families; and the young John Carrington. (There are other possibilities as well, such as the John and Ann McGann McGinty family, whom I find as coming from Ballykilcline; two men named Donlan; and a couple named Patrick Connor and Bridget Downey.)[3]

These evictees must have gone almost directly to Rutland when they disembarked from the Crown's ships in New York, since they appeared in

Vermont in the 1850 U.S. census. A few of them later moved on to Massachusetts, Illinois, Minnesota, and likely elsewhere. It was an era of great mobility and Vermont residents were no exception. A census analysis of the Irish in Northfield, Vermont, in 1850, 1860, and 1870 showed that three-fourths of the immigrants did not stay there long enough to appear in two consecutive censuses. The native-born appeared "only slightly less transient" (Sessions 1992, p. 242).

Other former residents of Ballykilcline—not just the evictees—were living in Rutland then as well, despite Scally's assertion that only one family had gone out of Ireland before 1847 (1995, p. 75). Bridget Wynne McLaughlin must have left the townland before the evictions and moved elsewhere in Kilglass before emigrating, because she gave her birthplace as Ballykilcline and reported that she had emigrated in 1847 but was not recorded as present during the evictions. Her sister Ann was married to Bartley McGuire of Augha (i.e., Aughamore), a neighborhood in Ballykilcline (Vandenburg communication, 2006). The earlier immigrants to Rutland included one named Patrick Colligan, Michael Costello, additional Hanleys, the Foleys, some Geelans, the Igos, the Maguires, and others, probably including a John Toolan and a man named Owen Mulligan. Some of their names fill Ballykilcline's rent rolls in the 1830s and early '40s. Some of the scores of Kilglass newcomers to Rutland must have had either direct or extended ties with these Ballykilcline families, but the records are not sufficiently detailed to document the relationships.

It is clear from naturalization records, though, that perhaps twenty-five to thirty Kilglass Parish men, some (like John Hanley) with families, had arrived in Rutland long before 1850. A number of Kilglass and Strokestown men became citizens in Rutland courts in the 1840s, demonstrating that a chain migration was under way even before the famine years.[4] Hanley was the earliest known of these new Americans.[5] He arrived by or before 1835. A handful more went to Rutland in the next few years and the rest in the early 1840s.[6] Since citizenship records provide information only about males, the actual number of people from Kilglass would have been far larger, because the men's wives and children usually came from the same parish. Notable too is the fact that these men must all have become citizens within their first five to ten years in the United States. Undoubtedly, there were other Kilglass immigrants around Rutland who did not naturalize as early, if at all, and thus do not even show up in the records.

For another fifty or more years, people from Roscommon with some of these Kilglass surnames continued to arrive in Rutland (Rutland Courts). Experience working with the Kilglass and Rutland Irish records suggests that any Carlon (Carolan), Colligan, Neary (Nary), or Mullera immigrant in Rutland in the late 1840s and 1850s most likely came from Kilglass or the Strokestown area, as did many of the Hanleys; some of them had lived in Ballykilcline. Immigrants named Carroll came from the Kilglass townland of Knockhall. Igos, Geelans, and Gintys (McGintys) in Rutland probably hailed from Kilglass, possibly Ballykilcline. Many individuals named Burns came either from a Kilglass family or at least, more certainly, from County Roscommon; the O'Beirne sept's ancient territory was at Jamestown, to the north of Kilglass, and the family had been a prominent one in the townland. The name O'Beirne in America often became Burns.

As Scally suggested, a conspiracy in Kilglass may have allowed some people to "trade places in the line" for emigration with evicted Ballykilcline farmers who got the bounty to leave but wanted to stay in Ireland. Some individuals listed as boarding in Liverpool were not on the manifests when the ships docked in New York, and shipboard deaths do not account for the missing (Scally 1995, pp. 221–225; Harris communication).[7] If an exchange is what happened, both parties to such an arrangement would have gotten what they wanted. If it happened, some Kilglass people in Rutland may have been indebted to Ballykilcline strikers for their passage to America. And if it did happen, the people conspired to achieve what they wanted despite the rules and watchfulness of their British overseers.

In Rutland, a number of Ballykilcline evictees sought citizenship early. They included John Stewart in 1853; the brothers William and Daniel Brennan in 1854; Edward McCormick in 1856; and William Neary in 1858, about ten years after he arrived.[8] Patrick Brislin of Strokestown filed papers in 1853, within ten years of his arrival.

Strike Defendant Bartholomew (Bartley) Neary, then about forty-five, appeared in Rutland in the 1850 federal census, but that seemingly was the last record of him. His son Michael lived there until at least the mid-1860s, and Bartley's brother William lived to see the turn of the century from a seat at the poor farm. It is likely that Bartley and his brother Patrick, also a leader of the rent strike, died in Rutland during the 1850s and are buried in unmarked graves.

William Colligan's family often welcomed the circuit-riding Catholic priest who visited Rutland occasionally in those early years and celebrated Mass in private homes (Hannon 1986, p. 53). Colligan was born about 1818 in the Kilglass townland of Ballymoylin (Rutland Courts); it appears that his brother Bryan came out of Ireland with him. In Rutland as at home, the immigrants aided one another. Michael Hanley, apparently a man of education and some means, extended loans to friends in time of need: $100 to John Hanley in 1844, perhaps so he could buy additional acreage that year; $159.20 to Pat Gentry (Ginty, McGinty) in 1847; $40 to Bernard Carolin (Carlon, Carolan);[9] and $43 to Patrick Cox, formerly of Kilglass (Bell communication, 1999; Harris et al. 1989–). Michael died on January 6, 1848, of ship's fever, which he likely caught from an immigrant, since he himself had then been in the United States for years.[10] It appears that he was either a brother or a cousin of John Hanley, since he is buried alongside the Hanleys' young daughter Catherine in the Pleasant Street Cemetery in West Rutland (Bell communication, 1999; Middlesex, Vt., record center). Newly arrived widower William Brennan the elder, born in 1780, died about the same time from the same cause, soon after his Crown-paid Atlantic crossing on the *Creole*, leaving six Brennans, aged eighteen to twenty-eight, to make their own way with guidance from their sister Sabina and her husband John Hanley. William's wife, Nancy (aka Anne) McGuire, had died in Ireland during the 1840s.[11]

Numerous Colligans from Kilglass settled in Rutland, and descendants put their knowledge of their ancestors' moves on paper in the 1960s[12] (they gave a phonetic rendering of the name of their home "hamlet," but the only Kilglass townland it possibly could be—based on a comparison of names and spellings—is Ballykilcline):

> The Colligan family originated in the County of Roscommon, Parish Kilglass of Strokestown . . . in a hamlet called Ballin-a-chine. All the men were known for their stature, being six feet seven inches and six feet eight inches, and most were red-haired. They were noted for being bright and daring, and given to outwitting their British rulers. Four Colligan brothers who have left descendants in Vermont came from this Colligan family. They were Bernard, William, Patrick and John. Both William and Patrick were married and had eight children apiece. They were in West Rutland as early as 1830 or 1831 and were employed as drill-sharpening smiths for (?) Searson [Slason?] and Barnes Marble Co. . . .
>
> John Colligan married in Ireland and had two children, Mary and Sarah. He was a schoolmaster who died in Ireland and never came to the U.S. However, his wife, Susan Carroll, remarried another John Colligan who was a cousin of her late husband and his three brothers. Susan and her second husband also came to West Rutland, Vermont and settled there. . . .
>
> Bernard Colligan didn't come to the U.S. as early as his brothers William and Patrick did. He stayed on the Colligan homestead in Ireland until a later date. It was he who owned the ancient Colligan freehold of 40 acres. It ran from a narrow frontage on the road far up into the hills. . . . Bernard lived in Ireland until 1847. In May of that year, he emigrated with his wife

and six children. They arrived in West Rutland, Vermont in July. Bernard died later that same month of bubonic plague. His wife, Anne, and six children, the oldest of which was ten or eleven[,] remained in West Rutland.

One of several traditional stories that surrounds Bernard Colligan is his flight from the law in Ireland before he came to the U.S. It seems that for "some offense against the crown" Bernard became a fugitive "over the mountains" in Galway. What exactly this offense was is unknown. . . .

For some years he acted as an itinerant blacksmith and farrier (horseshoer and veterinarian) "over the mountains," coming home intermittently with poached deer, hares, etc. to supplement the family's meager diet. He took the name of McLaughlin during this time. It may have been the same surname that his mother had, however this is unknown. (Butler letter, March 12, 1969)

The family history of the Colligans told about many difficulties encountered by Irish immigrants on both sides of the Atlantic and captured the Irish animosity for the British ruling class at home. It also demonstrated the family and "chain" nature of migration before and during the famine. Noteworthy too is the date supplied for Bernard's emigration: May 1847, when so many local families were evicted and sent across the Atlantic by Denis Mahon and Crown agents.

A Bernard Colgan (Colligan) was among those evicted from Ballykilcline: he was the eight-year-old son of one of the two Patrick Colgans there and that Patrick's wife, Anne. A twenty-five-year-old Bernard Colgan showed up on the 1840 tenants' list for Ballykilcline, but he was gone before the evictions occurred. In 1842 a Bernard Colligan appeared on a British government list of owners of illegal firearms; he lived in Knockhall, which is next to Ballykilcline; he may be the Bernard of the 1840 tenants list (Dillon letter, March 25, 1842) and could have been the man who died in Rutland. Perhaps the Bernard of the letter saw what was happening in 1847 and decided that it was time to join his brothers in the United States. Perhaps he voluntarily moved on, or the law, the landlord, or the worst year of famine drove him to it. In 1870, Rutland was home to a Bernard Colligan, born in 1811 (U.S. Census, Vermont, 1870). He, alternatively, could have been the man who lived in Knockhall and owned a gun.

The writer who documented the Colligan history said that John and Susan Colligan's two daughters were schooled at a convent in Montreal, where they learned fluent French. One of them received musical training and became the organist at St. Bridget's Church in West Rutland, a post she held for forty years (Butler letter, March 12, 1969).

Another fugitive who arrived in Rutland from Strokestown was Patrick Brislin. In Roscommon, Brislin had been arrested in connection with a raid for firearms and accused of belonging to a secret society, so he fled the country rather than risk transportation to Australia. Brislin was living in Rutland by 1850 (U.S. Census for Vermont, 1850). A few years later he witnessed the citizenship filings for two Ballykilcline evictees (Rutland Courts); surely he had known them in Roscommon as well. In 1860, Brislin had a family and $975 [$23,625 in 2005 dollars] in assets (U.S. Census, Vermont, 1860).[13]

In Rutland, some portion of Ballykilcline and the larger parish of Kilglass was reestablishing itself as a community through the 1840s, while Ballykilcline unraveled in Ireland. More than the lakes and hills looked familiar to these strangers in this new place.

RUTLAND IN THE 1850S

The Irish were not the only newcomers to Rutland in the mid-1800s. At least a few residents had been born in French Canada, England, or Scotland; one came from Norway and another from Portugal. To the west in Castleton, where slate was becoming an important product (the first eight slate businesses opened in the 1850s), a significant influx from Wales was under way: workmen were transferring their skills from a huge slate operation in Dinorwig to Vermont's slate district, which also employed the Irish (Hancock 2001, p. 21). A historian of the Welsh in Poultney and Fair Haven has compared the Welsh and Irish immigrants: "These skilled workers were likely conscious of their working class status and able to formulate criticisms of the developing capitalist economy. In turn, the Irish came from a tradition of militant class conflict and solidarity. This prepared them for trade union activity in industrial America, even though many of them were unskilled initially" (Hancock 2001, p. 2).

There is no sign that John Hanley worked to extract either marble or slate, but at least one son and a son-in-law worked in the marble quarries. John and Sabina acquired land for farming in the early 1840s, and it was worth $500 [$12,900] in 1850, giving them the status, along with one other farmer whose real estate assets equaled theirs, as the wealthiest Irish immigrants by property value. In fact, since the real estate of all 760 Irish-born Rutland residents was valued at $1,600 [$41,279], which belonged to just four families (U.S. Census, Vermont, 1850), the Hanleys had nearly a third of the land wealth of all Irish natives in Rutland that year. Their other assets then are unknown, since the 1850 census did not inquire about personal cash or the value of household goods; not until ten years later did it ask about personal assets.

At that time, the Hanleys were one of only a half-dozen Irish-born families who had the resources to make a living at farming, which they pursued near Hanley's Mountain on Whipple Hollow Road in what is now West Rutland. When they bought seventy acres of land in the early 1840s, the Hanleys wrote home to Ballykilcline to share their good news, boasting that the property "was so large that neither man nor beast could walk over it in a day" (qtd. in Hannon 1986, p. 51). They later bought twenty-three acres more. Whether they bought their first parcel of land out of funds they brought with them or money they earned in Vermont or borrowed from Michael Hanley is not clear. But the famine immigrants from Ballykilcline and Kilglass, and elsewhere as well, apparently brought little money with them to their new life (U.S. Census, Vermont, 1860), since they did not buy property early, and worked at wage labor, and most had accumulated little by 1860 when the census form separated assets into real estate and personal estate. The wages paid to a laborer—the occupation of most Irish immigrants at least for a time—were only seventy-two cents a day with room and board, or ninety-seven cents without food and a place to stay [$18.38 and $24.76, based on conversion from the year 1848]. Farmhands made even less: about $13 a month (*Vermont Business Magazine* website). These wages were roughly in line with the average daily pay nationally: "[Claudia] Goldin and [Robert] Margo['s] (1992) study of wages paid to civilians by the U.S. Army is the most comprehensive source of information of wages in the mid-nineteenth century. They found that the average daily wages for laborers was $1.08, while artisans were paid $1.43 and clerks $2.35. Wages seem to have been little different in New York City in 1850. [Stanley] Lebergott (1964) reported that unskilled workers received ninety cents per day, carpenters $1.38, and female domestics $1.05 in addition to room and board" (O'Grada 2002b, p. 9).

The United States at that time saw unusual growth. The gross national product was up; gold found in California had created a rush there; manufacture was developing, and agriculture was shifting west. "Output per worker in manufacturing grew thirty percent or more in each region during the 1850s, and the size of farms, as measured by capitalization, grew seventy percent or more outside the South." In the same decade, the portion of unskilled workers in the labor force rose 10 percent. The farming sector grew as well, but that of skilled and white-collar workers dropped. Economist Joseph Ferrie interpreted the signs: "Urban workers in the Northeast (particularly in manufacturing) faced difficult circumstances throughout the decade," and the ability of workers to move between sectors became harder. Then the Panic of 1857 struck, followed by a slight recovery before the economy went into a recession just before the Civil War (Ferrie 1999, p. 37).[14]

Nevertheless, Ferrie found upward mobility among the Irish, British, and German immigrants he studied: "By 1860, any differences in wealth between the Irish and the British and Germans that could not be accounted for by occupation had been erased. Thus, although the Irish had on average thirty-five percent of the wealth of the British and Germans in 1850, by 1860 that deficit had shrunk to statistical and substantive insignificance after accounting for occupation. The remaining deficit could be explained by the large number of Irish immigrants who were unskilled workers, rather than by the overall poverty of the Irish" (Ferrie 1999, p. 189).

In short, the Irish, for all their troubles, were doing fairly well. Only 4 percent of the immigrants who lived in the East in 1850 had any real estate, however, and it was worth only $33.32 [$860]; nearly 20 percent of western immigrants owned property then, and its average value was $355.44 [$9,170] (Ferrie 1999, p. 69). Generally, Ferrie's data show that up to 1860 the asset gap widened between unskilled workers and those higher up the ladder, and that the immigrants who went west accumulated greater wealth than those who stayed along the East Coast.

That geographic differential seems borne out in the case of the Ballykilcline immigrants. For instance, evictee Patrick Mullera, the son of John and Anna Rowley Mullera of Ballykilcline, worked on the railroads in Orange, New York, for eighteen months after arriving in the United States. He spent time next in Kentucky and then returned to New York, this time to Utica, before moving to Clayton County, Iowa, in 1857, where he bought a farm. But he left his land to spend four years in Kentucky and Illinois before returning to his property in Iowa. Patrick married and had two children, one of whom apparently died young. In 1870, census takers recorded that his farm and personal assets were worth $5,200 [$80,281]. Patrick was a citizen who could read and write. An 1882 county history says his property was "265 acres in all, mostly under cultivation." He was a Democrat and "one of the popular men of the county." His older brother, Arthur (who had left Ballykilcline in the 1830s), lived with Patrick's family in 1880, as did a widow named Lannon, her children, and a farm laborer named McDermott. Families with other surnames from Kilglass—Hanley, Moran, Donlon, O'Connor, McLaughlin, Feeney—lived nearby. All these names were also present at some time in Rutland (U.S. Census, Iowa, 1870, 1880; *History of Clayton County, Iowa* 1882). Patrick's farming wealth in 1870 ranked him, in comparison with many of his former neighbors in Rutland, in the top tier of identified evictees for accumulation of assets.[15]

By 1860, some 40 percent of the unskilled workers Ferrie studied "owned some personal property," and "immigrants possessed an average of $1,327 [$32,154] in 1860 after an average of fifteen years in the United States" (Ferrie, pp. 189, 108, 129). Unfortunately for the ability of many Irish to build assets, they disproportionately remained in the East.

Earning a Wage in Rutland

Most of Rutland's Irish newcomers—predominantly single young men— found work at first as common laborers, often in railroad building, which began in Vermont in 1846 (Sessions 1992, p. 239). Rutland's Irish in 1850 included 366 men who were laborers (U.S. Census, Vermont, 1850). They boarded usually with Irish families, but sometimes lived in the homes of Rutland's Yankee natives, where the women served as domestic help (although the 1850 census commonly listed no occupation for them), and the men worked as either servants or farm laborers. Among them were these Kilglass natives: Ann Colligan, age 22, lived in the home of an Episcopal clergyman; Margaret Winters, 23, and Margaret Foley, 17, were counted in the house of marble man William F. Barnes, as was John and Sabina Brennan Hanley's son Gilbert in 1860; Kilglass native Peter Riley was a gardener in 1860 for marble man Henry Sheldon; Honora Winter's daughter and namesake appears (under the diminutive Ann) in the home of attorney Charles Williams (U.S. Census, Vermont, 1850). In 1860, Catherine Foley worked in the home of marble man William Gilmore; Archibald Hanley was a farm laborer there; and marble dealer William Ripley employed Margaret Hanley, John and Sabina's daughter, in his house (U.S. Census, Vermont, 1860). Domestic service was comparatively well paid, and the conditions of work offered advantages that did not come in millwork or the needle trades. Moreover, the Irish were advantaged in the service marketplace because many of them spoke English (O'Grada 2005). Thus, Kilglass people had an inside look at the lives, homes, and habits of some of Rutland's social leaders, and one wonders whether they purposefully pursued these connections with the local elite rather than take jobs in less visible households or enterprises, and how doing so influenced their view of life in their new country.

Although many of Rutland's Yankee population in 1850 had land assets worth at least several thousand dollars, the spread of real estate value (with a few exceptions), compared with later years, was not great. By land value, the richest man in town then appeared to be a farmer named Avery

Billings, 66, a Vermont native whose farmhands included Ballykilcline immigrant William Nary (Neary) and Michael Costello, 14 (likely a son of Michael Costello from Ballykilcline). Billings's farm was then worth $45,500 [$1.2 million]. Attorney Reubin Thrall, 54, had more than $29,000 [$748,000] in real estate, and merchant George Hodges, 62, had land worth $25,000 [$645,000]. A handful of others each owned real property exceeding $12,000 in value [$310,000], including two merchants, a farmer, a physician, and a hotelkeeper. Marble man William Barnes reported $12,000 in real estate but also had $40,000 [$1 million] in capital in his business operation (U.S. Census, Vermont, 1850; U.S. Manufacturing Census, 1850).

Railroad Work

Early in the 1850s, railroad lines, built by the Irish, were completed around Rutland, making the area an important hub for transport to eastern New England, New York and points west via the Erie Canal, and Canada. Laborers' jobs building the railroads frequently were welcomed by the Irish as a great improvement over the poor labor conditions in Ireland. According to Kerby Miller, "Most famine emigrants left Ireland eagerly. . . . Indeed, once in America at least a few emigrants wrote letters full of gratitude toward former landlords whose financial assistance had enabled them to leave what one called 'the Gulf of Miserary . . . and Ruin.' " "I am now Employed in the rail road line earning 5s [shillings] a day," wrote Michael Byrne from Vermont to "your Honour" in Ireland. "And instead of being chained with poverty in Boughill I am crowned with glory" (qtd. in Miller 1999, p. 182).[16]

The workers were not always so content, though. Two hundred Irish men who were laying track for the Central Vermont railroad in 1846 had a serious encounter with U.S. authorities when they went on strike over wages due them but not paid. At the time, the immigrants earned fifty cents for a ten-hour day and also received board. When their protest turned violent, Vermont authorities called out the state militia against them, thus replicating the tactics used earlier by U.S. and Canadian authorities to put down canal workers' disturbances in objecting to unfair wages and working conditions. Vermont's railroad leaders had petitioned authorities to use police force against the strikers. Even years later, in the 1860s, the Central Vermont paid its section men twelve cents less than the average for day laborers across the state: a dollar a day (Sessions 1992, pp. 240, 242). In spite of the wage scale, the railroads got built. Five hundred miles of railroad track snaked through Vermont by 1855 (Way 1993, pp. 287–295; Railroad History website).

Harsh working conditions were not unusual in railroad and canal work, which typically capitalized on cheap, plentiful immigrant labor. Something similar happened just across the border in New York state during the building of the Troy and Boston railroad line: the contractors overadvertised for laborers, and when they showed up in great number from far places seeking jobs, with no finances to return home, the contractors slashed wages to fifty-five cents a day. When this happened, a Clare man recalled, the men struck because they could not live on so little. "Matters began to wear a threatening aspect. At length, the legal authorities were called upon, with military force, to drive them off (which is always the custom in such cases). [When] I went to see the condition of those that remained . . . a scene of suffering presented itself which made the heart sick. All along for miles was one continued scene of anguish and suffering, as if some peculiar curse was chasing the unfortunate people from Ireland" (qtd. in Miller and Wagner 1994, pp. 52–53).

Such harsh treatment from authorities undoubtedly earned a reputation in all of the immigrant communities and more than likely generated resentful political conversations. It also must have forged a sense of solidarity and quickly tarnished the "crown of glory" that had so excited Michael Byrne. Learning came fast in such circumstances.

Maintaining Networks

Still, the network of railroad tracks they put down at such great cost helped the Irish, too. Fannie Reilly Carlon, wife of John, returned home to Rutland for many summers from Indiana, presumably by rail, to visit her family; the birth records of most of her children testified to her travels. Some Ballykilcline people had settled directly in Illinois in the 1830s and early 1840s; descendants have noted that some of the men worked on local canals and were paid in scrip, which they later traded for farmland in LaSalle County (*Famine to Freedom* 2003). There were members of at least a few Ballykilcline families in both Illinois and Vermont; they included Hanleys, Nearys, and Carolans (Carlons).

Communicating with far-flung family and friends was difficult; nevertheless, the immigrants accomplished it. The *Rutland Herald* helped by reporting the names of residents who had mail at the post office. Ballykilcline and Kilglass names appeared on the lists periodically; they had connected across states and regions. Pat Geenty (Ginty, McGinty) had mail to pick up in January 1848, right after Michael Hanley, who had lent him money, died. Nearly eighteen months later, a letter waited for Michael Hanley himself. In April 1848, Patrick Cox had mail to pick up. In January

1849, Pat Colgan (Colligan), Patrick Kelly, and John Stuart all made the list. Patrick Kelly had a "foreign" letter awaiting him on April 4.

Another indication of the extent of the immigrants' communications comes from the ads that the Irish placed in the *Boston Pilot* seeking "lost" family members. Roscommoners in Rutland placed some of them. Starting in 1851, Michael and James Foley made use of the newspaper in a search for their son and brother, Thomas. One of their several ads read "Thomas Foley, parish of Kilglass, Townland of Knockhall sailed from Liverpool in Nov. 1847 for New York. When last heard of was in Albany to work for a farmer named Darbey Whelan. Contact his father, Michael, and brother, James. Address Michael Foley, West Rutland, Vermont" (Harris et al. 1989–, vol. 2). There is no indication in the record that they ever located Thomas. Although the ad says that the Foleys came from Knockhall, which adjoins Ballykilcline, the tenancy records of Ballykilcline show a Foley working a plot there in 1834 with Patrick and Michael Coyle; two years later a survey map of Ballykilcline adds "James" to the Foley surname as holder.[17] Ten years later, that parcel had been taken over by George and William Stewart.

James Maguire of Rutland resorted to the *Pilot* in 1845 in his search for Eleanor Maguire O'Hara, though their relationship is not described. She had been in Toledo when they last communicated; persons with information were instructed to contact either Maguire or John Hanby (probably Hanley) in Rutland (Harris et al. 1989–, vol. 1). When John Cox of Kilglass came to Boston in 1846, he advertised for his brother Pat, who had arrived in the spring of 1845 and gone to West Rutland (Harris et al. 1989–, vol. 1). Thomas Dervine of West Rutland sought his brother in 1861: "Bernard Dervine, of the Town of Slataughmore, parish of Kilglass, co. Roscommon. When last heard from, in 1856, was in San Francisco, California." Patrick Oats of West Rutland, born in Kilglass, sought his uncles, Michael and Thomas Oats, who had arrived in the United States in 1848 and spent time in St. Louis (Harris et al. 1989–, vol. 5).

Sometimes the immigrants' ads for lost children or siblings told of wretched fates in their new places. One such ad was placed by the son of a former tenant of Denis Mahon's. "In 1847 or 1848," the parents, Patrick and Mary O'Connor, had left two daughters with relatives in Ireland and arrived in Canada with son John, a small child. The couple made their way to work in Niagara, near Buffalo, New York, and saved passage money for their daughters in order to reunite the family. "This money . . . was the ruin of both father and mother; for, to possess it, they were both cruelly murdered by a brutal assassin. The little boy, only . . . miraculously escaped sharing the same barbarous fate." John O'Connor eventually reached New York City and, in 1871, placed an ad that told his story in an effort to locate his sisters "whose Christian names, he thinks, are Margaret and Bridget, or Elizabeth" (DeGrazia et al. 2001, p. 371).[18] It is not known whether John ever found them. Among the families evicted by Mahon in 1847, however, were three headed by men listed as "Patt Connor." They were evicted from holdings in Goreygloss, Castlenode, and Newtown, and their households totaled fifteen people (*Freeman's Journal*, April 1848, Bishop's List).

The newspaper ads show communication across great distances by giving the location of the missing relative "when last heard from"—New York, Ohio, Vermont, California, Missouri—indicating the dislocation and wandering range of the Irish in their early years in the United States. It was not inexpensive to place such notices: Harris, using figures from Oscar Handlin's study of the Irish in Boston (1941), calculated that it cost a laborer half a week's wage in Boston to do so (1996). That so many Irish advertised, then, testifies to the intensity of their family ties. The ads also were evidence of the chaos wrought in families by famine and emigration; they show that even husbands and wives, parents and children, and siblings lost track of each other.

THE ISSUE OF LITERACY

Their mail and their use of newspaper ads to search for lost family members indicate that a number of the immigrants were literate. Scally reported on the extent of literacy in 1841 among the more than 19,000 people who lived in Ballintobber North, the Roscommon barony that included Kilglass Parish: "Males who were able both to read and write outnumbered females by more than three to one (2,694 to 809). But among those who could read only, females were in the majority (1,837 to 1,647)" (Scally 1995, p. 249). These figures show that 37 percent of the people in the barony could read; 18 percent could both read and write. James Donnelly found that illiteracy among males in County Roscommon as a whole exceeded 60 percent in 1841 (2001, p. 3).

When O'Grada studied the Irish in New York in the 1860 census, he found that 8 percent of the men and 14 percent of the women were illiterate but also that those rates were lower than corresponding rates in Ireland. Its 1861 census showed that 28 percent of men and 31 percent of women between the ages of sixteen and twenty-five could not read or write, and the rates went up for an older age group: 35 percent for men and 51 percent for women between the ages of forty-six and fifty-five (O'Grada, 2005).

Because the assessment of literacy or the lack of it seemed an important indicator of the Ballykilcline farmers' ability to comprehend the issues of the rent strike and its legal context, a clue to how well they were equipped to navigate their new environments, as well as a gauge of agency, I hoped to gain information about their literacy as a factor not only for their life in the United States but also during their rent strike in Ireland. Although Irish records were inadequate, it seemed that U.S. records could overcome that deficiency, since federal censuses beginning in 1850 inquired about the ability to read and write, and my study had identified immigrants from Ballykilcline. (See tables 2A and 2B in the Appendix.)

I decided to examine the issue only for those individuals for whom documentation showed that they had lived or held property in Ballykilcline. Spouses for whom no evidence showed residence there, children who were very young at the point of immigration, and children born after a family moved to the United States were excluded from this dataset. The cohort was constrained in size also because the 1850 and 1860 federal censuses sought responses on literacy only for those over age twenty. In 1870, the government counted "cannot read" and "cannot write" answers separately, and again in 1880. In order to make the test as robust as possible, information was included on evictees who met the established criteria but settled elsewhere than in Vermont: Maryland, Illinois, Minnesota, and Iowa (tables 2A and 2B with analysis in the Appendix). The results showed that forty-four of fifty-eight individuals, or 76 percent of the studied group, were literate, and no contradictory evidence appeared.

Most of the people from Ballykilcline, then, were literate to some degree. But a large percentage changed answers between censuses, which may have had to do with their own understanding of literacy or perhaps how a census taker or a family member explained it when the question was raised. It appears, though, that they could read and write in greater numbers than others in the barony of Ballintobber North, as measured against Scally's and Donnelly's reports. Several factors may account for their greater literacy. Ballykilcline may have been exceptional; as Scally showed, a number of schools operated locally near the townland before the 1840s. Samuel Lewis (1837) reported fourteen schools, public and private, educating 740 children in the area. Two priests were associated with the townland: Father Peter Geraghty boarded with the Padians during the strike and Rev. Brian McDermott of Kilglass came from a family in the townland; as members of an educated class, they may have encouraged literacy in the residents. At least one sometimes schoolmaster, John McGann, lived in Ballykilcline.[19] John Colligan also was said to be a schoolmaster (Butler letter, March 12, 1969). One of the Donnelans was an aide to Attorney O'Ferrall. The number of schools and the occupations of people in or connected with Ballykilcline suggest that the townspeople may have been more literate than the general populace of the barony (additional study is warranted, however).

Roscommon immigrants in Rutland and elsewhere had another marked advantage over immigrants from other Connacht and Munster counties: most spoke English or were bilingual. "Only sixteen percent of those emigrating from Roscommon . . . were Irish speakers. [Isaac] Weld noted from a survey of the Rev. William Thompson conducted in the parish of Kilglass in 1816, that 'English is the language spoken by people in general though they all understand Irish, but it is not so much used among them as formerly'" (Coleman 1999, pp. 13, 14). That observation, made more than three decades before the Ballykilcline evictions, is further indication that Kilglass was well connected to larger worldly markets.

BUILDING COMMUNITY

During the middle and later 1850s, the Irish in Rutland focused on building their community—their families, church, and social organizations— and they welcomed and supported a newspaper, the *Rutland Courier*, which was pro-Irish and pro-Democratic. The *Courier* was founded in 1857 by John Cain, an immigrant from the Isle of Man, in opposition to the Yankees' entrenched, conservative *Rutland Herald*, which was run by old money and marble interests. Cain often spent column inches tweaking the *Herald*, which, he said, "has a class of readers that swallow down as bible truths and realities all the ridiculous inconsistencies and nonsense that appear in its columns" (*Rutland Courier*, Dec. 13, 1864). A more serious effort was later advocated by the *Courier:* "Every man that intends making this county his home ought to be a citizen thereof" (*Rutland Courier*, Sept. 16, 1864). Many Roscommon immigrants did not need Cain's exhortation: they were naturalizing early and in numbers by the mid-1850s, even before the newspaper established itself in Rutland, as had Kilglass men who arrived during the previous decade. They had learned well the Liberator's lessons at home that political power can change the terms of life.

By such actions, they were positioning themselves in the new socioeconomic and political structure, but even as they did so, they did not forget where they came from; chain migration and casual private help, such as the loans made by Michael Hanley, attest to that. No known records document the amounts of money returned home by the Kilglass immigrants or other Irish in Rutland, but continuing immigration pointed to their commitment. The amounts likely were significant, especially coming as they did from workers at the bottom of the wage scale. Many of the "assisted" immigrants in Tyler Anbinder's Five Points study of County Kerry's famine Irish were "sending money to loved ones in Ireland, either to help support aged parents or to pay for relatives' emigration" (Anbinder 2002, par. 63). The Irish viewed these obligations to support and "take out" family as a sacred trust. As one Roscommon immigrant wrote from Troy, New York: "All Friends[,] arrived here in good health, after a long and dangerous voyage of 50 days. We had only two deaths on board. We came to the city of Troy, we then went to Barney Murphy's. . . . [W]e all got employment. . . . [L]et us know how ye all are, or if any of the money that was sent from all parts of this country, for relief for Ireland, has reached as far as you. Although the Atlantic rolls between us, it has not removed my affection from you. . . . Owen Tansey'" (*Roscommon & Leitrim Gazette*, July 17, 1847). Rensselaer County's 1850 census shows three men named Barney Murphy. A 26-year-old laborer worked in the tannery of John Gary in Troy's Ward 5; at least eight others boarding and working there bore Roscommon surnames. He appears most likely to be Tansey's friend.

Remittances to Ireland

Employment had multiple meanings for Irish immigrants, among them both survival and aid to family and homeland. Of nearly $2 million [$45.7 million] in deposits at "the Savings Bank" in Boston in 1835, the *Boston Transcript* said that five-eighths belonged to the "improvident" Irish (Lord et al. 1945, p. 137). A decade later, Boston's Provident Institution for Savings held more than $3 million [$80 million] in deposits, and Lemuel Shattuck estimated that "more than one-half of the depositors . . . are Irish, or persons immediately connected with our foreign population" (qtd. in G. Potter 1960, pp. 512, 513).

Irish women were particularly diligent in helping their families: domestics and mill girls "made a staggering contribution to the Irish economy in the form of these remittances" (Diner 1983, p. 52). In one instance, the captain of an American ship hired two Irish girls who were traveling aboard to a new life in New York to work in his own home, and they stayed on for years. Over time, he said, they sent small sums home "sufficient to convey from Liverpool to the United States no less than thirteen persons, including their father, mother, brothers and sisters, and cousins to the third and fourth remove. Such instances were by no means uncommon."

Charles Mackay said that remittances arrived "by almost every packet that reached Liverpool." He continued, "Few, however, know the aggregate amount. I had occasion, when in Ireland, when visiting a large union work-house, containing between two thousand and three thousand inmates, to enquire if many such sums found their way to the paupers in that estab-lishment, and I was informed that from six to eight persons weekly on an average were enabled to leave the workhouse by this means, and to pay their passage to America" (Mackay 1849, pp. 22, 23).

Officials and historians have tried to estimate the total support that Irish immigrants gave to their home families; their efforts have produced a range of answers. The British Emigration Commissioners judged the value of the dollars that emigrants sent to Ireland in an 1873 report. They esti-mated that North Americans had sent $83 million [$2 billion, using 1860 as the conversion year] through banks and commercial houses, *in addition* to the money that they sent privately. The commissioners apparently looked at proceeds from both Canada and the United States (Knight 1999).

If no record exists for Rutland's immigrants' remittances, nevertheless there is testimony that these Irish did support their distressed families at home. In 1847, Land Agent Joseph Kincaid, who was familiar with condi-tions in Kilglass and in Ballykilcline, told Parliament about

> the numerous Instances of small Sums of Money being sent over by Persons who emigrated in former Years both to the United States and to Canada, to assist other Members of their Families to go out this year. I have had repeated Applications this year, in Cases where I did not think the Parties had a Claim upon the Landlord for the whole Expense of sending them and the Entire of their Families to America, to contribute as much as would send out One or Two of the Children, in the full Confidence that those Children would send over sufficient Money in a few Years to bring over the Rest of the Family, and I have done so. (Kincaid testimony, June 21 1847)

The case of Lowell, Massachusetts, which had a large working-class Irish population in its mills in the 1850s, may be instructive about remit-tances. Lowell's Irish numbered some 18,000 by 1860 (Center for Lowell History website), about five times the size of Rutland's Irish community then (U.S. Census, Vermont, 1860). Through one firm alone in 1866, the Irish in Lowell spent $12,000 [$152,281] on prepaid passage tickets so that family members could leave the old country; they sent another $32,000 [$406,000] to support relatives who remained in Ireland. One Lowell immigration agent accepted $140 [$3,392] "from an industrious Irish girl in one of our mills"; he called it a "striking instance of liberality"

(Mitchell 1988, p. 149), since the girl likely earned less than a dollar a day. If Rutland's Irish sent aid home at the same rate as the Irish in Lowell did through that one firm alone in 1866, then their remittances and family support would have totaled more than $8,000 [$101,520] that year.

The aid sent was not always an individual and private mission. In 1847 the Irish in Boston raised $200,000 [$4.9 million] to save their famine-ravaged countrymen (Handlin 1941, p. 152). In Fall River in 1841 a thousand Irish "formed an organization to send relief funds to their starving relatives back home" (Blewett 2000, p. 432). Through the famine and troubled times in the old country in later decades, the immigrants worried and organized to help alleviate Irish starvation and deprivation. Records in Rutland show periodic collections to aid the Irish at home even after 1900.

The databases being compiled from savings account records of the early Irish in New York, Lowell, Providence, and elsewhere may determine precisely what resources they tapped and the rate at which they accumulated funds despite their multiple obligations, their lack of work skills, and their low position in the job hierarchy. In his study based on New York's Emigrant Industrial Savings Bank (EISB) records, Anbinder learned that the poverty-stricken immigrants assisted from County Kerry's Lansdowne estate to the notorious Five Points area of New York City amassed surprising amounts of capital in their first ten years in the United States (2002, p. 15). Gerard Moran pointed to the emigrants assisted from Lord Palmerston's estate in Sligo, who returned 2,000 pounds to family in Ireland within two years of landing in the United States, and to the destitute Lansdowne settlers who sent an equal amount home in their first decade in New York. Moran found that such funds returned to Ireland were a primary support of emigration after 1850, to the extent that "as a result, landlord enthusiasm for assisted passage declined" (Moran 2004, pp. 120, 220). The landlords saw that they could step aside and let the emigrants take care of their own. The "surplus" populations were leaving without their help.

The commitment to savings on the part of the Irish is illustrated by Cormac O'Grada in a study of panic behaviors by depositors of the well-known EISB, which was established in 1850 in New York City by the Irish Emigrant Society. O'Grada delivered figures derived from Alan L. Olmstead's work on New York City banks, representing the average deposits and the numbers of accounts for the EISB and for all U.S. mutual savings banks. By 1855, Irish-born depositors at the EISB had, on average, more funds in their accounts than did the depositors at all savings banks: they had saved an average of $224 [$5,220] per account as opposed to $196

[$4,568] for all such U.S. accounts—a remarkable achievement for recent immigrants. Nor was the finding a fluke: six years later EISB clients had accounts averaging $260.26, whereas $226.98 was the average for all Americans (O'Grada 2002b, p. 8).

The Church in Rutland

In 1853, Louis de Goesbriand became the first bishop of the Burlington Catholic diocese in Vermont. He recruited priests from as far as Ireland and Brittany and brought in Canadian clerics to create church infrastructure across the state to replace the traveling priests of the previous decade or more (Resch 1989, p. 155). The following year the bishop established St. Peter's Parish in Rutland and appointed its first pastor, Rev. Zephyrin Druon, who built a frame church and a school in 1855. Druon was responsible for Catholics throughout southern and western Vermont. In 1856, a French priest, Rev. Francis Picart, became Rutland's pastor, but after a year he moved on to St. Bridget's in West Rutland. He undertook the first parish census there and documented the size of his congregation: 1,294 people in 265 families. Father Picart's census also included the women's maiden names and identified the marble companies where the men worked (St. Bridget's Parish Census). The parish established a school, which two years later had 126 students; a new building opened in 1860 with 200 pupils.

Rev. Thomas Lynch, Dublin-educated and not yet thirty years old, succeeded Picart at St. Bridget's (a picture shows him with a broad forehead, a receding hairline, sharp eyes, and a tight cast to the mouth). Father Lynch hired an architect from Brooklyn, New York, to design a new church, and in June 1860 the building began. Parishioners did much of the labor after their twelve-hour workday in the quarries; marble was donated by Sheldon & Co. and carried by oxcart to the site. The Gothic structure was the first Catholic church in the state to be built of marble, its walls two feet thick with fresco decorations. It cost $13,000 [$315,000]. Though by then the parish was one of the largest in the state, nevertheless about $5,500 [$133,269] of indebtedness accrued during the construction. Assuming that by then the parish had grown to three hundred families over the previous three years and that congregants' support had financed the $7,500 [$181,731] already paid, then each parish family must have contributed an average of $25 [$606] to the cause—more than a month's wages for a quarryman.

With the parish taking shape, and despite burdensome obligations elsewhere, Father Lynch turned to social and cultural affairs as well. St. Bridget's established a debating group, a night school, a circulating library, a cemetery, and the General Sarsfield Band, whose specialty was Irish music. His name honored military leader Patrick Sarsfield who fought for James II, but lost at the Battle of Boyne in 1690. Picart and Lynch successively presided in the West Rutland parish until well after the Civil War (St. Bridget's Parish Centennial Pamphlet).

There and at St. Peter's in Rutland village, the Irish community marked life's births, marriages, and deaths. Most Irish immigrants married other Irish; in fact, trouble could ensue with family if they chose partners outside their own group. The settlers from Ballykilcline, for the most part, followed tradition, many of them choosing partners who had come from their own townland or parish in Ireland.[20]

One notable exception was Patrick Colligan, born about 1839, who went off to the Civil War a single man, reenlisted twice, and in 1869, while traveling through Missouri, married a Protestant woman who was divorced from her first husband. They returned to West Rutland, where he worked as a blacksmith, and they had a family of seven children.

Another match that stands out was the one between Annie Kelly and Edgar A. Batchelder in Dorset. Annie, the daughter of an Irish marble cutter named James Kelly (U.S. Census, Vermont, 1870), born in the 1820s, may have been part of the Kelly family of Ballykilcline. Vital records show his roots were in or near Strokestown (Lamson communication, summer 2007). She met Edgar when she worked in his family's home. Their families' reactions to a marriage that crossed social lines were strained on both sides, as their daughter recalled:

> My Father was a Congregationalist. My mother's parents were very strict Catholics. They did not know of the marriage at the time. When her parents did find out they were furious. Her mother, especially, never got over the fact that her daughter married out of the faith. They finally did forgive her, but it took a long time. My mother's sisters never did relent. For the same reason the relationship between my grandparents Batchelder and my parents was no less strained. In fact, my Grandmother never, as far as I can remember, came down to my parent's [sic] farm. Mother went up there, but never received much welcome. In time because of Father's good nature, there was a detente between the families, although the women never were themselves. (Lamson communication)[21]

With such strong traditional feelings on both sides, it is not surprising that evidence of few such first-generation marriages across religious and cultural lines appeared in the federal censuses.

On cursory inspection, it seems that generally, Irish immigrant couples who married subsequently died as husband and wife and were buried together, even though divorce was not uncommon among Rutland's residents. State data for 1873, for instance, discloses that Rutland County had one divorce for every seventeen marriages (*Seventeenth Registration Report*, p. 118). I discovered only one instance of divorce among the evictees and no case of spousal desertion (though I did not undertake a specific canvass for such issues).[22] Numbers of offspring ranged from none up to the eighteen children of quarryman Michael Hackett and Margaret Hanley, the daughter (and next-door neighbor) of John and Sabina Brennan Hanley (Bell communication, 1999).

In 1868 a young doctor named John Hanrahan arrived in Vermont and tended many of the Irish through births, illnesses, accidents, and death. Dr. Hanrahan was a Limerick man who had done duty as a Civil War surgeon; he was captured by the Confederates and imprisoned in Richmond, Virginia. In Rutland, after the war, the doctor was not only a respected caretaker but also a political and civic activist, a leader for years as a village trustee, Democratic convention delegate, and member of numerous organizations (nineteen are named in his obituary). He served as postmaster for a time, and under President Grover Cleveland he was appointed head of the U.S. Pension Examining Board. He was also viewed as a committed Irish nationalist. "As a physician in the days when doctors made house calls, . . . he must have spent long hours on the road, serving the widespread Irish community. In return for his devotion, they responded with intense loyalty in their civic life" (Short 1984, pp. 7, 8).

When Hanrahan visited his patients, what he saw most frequently were cases of consumption, pneumonia, and fevers, which were the most prevalent causes of death and accounted for about 25 percent of all deaths in Vermont between 1857 and 1873. These data were compiled for state legislators in a report about births, marriages, and deaths in 1873; it provided early data as well for comparison. Rutland County had the highest number of deaths from scarletina in 1858. Although the figures for some diseases were disheartening, there seemed to be a perceptible decrease in deaths from consumption despite a steady increase in population. On the other hand, more than half of such deaths were of people under forty years of age, more among young women than young men. In Vermont as a whole, the average age at time of death for each five-year period between 1857 and 1873 ranged from 33.88 years during the Civil War years to a high of 37.33 at the end of the time span. Unfortunately, the report did not deal with accidental deaths as a separate category; they were subsumed under the heading of "Violent" diseases or deaths. It is impossible, therefore, to extract numbers for workplace accidents, though many were captured in newspaper accounts as matters of public interest (*Seventeenth Registration Report*, pp. 122, 132, 119, 135).

By 1870, the population of Rutland County had risen to 40,651. Some 558 children were born that year to Rutland parents who were native-born Americans and another 449 to foreign-born parents. Officials noted that "the proportion of American births . . . is increasing while that of foreign births is decreasing. And this ratio varies so slightly from year to year, or from one decade to another, as to afford no just ground of apprehension that the Foreign population will outnumber the American for many years to come" (*Seventeenth Registration Report*, pp. 18, 113). The remark suggests some trepidation in Vermont over the rising immigrant populations.

The Hanleys Defend Their Borders

After they had purchased their farm on Whipple Hollow Road, the Hanleys stayed there; in fact, some of the property remained in family hands in the early twenty-first century, perhaps justifying the elation that John Hanley expressed over its acquisition. Though the Hanleys were not present in Ballykilcline for the rent strike, they too vigorously defended their property in person and at law when they deemed it necessary. To the Irish, land was a precious commodity.

For example, the March 1862 term of the county court witnessed a suit and a countersuit between a Samuel Butler, a neighboring farmer, on the one hand, and John Hanley, son Gilbert, and son-in-law Michael Hackett, on the other. Butler had accused the Hanleys and Hackett of entering his property on June 8, 1861, "with force and arms" and of stealing "twenty rods of fence, one thousand fencing poles and five hundred stakes" worth $200 [$4,006]. Butler also charged that they had assaulted him and "beat, bruised, wounded and evil treated" him, with damage amounting to $300 [$6,009], costs that he sought to recover.

A month later, John Hanley filed countercharges that Butler, on May 1, 1861, had entered *his* farmlands "with force and arms" and "cut down, prostrated and destroyed . . . 500 Basswood trees, 500 Maple trees, 500 Beech trees, 500 Hard-haek [*sic*] trees, 500 Butter-nut trees, 500 Ash trees, 500 Birch trees, 500 Walnut trees" worth $500 [$10,015] and "carried away the wood and timber." Hanley demanded compensation (*Samuel Butler v. John Hanley et al.*, 1862; *John Hanley v. Samuel Butler*, 1862). John Prout represented Butler; R. R. Thrall was Hanley's attorney.

The record of the disposition of these cases unfortunately has not been located. Nevertheless, Hanley's actions showed his willingness to use the courts to protect his property and also take on a native Vermonter—to some degree perhaps the land battle in Ballykilcline in miniature. Hanley did not go meekly or passively to a decision in Butler's suit against him but instead took the offense. By this time, of course, he had been in the United States for more than twenty-five years, and he knew—and asserted—his rights. But the cases also suggest that, as likely happened often enough in Ireland, his first choice would have been to lash out directly and in person, with family help, against a perceived injustice rather than to take the matter straight to the courts, which the Irish had so distrusted in their home country. It is possible to see hints of an Irish faction fight in Hanley's initial response to what he saw as a wrong. One wonders what, if anything, it cost him.

4

To Battle with a "Two-Edged Sword"

꧁

> America is Irland's refuge Irland's last hope destroy this republic and
> her hopes are blasted[.] If Ireland is ever ever [to be] free the means to
> accomplish it must come from the shores of America. . . . When we are
> fighting for America we are fighting in the interest of Irland[,] striking a
> double blow [and] cutting with a two edged sword[.] For while we strike
> in defence of the rights of Irishmen here we are striking a blow at Irlands
> enemy and opressor.
>
> —Civil War soldier Peter Welsh, *in Kevin O'Neill*, "The Star-Spangled Shamrock:
> Memory and Meaning in Irish America"

> The diasporic imagination—that sense of undying membership in, and
> unyielding obligation to, a distant national community.
>
> —Matthew Jacobson, *Special Sorrows*

WHEN THE British went after Young Ireland's firebrand leaders in
Dublin in 1848, John Cain made certain that his *Rutland Courier* readers knew about it: "The Government have [*sic*] arrested W. S. O'Brien,
and Messrs. [Thomas Francis] Meagher and [John] Mitchel [*sic*], for sedi-
tion" (April 12, 1848). Cain's columns kept the Irish in Rutland informed
about what happened at home.

In their major battles after 1857, Rutland's Irish had the *Courier* on
their side. Cain was a Democrat who attended national conventions and
who pushed civic activism and the party's line in his columns. Cain, an
immigrant from the Isle of Man in 1832, "espoused the Democratic views
of Jefferson and Jackson, and valiantly defended the doctrines of that
party and became prominent in its ranks." An architect and builder, he
also served as Rutland's postmaster and ran for Congress (*Isle of Man Family History Society Journal*, July 1896). Vermont, however, was one of only
two states that had voted Whig in every presidential contest from 1836 to
1852, David Potter has pointed out. The burst of immigration in the late
1840s and early '50s seriously disrupted American life because so many
people came from a single country, so many were poor, and they were

overwhelmingly Catholics stepping into a Protestant society. "It was in the midst of serious tensions, therefore, that the immigrant Irish began their participation in American political life. One of the earliest steps . . . was choosing between the Whigs and the Democrats" As time told, the Irish became "unswervingly Democratic" (D. Potter 1976, pp. 241–243, 436).

In his newspaper, Cain pressed the Irish to naturalize and explained the process of citizenship involved. In 1864 he ran a column headlined, "Who Are Citizens" (*Rutland Courier,* June 3, 1864). In the 1840s, white males had almost universally acquired the right to vote in the United States; curbs on voting by Catholics were dropped; and in some places even white men who had not yet become naturalized citizens were allowed to vote. Two states retained property qualifications for voting, but they had disappeared by 1856 (Browne n.d.). By then, David Montgomery argued, "A man's wage contract had taken its place alongside property ownership and race as a badge of participation in the polity" (1993, p. 22).

As editor, Cain sided with the Irish workmen in labor disputes with marble owners. He criticized the administration's efforts in prosecuting the Civil War, even though Vermonters had greatly supported Abraham Lincoln at the time of and after his inauguration (Vermont Civil War website). As the war dragged on, Cain was especially harsh on Lincoln and the Republicans: "That this incompetent Administration will very soon again call for more men as food for gunpowder, and more money to squander on partisans, to secure Abraham's reelection, no man who watched the slaughter of our armies for the last two months, can doubt. . . . We leave the Democracy of other towns to take such measure as they best can, to evade being forced into our armies and to decide 'ways and means' to avoid being forced to risk their lives for the equality and the superiority of the 'Honorable gentleman from Africa'" (*Rutland Courier,* June 24, 1864).

The Irish had not elected Lincoln; he drew votes from Protestant immigrants but got few from the Irish and German Catholics. It was the natives who delivered the presidency to him (D. Potter 1976, pp. 435–436).

Protesting the Conscription Act of 1863

The Lincoln administration's war policies did not rankle Cain alone. Rutland was one of a handful of places around the country that erupted in violence several months after the Conscription Act of March 1863 required all physically fit men aged twenty to forty-five either to submit to a military draft, to furnish a substitute volunteer, or to pay $300 [$4,814]. The poor and immigrants, largely Irish in Rutland and other cities in the

East, who could not afford to buy their way out of service, saw it as a class issue, "an attempt to force poor men to fight a rich man's war" and to free slaves who then would compete with them for scarce jobs in a gruelingly competitive economy (New York City Draft Riots website). The most violent eruptions took place in New York City over four days in July, causing widespread injuries and damage and a thousand deaths by mob action, including the lynching of many blacks. "Irish boys, who made up about fifteen percent of the Union army, were suffering horrific casualty rates since they were commonly used as frontline troops against better-trained and better-led Confederate soldiers" (W. Stern 1997).

In Rutland that season, when enrollment officers visited the quarries to take down the names of those eligible for the draft, they faced several hundred angry men.

> Jerry Connell, a blacksmith, employed at Adams and Allen's marble quarry, at West Rutland, having been reported by the enrolling officer for obstructing the enrollment, in refusing to give his name or any other information when legally required to do so: it became the duty of the Provost Marshal . . . to summarily arrest him. . . . [Provost Marshal Crane] then returned his pistol and did not again display it until surrounded by about two hundred men, and his life endangered by the shower of marble chips hurled upon him by the mob, some of which took effect, when he did again draw the weapon, and, from the wagon in which he had taken refuge, fire two shots at men whom he saw hurl stones at him. (*Rutland Herald,* July 2, 1863)

William Y. W. Ripley, then off at the Civil War, wrote that Crane "tried hard to shoot the ring-leader, but was over-powered and carried off by his own Posse, after having emptied his revolver" (Eisenschmil 1960, p. 129). In his own account of the incident, Crane said, "There are in and about the quarries about one thousand laborers, all Irishmen, . . . organized and determined to resist the enrollment and draft" (This Week in the Civil War website).

On July 31 a man named Hugh Corey was arrested. He later was excused from the draft because of a jaw problem, but in October he was convicted of assaulting the provost marshal, sentenced to jail, and fined. In another case, Jerry Connell was acquitted when it was discovered that the Conscription Act did not require any man to provide his name. In the meantime, the local marshal formed a Home Guard of two hundred men who drilled at night (Eisenschiml 1960, p. 143).

It is difficult to imagine that Kilglass people, many of them quarry men, would have or could have avoided these conflicts. William Ripley described the incidents in letters to his brother that month: "We have had an exciting time here for the past few weeks. I wrote to you about Crane being stoned off the Quarries when he went there to enroll the Irishmen. That made a great breeze at the time. Everybody was indignant and everybody said it was a shame and that the rioters ought to be punished, and everybody damned Crane because 'he did not do something.'" Citizens were asked to step into the fray to help Crane uphold the law, but, Ripley said, nobody immediately came forward: "One lived there or near there and did not wish to embroil himself with them. Another had a barnful of hay on his meadow liable to be burned by them if he made them his enemies, and so on. Well, Crane got two hundred men, the presence of which force developed such a wonderful amount of courage in our townpeople that they immediately set to work and formed a Home Guard. They drill every night" (Eisenschiml 1960, p. 143).

On July 23, one day after the draft calls were issued at Town Hall, the *Rutland Herald* published the names of 263 conscripts (some of whom later were excused from serving). Approximately 29 percent of them appear to be Irish names; they include Michael Costello, Dennis Cox, Edward Duffy, three men named Farrell, Dennis and John Foley, William Hanley, John Kelley II and Thomas Kelley, two McCormicks, a McDermott, John McKeough, and Peter Nary.

According to one calculation, nearly two-thirds of the 2,948 Vermont men who were drafted before the state could meet its one-regiment (780 men) quota bought their way out of serving, far higher than the 42 percent who did so nationally. Another 22 percent (660 men) hired a substitute, so just over 12 percent (361) of the men drafted in Vermont, actually served in the war (Vermont Civil War website). In total, though, 34,555 Vermont men—many of them volunteers or substitutes—did war service. In 1863 the state paid each $7.00 a month, in addition to their federal pay (*Vermont Business Magazine* website).

Protesting what they saw as inequities in the Conscription Act did not mean that the Irish evaded service; numbers of them enlisted, including men from St. Bridget's Parish who were Kilglass natives. They included Patrick Colligan, who enlisted three times: once in an infantry unit, once in the cavalry, and then in a Veteran Volunteer unit. Colligan served his Union duty as a blacksmith, for a time in Virginia. When he left the military on August 9, 1865, at Burlington, he carried with him diseases contracted during the war—malaria and asthma—which forced him to stop working in 1908 (Powers communication). Men from West Rutland who fought in that war were involved in action to block Pickett's Charge

at Gettysburg (St. Bridget's Centennial Pamphlet). The Second Vermont
Volunteer Regiment, which had members from Rutland and surrounding
communities, saw action in the Cold Harbor, Wilderness, and Spotsylva-
nia battles. One soldier was a John T. Kelly, who served from September
1862 until June 1865 and left a diary of his career as a soldier covering
the year 1864. Although there were Kellys from Ballykilcline, this soldier's
familial background is not known (Kelly 1994).[1]

Rutland men with ties to Ballykilcline who served during the war, in addition to Colligan, included John Winters, Gilbert Hanley, James C. Kelly,
and James McGuire (*Revised Roster* 1892). Half the men in Vermont of the
proper age served as Union soldiers, and proportional to its population
size, the state lost more men killed in battle than any other except New
Hampshire (Washington 1992, pp. 165–174). Although Colligan and the
others did return to West Rutland, too many local sons ended in wartime
graves; however, James McDermott, the son of Hugh, a leader of the strike
in Ballykilcline, is the sole evictee so far known to have lost his life in that
war. James had lived in Ohio with his wife and at least one son.[2]

A Wisconsin soldier whose roots may have been in Ballykilcline also
served but, by happenstance, was labeled a deserter for years.[3] Patrick Hanley, born in Roscommon to Michael and Mary Gill Hanley in 1841, had
moved to Wisconsin from Sullivan County, New York, by the early 1860s.
For a $25 bounty, Patrick enlisted in the Twenty-eighth Wisconsin, Com-
pany H, in August 1862. For several months he trained at a Milwaukee
army camp and then took leave to visit his family before shipping out. On
his return, he discovered that his unit had left without him, and eventually
Hanley was labeled a deserter. He tried unsuccessfully to follow his unit
and then went to Chicago to sign up anew but was rejected because of some
health issue. Months later, though, the Navy accepted him for the Missis-
sippi fleet. Aboard the U.S.S. *Covington*, Patrick had a role in the Red River
Campaign to access Texas in order to secure cotton and divide the South.
In a battle at Alexandria in 1864, Patrick was one of thirty-two men to survive from a crew of seventy-four. Later, he took part in the siege of Mobile
Bay aboard the U.S.S. *Kickapoo*. In 1898, the U.S. Congress voided his deserter status and conferred an honorable discharge on Patrick Hanley, who
had sought it, in part, "on account of his children." A former captain in the
Twenty-eighth Wisconsin had told Congress that Patrick "was a good soldier, no way disorderly, and was, I verily believe never reprimanded by any
of his superior officers. . . . I found him dutiful, orderly, and a manly young
man." Patrick died in 1907 and is buried in a veterans' home graveyard in
Waupaca (28th Wisconsin website; Bunzel communication).

It is hard to know the precise motivations of the Rutland Irish who served in the war. Kevin O'Neill, on the basis of soldiers' correspondence, pointed to the mixed emotions and dual allegiances of the Irish. The Rutland soldiers undoubtedly shared attitudes with other Irish immigrants who served, especially men like Peter Welsh, who wrote in a letter about his views of military duty:

> Here we have a free government[,] just laws and a Constitution[,] which guarantees equal rights and privelages [sic] to all. Here thousands of the sons and daughters of Ireland have come to seek a refuge from tyranny and persecution at home . . . Here Irishmen and their decendents [sic] have a claim[,] a stake in the nation and an interest in its prosperity. . . . We have the same national political and social interest at stake not only for ourselves but for coming generations and the oppressed of every nation. . . .
>
> England [which was supporting the Confederacy] hates this country because of its growing power and greatness. She hates it for its republican liberty and she hates it because Irishmen have a home and a government here. . . . England hates this country because we have out riveled [sic] her as a naval power and are fast outrivaling her as a commercial power. There is but one step more which a few years of peacefull [sic] progress will accomplish[,] that is to surpass her as a manufacturing nation and Englands [sic] star of asendency [sic] will have set to rise no more. Such motives have influenced me . . . to strike a blow for the rights and liberty of Irland [sic]. (O'Neill 2001, p. 127)

The influential *Boston Pilot* had urged military service upon the immigrants for the sake of the Union: "Catholics have only one course to adopt, only one line to follow. Stand by the Union; fight for the Union; die for the Union" (qtd. in O'Neill 2001, pp. 123, 124). O'Neill argued that military service was a transforming experience for the Irish immigrants individually and for Irish society in the United States: "Their sacrifice earned the larger community acceptance. But perhaps just as importantly it gave a generation that had begun life with the terror and humiliation of the Great Famine an opportunity to redefine themselves as a heroic group who were the authors, not the subjects, of one of the great defining moments of a nation" (2001, p. 135).

But he also recognized that the experience "militarized" some Irish and caused "moral and political acceptance of massive violence as a legitimate instrument of a just political cause; the belief that in the end only violence really produces results, and that individual self-sacrifices can redeem a people" (O'Neill 2001, p. 137). Thereafter, numbers of Irish, many of them ex-soldiers, worked in the nationalist underground for Ireland's freedom in an effort to leverage their new military experience against their old enemy.

ORGANIZING FOR IRELAND'S FREEDOM

Various efforts on behalf of Ireland that aimed to strike at England had been discussed and initiated but then collapsed throughout the late 1840s and early '50s. This notice, for one, was reported in the *Rutland Herald* in 1848, after a meeting in St. Louis:

> GRAND IRISH AGITATION SCHEME
>
> A plan of operations was submitted in which it was proposed to hold a national convention of the friends of Ireland in the United States and Canada, at Albany, New York on the 3d Monday of next July for the purpose of organizing a system of agitation in behalf of that suffering country. It was also proposed that a fund of one hundred thousand dollars be raised, said fund to be placed in the hands of seven citizens of the United States, of known integrity to be invested in United States securities, the interest of which would be devoted to disseminating intelligence in regard to the ruthless oppression exercised by the British government against the Irish nation. (*Rutland Herald,* March 22, 1848, p. 3)

But organizing for Ireland's freedom began seriously in 1859 and focused on more than "disseminating intelligence." Coinciding with the war years, an Irish nationalist organization called the Fenians grew dramatically in immigrant communities across the United States. Eventually, more than 50,000 Irish were enrolled in the cause, and their sympathizers grew to the hundreds of thousands (Fenian Brotherhood Collection). The Fenians' goal was to free Ireland from British rule. As the Rutland senachie—storyteller, poet, and historian—James Patrick Carney, a Tipperary man who had immigrated after trouble with the authorities in Ireland, told it:

> I am old Grania, and my country have suffered sore;
> I am looking out for assistance from the West, or Columbian shore . . .
> There is Col. John O'Mahoney with his well armed Fenian Band,
> For to hunt John Bull, the tyrant, the oppressor of Old Ireland . . .
> Fair play and Liberty we must have; poor Ireland you must be free.
> (Carney *Violet-Book*, p. 15)[4]

The Fenians held a large meeting in Rutland in 1864 at which the organization's New England leader, or "center," W. J. Hynes of Springfield, Massachusetts, delivered a call to action. (Hynes later became a director of the freedom-fighting Clan-na-Gael in Chicago, where he then practiced law [Le Caron 1974, p. 123]). A *Courier* reporter attended the meeting and recorded the formation of the local circle and the selection of its officers:

ORGANIZATION OF THE FENIAN BROTHERHOOD IN RUTLAND—

According to notice, W. J. Hynes, Esq., central organizer of the Fenian Brotherhood for New England, addressed a large and intelligent audience at the Town Hall, Wednesday evening, Dec. 28th. Subject—"The Irish question, and the nature and objects of the Fenian Brotherhood." The lecturer was introduced by Jno McKeough.

At the close of the Address, the following officers were unanimously elected, Jno McKeough, Centre; Jno. Carlon, Secretary; Michael Slattery, Treasurer. Jno. Fitzgerald, Timothy Spellman, Patrick Flannery, Safety Committee.

Jno McKeough, Centre
Jno. Carlon, Sec'y (*Rutland Courier*, Dec. 30, 1864)

Link with the Fenians

Two of the officers—Carlon and McKeough—likely had Kilglass roots. Evidence suggests that Carlon was connected to the Ballykilcline family of that name. Three men and a widow named Keough were listed in the Tithe Applotment Book records in Kilnaghamore in Kilglass;[5] the question is whether John McKeogh was part of that family.

At least two Carlons (originally Carolan)—Owen and John—had farmed as joint tenants in Ballykilcline. A John Carlon family was evicted and emigrated from the townland but went to Illinois. Various Rutland records show that most of the Carlons who relocated there came from Kilglass; two were natives of adjacent Kilmore. The Rutland Carlons included two men named John; one born before 1800, the other, whose father's name was Patrick, born about 1838 (Offutt communication). They lived in separate units in the same house in 1860.[6] A decade later the immigrant Owen Carlon, son of Owen of Ballykilcline, had replaced the younger John in that house (U.S. Census, Vermont, 1860, 1870). The two Johns almost certainly came from Kilglass and perhaps were grandfather and grandson or uncle and nephew. It is not clear from the record which man was the Fenian, but since Fenianism was a young man's organization, it was surely the younger John Carlon who was the organization's officer. Moreover, the older man, then in his seventies or eighties, was illiterate and therefore would have had a difficult time serving as a record-keeping secretary.[7]

Nearby, the area around Albany and Troy, New York, which was linked to Rutland by several rail lines, was a hive of Fenian activity. Rutlanders often traded in the upstate New York cities, not far from the state border. In 1866, Troy had "about one thousand" Fenians organized in a number of "circles" named for Irish nationalists, such as the James Stephens Circle (Nicholson letter, Sept. 20, 1866).

Another potential link that may demonstrate Kilglass people's concern for Ireland's freedom came from a Fenian named John Roche (LeCaron 1974, p. 66) of Troy, who rose at a Fenian meeting in Philadelphia in 1868 and publicly accused General John O'Neill's top aide, Henri Le Caron, of spying on the organization for the British. In fact, Roche was right: Le Caron, whose real name was Thomas Miller Beach, was perhaps the top British agent spying on the Fenians, but he had so embedded himself with them and with O'Neill that the convention rejected Roche's charges and even reprimanded him for making them (D'Arcy 1947, p. 307).[8] For another twenty years or so, Le Caron continued to spy on the Fenians and successor nationalist organizations such as Clan-na-Gael and the Land League, at whose convention in 1883 in Philadelphia a "Brother Roach of Troy" served as a temporary secretary (Le Caron 1974, p. 214). Some evidence suggests that Roche may have been a Kilglass native: a "Missing Friends" ad showed that a woman from Kilglass Parish named Catherine Roche was ill in a Troy hospital in 1853 (Harris et al. 1989–, vol. 2).[9] For now, though, the link is speculative.

Le Caron continued reporting to the British for years about the Fenians, such as their plans to invade Canada, and enabled authorities to foil their efforts. Only when he wrote his autobiography years later was Le Caron's real role disclosed (D'Arcy 1947, p. 307).

Fenian circles were known to exist as well in LaSalle County, Illinois, where Ballykilcline people had settled. Catholic University's archive of Fenian documents contains letters from LaSalle group leader John Forristal to central Fenian officials. In one letter, Forristal reported that he had sent $463 [$5,937] to the central officers from LaSalle and complained about the local clergy's attitude toward Fenian activity: "The Catholic clergy are making a crazy opposition against the Fenian Brotherhood. Missionaries are going from town to town preaching against Irish nationality, I can assure you with very little success. The time will certainly come when they will wish they had not medled [sic] in political affairs. We at all events are prepared to persevere until we bring the cause of Irish nationality to a successful issue, or if not the Irish race will become extinct" (Forristal letter, June 28, 1864).

The Invasion of 1870

In his autobiography, describing his exploits as a spy, Le Caron explained his role in the Canadian invasion of 1870:

> I distributed fifteen thousand stands of arms and almost three million rounds of ammunition in the care of the many trusted men stationed between Ogdensburg [New York] and St. Albans [Vermont]. Some thousands of these guns were breech-loaders, which had been re-modelled from United States Government "Springfields." ... The depot from which the bulk were packed and shipped was "Quinn's and Nolan's" of Albany. Quinn was a United States Congressman and Senator of the Fenian Brotherhood; and Nolan, that very Mayor Nolan so prominently mentioned by Mr. [Charles Stewart] Parnell. ... [M]y new position enabled me not only to become possessed of the originals of every document, plan of proposed campaign, &c, but also specimens of the Fenian army commissions and uniforms of the time, which of course I conveyed to the officials of the Canadian Government. (Le Caron 1974, pp. 74, 75)

Le Caron singled out two advantages of this planned invasion over the previous unsuccessful efforts: secrecy and preparedness. The preparations included engaging "a number of ex-military men of undoubted ability" and placing supplies for 12,000 men "on the ground" at the sites of intended action. In his (perhaps self-serving) view, if the Canadians had not been forewarned, the outcome would have been "undoubtedly serious." Le Caron watched at Franklin as the well-prepared Canadians routed the Fenians and arrested their General O'Neill, who later was held for violating international neutrality laws. A second planned action in Vermont sputtered out at St. Alban's when thousands of Canadian and U.S. troops arrived there, making engagement impossible. In a brief skirmish at Pigeon Hill, several Fenians died, and a handful of them were captured (Le Caron 1974, pp. 82–89).

The United States sent General George C. Meade from Maine to protect the frontier at Quebec and Ontario, and he prohibited "the railroads and express companies from transporting Fenians and their arms to the border." Later, two Fenian generals met with Meade and heaped scorn on the U.S. role in the confrontation: "We have been lured on by the Cabinet, and used for the purposes of Mr. Seward—They encouraged us on to this thing. We bought our rifles from your arsenals, and were given to understand that you would not interfere" (Libby 2004, p. 248).

Thus ended the Fenians' strategy to weaken England by making a base in Canada from which to launch a battle to free Ireland. What the Fenian

threat did instead, according to Gary W. Libby, was strengthen the movement for provincial confederation in Canada as a form of protection;
confederation was accomplished a year later (2004, pp. 249, 250).

What roles, if any, McKeough, or even Carlon, who by then lived in
Indiana, might have played in the attempted Canadian invasions are not
known. Even if he had no battle role, McKeough may have helped to position weapons and manpower along the Canadian border for the planned
invasion. Oral history in Rutland says there were several local circles and
that trainloads of Fenians from other parts of New England came through
the town by rail at the time of the invasions. But it is the fact of their involvement in Fenianism at all, rather than what they may have done as
Fenians, which is of paramount concern here. Neither membership rosters
of the Vermont Fenians nor reports of their activities are known to exist,
but these clues may point to the as yet undocumented involvement of other
Kilglass men who lived in northern and central Vermont and New York.

Involvement in Fenianism by men from Ballykilcline and Kilglass should
be no great surprise. Given the fractious state of affairs they left behind in
Roscommon, the level of secret society activity there, and the intensity of
their opposition to British authorities, it would be more difficult to believe
that none of them was active in Irish nationalist activities in the United
States, particularly when they lived so close to the centers of action in the
Fenian cause along the Canadian border. The Fenian organization and
its successors came close to correspondence with the secret societies at
home, which were effective in achieving many of their members' goals,
and evidence showed them active around Strokestown. As well, the Fenian
battles along the Canadian border virtually coincided with some of the
Irish workers' collective actions against the marble company owners. The
Irish may well have seen them as similar contests on different fronts.

Historian Matthew Frye Jacobson observed the fusing of economic interests and nationalist feeling that occurred among nineteenth-century
Irish immigrants: "Labor politics and nationalism among the Irish in
America now achieved a new and dynamic affinity. The immigrants'
harsh existence in the mines and factories of America fueled an interest
in the new economic bent of Irish nationalism as represented by mounting land agitation; and conversely, Irish nationalism became the language
in which many labor leaders appealed to the Irish laborers on behalf of
unionism or socialism. . . . The call to American working-class action
rested on the basis of Irish colonial memory." Jacobson pointed also to
the tight bonds that developed later between the Knights of Labor and
nationalist organizations and leaders. In fact, Knights leader Terrence

Powderly held official positions with Clan na Gael and the Scranton Irish National Land League (2002, p. 28). And the Knights came to Rutland to organize quarry workers in the 1880s.

In his analysis of midcentury Fenianism in Britain, John Newsinger examined its social composition and found it based in the working class and, more specifically, in the skilled trades and artisanal culture. It may be that Rutland's Irish immigrants inclined toward Fenianism more as a result of their experience in their first two quarry strikes—as they themselves morphed from tenant farmers to workers with newly acquired wage skills, thus strengthening their sense of cohesion—than otherwise might have been the case. Newsinger said the evidence supported James Stephens's view that the Fenian members were highly democratic—"the farmers' sons, the mechanics, the artisans, the labourers and small shop-keepers" (1994, pp. 29, 30).

A peculiar Rutland footnote to the Fenian actions against Canada came from marble owner William Ripley's family. Ripley's youngest son, Charley, who had a taste for adventure and traveled west looking for it, found it in a Fenian raid on Canada staged from Buffalo, New York, where the marble magnate's son "took part in what he called 'a brisk little battle'" before wandering on to Chicago. Which side he took in the engagement was not stated (Eisenschmil 1960, p. 321).

The Fenians' attempts to invade Canada got short shrift from John Cain's *Rutland Courier*, however, which commented in 1868 on "another move being about to be made by the Fenians for the invasion of Canada. If the *Courier* has been silent on this subject, it is from the fact that we consider the invasion of Canada by any number of men from the States, as a brainless project and unworthy [of] serious consideration. . . . The Fenians' only chance is in the event of a war between Great Britain and [the] United States" (*Rutland Courier*, June 19, 1868). That war, of course, never happened. U.S. politicians kept a sharp eye on Fenian activities but feared to oppose them outright because of the growing political power of the Irish across the country. Even before the mighty famine immigration, "by 1844, the Irish were the most solid voting bloc in the country, except for the free Negroes" (Ignatiev 1995, p. 75), surely a result of the immigrants' legacies from Daniel O'Connell and their experience with "combinations" of several sorts.

Federal officials took advantage of the Fenian issue to draw out concessions from the British over relations between the two countries, particularly regarding the apprehension of residents and citizens of another country. The United States found that the Fenians' "nuisance value against the British diplomatically was too handy to throw away" (Kee 1972, p. 29).

5

Family Paths

&

> The drama of people struggling with conditions that confine them through cycles of limited life spans is the heart of all living history, and the development of that drama itself . . . must provide the framework for any interpretation of history.
>
> —Bernard Bailyn, American Historical Association Presidential Address, 1981

> How, in what ways, with what success, does an individual interact with, create a life from, and possibly alter a culture and a society not of their own making, one which they largely inherit?
>
> —Nick Salvatore, "Biography and Social History: An Intimate Relationship"

An individual's actions and a family's choices after eyeing the paths open to them may reveal their conflicts, priorities, memories, and daily experience in making their way. How the tenant farmers of Ballykilcline behaved around Strokestown, where perhaps their greatest losses occurred, may tell what the subsequent record does not, but what happened thereafter may shed light on what came before. The remainder of the farmers' lives is significant in their story. Their later years were lived where they were freer to act openly for themselves and where their stories come closer to narration in their own voices, since their U.S. records were less filtered through the eyes and voices of their opponents than were the Irish records. In America they spoke for themselves. Where they chose to invest themselves demonstrated what was important to them, showed what they valued. How they aided one another helped to explain the survival strategies of the Irish as they put aside and emerged from a collective trauma, an experience that sociologist Kai Erikson has described as a "blow to the tissues of social life that damages the bonds linking people to each other and impairs the prevailing sense of community" (qtd. in G. Stern 1976, p. 235). Recovery after trauma, according to Deborah Peck in an essay about the famine's psychological legacies, requires a safe environment (2002, p. 169).

Here then are brief accounts of a number of families, most of them evictees and several others who emigrated from the Kilglass and Strokestown neighborhoods surrounding Ballykilcline. The focus on the stories of these particular families—and those of the Hanleys, Brennans, and Colligans who remained around Rutland and whose lives are described in other chapters—stemmed from the fact that their records "talked." That is, the information gathered about them from descendants and public records was sufficiently detailed and weighty to tell something about who they were, what they did, what happened to them (and sometimes why) over time in one or both locations. These families also represented a range of experience: in some cases they exemplify the most common choices of the immigrant Irish (e.g., settling in East Coast urban centers); in others, they took roads less trodden. Although most of them passed through or settled in Rutland, the accounts about the Padians, who were evicted from Ballykilcline but went elsewhere, and the McCormicks and Rileys, who had roots in Kilglass-area townlands and whose surnames were present in Ballykilcline but who so far have no documented links there, were fleshed out enough by descendants to be presented here. Their surrogates' lives come out of similar experience and speak to diverse aspects of the immigrant position, warranting inclusion here because of the stories they tell. In large measure, these profiles were built on the descendants' efforts to learn their own history.

The accounts of all these families allowed views of the Ballykilcline and Kilglass people's experience in multiple other geographic contexts (both England and the northeastern, midwestern, southern, and north central United States) and in a variety of sociopolitical circumstances. The cases drew in a family of evictees who held themselves loyal to the southern cause in the great divisive issue of their early life in the United States—the Civil War. Another family made its way on the American frontier where the McGintys' son was kidnapped by Indians in what likely was the family's third or fourth American home place. These life stories include accounts of three men—John McGann and Patrick Brislin here, but also Bernard Colligan (see chapter 3)—whom British officials had labeled as criminal suspects in Ireland. Two of them had emigrated as fugitives from the law; McGann just barely escaped that designation. Their stories make it possible to see how their alleged actions in Ireland carried over in an American setting. For McGann and Brislin, Irish police records gave details about their particular predicaments in the Irish scene. One of the profiled families in Rutland was led by matriarch Honora Igo Winters, who was the center of a web of relationships in her new home

Twelve Families, Their Roots, Places of Settlement, and Special Notes

Name	Roots	Settlement	Special Notes
McGanns	Ballykilcline	Minnetonka, MN	John, seasonal worker, a suspect in Mahon's murder; McGinty relationship; siblings move together; famine deaths
McGintys	Ballykilcline and Kilglass Parish	Rutland, VT; LaSalle Co., IL; Minnetonka, MN	possible subterfuge in getting Crown passages; 3 places of settlement in U.S.; husband likely also from Ballykilcline; siblings move together; frontier experience—son taken by Indians; multiple sources
Winters	Ballykilcline	Rutland and Dorset, VT	Honora Igo Winters, matriarch of extended family network; chain migration; daughter emigrated early; 2 sons, quarry men; son John, Civil War veteran; daughter, grandchild missing from U.S. records; newspaper account of Nancy Winters McGuire's death
James Mulleras	Ballykilcline	Rutland, VT; LaSalle Co., IL	extended family dispersed in U.S.; early immigrant (Arthur); Rutland marble workers; child, adult deaths; daughter divorced; reused Christian names; history from court records
Carolans (Carlons)	Some Ballykilcline; some Kilglass	Rutland and Dorset, VT; one then to LaSalle Co., IL, another to Indianapolis; one family direct to LaSalle; parents remain in Ireland	extended family network; John's Fenian, business, and political activity, some quarry men; the move west from VT; newspaper, book sources
Brislins	Strokestown/Kilglass	Rutland, VT	Patrick a criminal suspect in Ireland, called a secret society member; Irish police records; wanted Mahon dead; marriage, friendship links with Ballykilcline; helped evictees to U.S. citizenship

Twelve Families, (*continued*)

Name	Roots	Settlement	Special Notes
Padians	Ballykilcline	Texas, MD	rent strike leader; much church involvement; southern politics and behavior in Civil War; son emigrated later; son rose in NYC liquor sales and politics; records from a church and family history
McCormicks	Kilglass-Strokestown area; surnames in Ballykilcline	Lancaster, UK; Albany, NY	pattern of settlement: time in England, chain migration to NY; insights from famine experience; urban choices, millwork; deaths at an early age; children took in young siblings
Rileys	Kilglass; parents' surnames in Ballykilcline	Providence and Burrillville, RI; several to Hampton, CT; one to Warwick, RI; one to Willimantic, CT	chain migration to RI; priority for son's education; daughter a nun in hospital work; church roles; Yankee town relationships; millwork, farming; guardianship of deceased brother's young children; siblings move together
Hanleys	Ballykilcline	Rutland, VT; LaSalle Co., IL	early emigration; senior figures in Rutland; large family; marble workers; Civil War veteran; death of Michael Hanley from ship fever; Rutland land battle in court records; early assets (1850); M. Hanley will
Brennans	Ballykilcline	Rutland and Poultney, VT	large family; marriages within the group; success by farming; education priority; Jane's son a priest; father died of ship's fever in VT
Colligans	Ballykilcline and Kilglass	Rutland, VT	chain migration; Civil War veteran; marriage across cultural lines; story of illegal activity; convent education for daughters a priority; VT death from ship disease; quarry man; written family history, war record

place. The table in this chapter gives a capsule view of the distinguishing characteristics of each family's experience.

Further, taking a view that spans two decades makes clearer the diversity and commonalities of how they lived in a new world that was in some sense forced on them, though in fact a number of the evictees reluctantly came to embrace the move to the United States. Listen for the echoes in these stories. For these Irish, out of a sense of collective history and purpose and out of intimate knowledge of common loss and uncommon trauma, shared identity and allegiance became powerful forces in their lives and social relationships.

The McGanns and McGintys

When John McGann was evicted from Ballykilcline and left Ireland, he was single, twenty-four years old, and the head of his family. In Ireland he had been, in Scally's words, "one of the smaller cottiers who had not been prominent in the rent strike" (1995, p. 175). In 1845, McGann had spent time in Munster province, to the south, as a country schoolmaster. As the famine progressed, though, he had worked as a timekeeper on the public road works in Kilglass Parish. He was five feet, five inches tall (Fox memo, Nov. 26, 1847).

John's family suffered significant losses during the famine years. About 1840 the McGann household included his parents, John, 70, and Mary Cox McGann, 50; his brothers, Phelim, 25, Luke, 12, and Anthony (called Atty), 10; his sister Mary, 20; and a niece named Mary, 6 (List of Tenants). When the McGanns emigrated eight years later, the family consisted only of John, Atty, Luke, sisters Mary, 15, and Annie, 26, and one-year-old John McGann, whose relationship was not specified (Coyle 1994, p. 33).

John's father died a famine victim in the summer of 1847, and some of his brothers suffered with fever in that season when Ballykilcline was torn apart (Fox memo, Nov. 26, 1847). Phelim and their mother disappeared from the record, although a police memo in November 1847 alluded to Mary Cox McGann as though she were still alive. The evicted Mary likely was the niece, since the sister Mary could not grow younger as time passed. One Mary was missing—she may have died or married off the land or within the townland, where she may have been listed as an evictee under a new surname and thus be unrecognizable in the written record.

The sister Annie and baby John raise questions as well, but evidence suggesting answers can be found in Vermont and Minnesota records. John and Luke McGann settled in the mid-1850s in Minnetonka, Hennepin

County, Minnesota. John's farmland adjoined property owned by a John and Ann McGinty. John McGann and the McGintys are buried in nearby plots in St. Mary's Cemetery in Minneapolis. Census records show that two of the McGinty children were born in Vermont. The 1850 Rutland census lists the couple and their children; the children's names (some of them uncommon—for example, Henry, which was little used by the Irish) and ages closely match those of the family in Minnetonka. Another McGinty child, according to a Minnesota census, was born in Illinois, where Bally-kilcline farmers had settled in LaSalle County.

The McGintys had spent time in Rutland before heading west. In Vermont, John McGinty applied to become a citizen, and his papers said that he was born in Roscommon. The facts suggest—though no record yet has substantiated it—that Ann McGinty was born Ann McGann in Ballykilcline and is the Annie on the Ballykilcline eviction list. Further, Ginty/McGinty is a surname from Ballykilcline. Indeed, the McGintys named their oldest son Patrick, perhaps after the "P. Gint" who appeared as a landholder on an 1836 survey map of Ballykilcline (Brassington and Gale). If the couple followed Irish custom for names, then Patrick was John McGinty's father's name.

Ann was not listed in the McGann household in 1840. From the fact that the McGintys' oldest child was born in 1838, it appeared that she had married John McGinty earlier; he probably lived then in adjacent Knock-hall (1860 U.S. Census, Tithe Applotment Books).

As he trudged out of Strokestown in 1848, John McGann had special reasons to celebrate as well as mourn leaving Irish soil. It seems likely that Ann had not qualified for a ticket paid by the Crown, which turned away numbers of others' claims for passage; nevertheless, Ann went out with her siblings and was listed as an evictee. It also seems likely that the baby named John was her son, who may have been listed as a McGann as a cover to secure the travel bounty. The Crown passages secured for Ann and the child lend credibility to Scally's suggestion of a conspiracy among the evict-ees to take the British bounty and trade places in the line to leave Ireland, achieved by secretiveness in camouflaging individuals' identities or special help to the family from an insider on the travel arrangements. The infant John apparently died in transit, because later records showed that the first child born to the McGintys in Vermont also was named John (U.S. Census, Minnetonka, Minn., 1860). The Irish sometimes used a given name a sec-ond time after an earlier child so named had died (see other instances of the practice below). If these speculations are accurate, Ann's husband and other children may have traveled as Crown passengers under the names of legitimate evictees who received the bounty to leave but who, choosing instead to remain in Ireland or England, sold their spots on the ships.

How much subterfuge was required for the McGanns to accomplish their plan for leaving and to secure paid passage for Annie and her child is unclear. It certainly must have helped that their mother was a Cox (Outrage Papers, police report), since it was bailiff and Crown agent Johnny Cox who escorted the Ballykilcline people to Dublin; he might have gone out of his way to help members of his own extended family. Cox was the sole "official," as Scally pointed out, who was in a position to know the tenants personally; in fact, Cox's brother lived in Ballykilcline (Scally 1995, p. 73). John McGann spoke up for Cox in Liverpool when his neighbors criticized the Crown agent; he signed an affidavit and added a postscript: "All the complaints that were got up were for the purpose of injuring Johnny Cox" (Scally 1995, pp. 174, 175). Did McGann do so because he was especially indebted to Cox, possibly a relative, for allowing Annie and her infant, and perhaps others in her family, to leave at Crown expense?

But payment for passage was not their only obstacle in leaving. John McGann was an early suspect—though not the only one—in Mahon's murder. The clues that pointed in his direction are not clear from the police record, although it was no surprise that authorities' suspicions quickly turned to the troublesome townland. Police decided to investigate McGann more thoroughly: "Nov. 26th, '47. . . . I have made a strict and general enquiry along the sub Districts of Rooskey [Ruskey] and Kilglass after a man named John McGann who is supposed to be one of the party who was concerned in the Murder of the late Major Mahon . . . I will keep a constant watch. . . . Michael Fox" (Fox memo, Nov. 26, 1847).

On the other hand, Fox added that John's "family are under a good character and I have been given to believe by Constable Rodgers who is well acquainted with the family that this person would not be likely to be concerned in the fatal deed." He told his superiors that the McGanns had prepared to go to America at the previous harvest "but were disappointed. I think they have no intentions of going at present as they appear to be poor and not possessed of sufficient means to go out" (Fox memo, Nov. 26, 1847).

Days later, a constable filed this report:

Confidential
25/297 [797]
County of Roscommon
Cullagh 5th December 1847
    . . . having consulted with Sub Inspector Blakney, he directed me to proceed to this Post for the purpose of keeping a sharp lookout on a man

named ____ Cox who is supposed to be one of the persons concerned in the Murder of the late Major Mahon of Strokestown. . . .

There are numbers of the name of Cox in this neighborhood, but not having the christian [*sic*] name or description of the person accused it was impossible to say which of them was the man named, and that I did not hear of any of them preparing to immigrate to America, also gave the following names of John Cox, James Cox, John Cox, Thos Cox and Peter Cox which I selected as being the most likely to be concerned in the Murder of Major Mahon, and my reason for stating so is that I find they are very intimate with a man named Andrew Connor of Graffoge, who is suspected to be in the confidence of the ill disposed in this neighborhood. . . .

Martin Carrick, 2d Hd Cont, D, Stud, 9/12/47
(Carrick report, Dec. 5, 1847, Outrage Papers)

The police pressed their murder investigations that December as Parliament passed a coercion bill for Ireland. Many of Roscommon's Protestant gentry panicked and fled after the deaths of Major Mahon and Rev. Lloyd. Authorities still had McGann under surveillance weeks later, but interest in him waned for lack of evidence. Apparently none of the witnesses had made explicit charges against him, despite heavy surveillance by "a sharp disposable man" (Blakeney report, Jan. 2, 1848, Outrage Papers). For lack of charges and depositions against him, McGann was not apprehended.

Early in 1848, John McGann and his family left for Dublin, Liverpool, and America. They took passage from Liverpool on the *Channing* on March 13 and landed in New York City on April 17 (Ballykilcline website). It is not clear where John spent his first years in the United States, but the McGinty family went to Rutland, where they had two more children in 1850 and 1852. McGinty applied for U.S. citizenship in 1851 in Rutland, probably alongside a brother named Owen, who filed on the same day. John and Ann had seemingly named a daughter after Owen's wife, Winnifred. The McGintys then moved to Illinois, where another son was born in 1854 (U.S. Census, Vermont, 1850; U.S. Census, Minnetonka, Minn., 1860; Rutland Courts).

In the mid-1850s, the McGintys were the first Irish settlers in Minnetonka, about ten miles west of Minneapolis in Hennepin County, where others from Vermont and even immigrants from Bohemia also bought land.[1] John and Luke McGann soon joined them on this frontier. The McGintys purchased farmland from the government at $1.25 an acre and built along an old trail used by Indians, who helped themselves to potatoes in the family's underground storage pit as they passed by. At one point the Indians kidnapped their young son Dennis, and he was gone for a year before he escaped and made his way home (Johnson letter, Feb. 17, 1977). In 1860, John McGann and John McGinty had adjoining farms. Luke, still single, lived with his brother, whose wife, Ellen, was second-generation Irish and had been born in Pennsylvania. John and Ellen had assets of $675 [$16,356]; Luke had $600 [$14,538]; and the McGintys had $750 [$18,173] (U.S. Census 1860). Their assets then exceeded those of many Rutland quarry men from Kilglass who had arrived in the United States at the same time.

Twenty years later, in 1880, John and Ellen had six children ranging in age from 4 to 19. One of them was named for John's brother Anthony (Atty), who does not appear in the known U.S. record. By that time, though, John was ill: the federal census reported him "maimed, crippled, bedridden or otherwise disabled." Whether his debility stemmed from the lung disease that killed him a few years later, or from a farm accident, or from something else altogether is not clear. Luke was 50 years old, and his Irish wife also was named Ellen. They had five daughters, including 12-year-old twins. Luke worked as an expressman. The 1880 census showed Ann "McGenty" as a widow at 65, with three sons and a daughter still at home on the farm. Three teen-aged nieces (their surname was Kain), all Minnesota natives, lived with her family, but whether their relationship was on the McGann or the McGinty side is not known.

The only Gintys officially named as evictees who received Crown passage to New York were Margaret Ginty, widow of Edward, and her children Bernard, 14, and Bridget, 16, who may have gone to Connecticut. Another hint of John McGinty's Ballykilcline connection was that his youngest son's middle name was Edward.

John McGinty was 77 when he died of a cold and old age in 1877; Ann lived until 1881, when she had a fatal bout of asthma. John McGann was 63 in 1886 when he succumbed to bleeding from the lungs (Minnesota vital records).

In the 1920s, John and Ann's son Dennis sold a portion of his farmland to a Minneapolis businessman who erected a "chateau-style mansion" with sixty-three rooms. Dennis's son Roy became the groundskeeper of the place. In 1944 the McGinty lands became the world center for the Cargill Companies, and Roy continued working for the firm. After World War II, Roy planted 250,000 pine trees on the property, which townspeople later viewed as "a McGinty legacy" (Dickson "Legacy," Nov. 29, 2000).

A second McGann family evicted from Ballykilcline had also arrived in New York on the *Channing* in April 1848. The head of household was

Mary McGann, and traveling with her were six children ranging in age from one to eighteen years. Mary was the wife of Thomas McGann Jr., who appeared on the 1840 rent roll in Ireland. Since he was not listed as an evictee and never appeared in U.S. census records, the presumption is that Thomas died in Roscommon during the 1840s. In the United States, Mary and her children were listed on the 1850 federal census in Dutchess County, New York; the 1860 census shows this McGann family living in Boston. But the record so far does not explain why they moved to either place. One theory is that Mary may have moved to be near her own relatives rather than her late husband's (Cassie Kilroy Thompson communication, 2006), but her maiden name is not known.

THE WINTERS

Honora Igo Winters was the sixty-year-old widow of Lawrence Winters when she was ousted from Ballykilcline by Crown authorities and emigrated along with her children: Thomas, 30, Margaret, 24, Honor, 18, and "traveling with them, Catherine," one year old (Coyle 1994, p. 33). The family landed in New York and seemingly went directly to Rutland, where Honora's daughter Nancy and family had lived for several years. Nancy Winters McGuire and husband Daniel had emigrated sometime after 1838.

But the list of evictees omitted at least two members of Honora's family: the 1840 Ballykilcline tenants' list showed a daughter Catherine, 20, and a son John, 9, neither of whom traveled among the Crown's emigrants. Neither that daughter nor the granddaughter, both named Catherine, appeared in Rutland records under the name Winters; what happened to them remains a mystery. Daughter Margaret was missing from the 1840 tenant list; perhaps she was a domestic helper who was living elsewhere at that time. Why was John Winters missing at the time of eviction and emigration? He did not show up in Rutland for years, yet during the Civil War he served with Union forces in Company F of the Thirteenth U.S. Infantry (Vandenburg communication, 2002).

The Winters family had a web of relationships in Rutland with Wynnes and Igos. Bridget Wynne was born in Ballykilcline in 1834, emigrated in 1847 (though not as an evictee of the Crown), and married Patrick McLaughlin of Kilglass in Rutland (Tithe Applotment Books, Rutland vital records). Her sister Ann was married to Bartley McGuire; both had lived in Ballykilcline but settled in Rutland (Vandenburg communication, 2006). The Wynnes were the daughters of Terrence and Bridget

Winters Wynne, who lived in Ballykilcline in the 1830s. Through their mother, the sisters must have been related to Honora's late husband. And Rutland immigrant Michael Igo probably belonged to Honora's extended family, since her maiden name was Igo. Michael's wife was Catherine Geelan, a sister of the young William Brennan's spouse. A third Geelan sister, Mary Ann, was married to a man named Regan and also lived nearby.

Ten Geelans had called Ballykilcline home, but the sisters' way across the Atlantic was not aided by Crown money, according to official accounts. The father, Thomas Geelan, claimed that he had paid to hold one acre of land in the townland, but officials grouped him with "landless" cabiners, and his request for the allowance to emigrate was denied (Scally 1995, p. 120). Even today, Geelans who live at the edge of Ballykilcline embrace a family memory of the three Geelan sisters who went off to Vermont (Geelan communication).

Honora Winters' son Thomas worked in the quarries in 1857 and was enumerated in St. Bridget's Parish Census as "Co Boss"—probably a position with Rutland Marble Co. Since in later years he appeared in the census simply as a laborer, one wonders whether he eventually chose other work or whether he had compromised his quarry position by activity in one labor strike or another or by something more mundane. By 1860, the census showed, he had saved $450 [$10,904].

Through marriage, the Winters offspring affiliated with Carrolls (Thomas), McLaughlins (daughter Honora), and Maloneys (John). Margaret's marital status is unclear. The Carroll connection certainly was a Kilglass relationship; several Carrolls from Knockhall, adjacent to Ballykilcline, had settled in Rutland. The McLaughlins may have come from Kilglass. From these marriages, Honora had nine grandchildren, and four more in Nancy McGuire's family.[2]

In November 1874, Nancy Winters McGuire died under mysterious circumstances after driving alone in her buggy from Mendon to West Rutland to sell butter. She also had visited friends in Rutland, left there "in good health and spirits, and in less than an hour arrived at her home a mangled corpse," causing a sensation (*Rutland Herald*, Nov. 18, 1874). It appeared to the town's newspaper "as if a murder had been committed," but a physician later ruled her death due to heart disease and her contusions caused by her fall in the buggy. Sixty-eight carriages turned out for her funeral procession (*Rutland Herald*, Nov. 19, 1874).

Evictee Honora Winters outlived the daughter she had followed to Vermont. She survived into her nineties and died in 1879. Descendants of Honora and Lawrence Winters remained in Rutland into the twenty-first century. Other family members eventually moved on to Boston and Providence (Vandenburg communication).

THE MULLERAS

Twenty-one Mulleras were evicted from Ballykilcline, apparently descendants of John and James Mullera, who, the family believes, were either brothers or first cousins. The senior John died in 1847 (UK Moving Here website), and his wife stayed in Ireland. Their son Arthur, born in 1814, left for America in 1834; he was one of the earliest known emigrants from the townland to the United States. Arthur lived for a time in Paris, Kentucky, along with several neighbors from Ballykilcline, and likely was there in 1847 when his brothers John and Patrick arrived in the United States. This John with his wife, Sarah, and five sons lived over time in New York, Kentucky, and Elkader, Iowa. At the end of his life, Arthur moved in with Patrick's family in Elkader.

Evictees James and Bridget McManus Mullera, the other branch of the family, were living in Rutland in 1850, where the census recorded them under the name "Mularr." With them were their children: James, Thomas, Denis, Bridget, and Annie. The father, James, and 22-year-old Thomas worked as laborers. Thomas also spent time in the marble quarries.

In court testimony on the will of Denis years later, James and Bridget's grandson James McGuire testified under oath that the couple had had a family of twelve children, some of whom were stillborn and four of whom had died in childhood. The couple used the dead children's names a second time for later offspring. McGuire also claimed that a son had died in 1858 in Vermont; he mistakenly called that son Thomas when he evidently meant James; son James's death in Vermont was confirmed by another family member, but the evidence suggests that he actually died in 1848 (Alberts communication).

By 1859 these Mulleras had relocated to LaSalle County, Illinois, where other Ballykilcline families had put down roots as much as a generation earlier. The patriarch, James, died there in 1859. Thomas married Mary Kelly, whose native place had been Strokestown, and they had eight children (Alberts communication). In 1860 the widow Bridget Mullera lived in son Denis's household. Denis's sister Bridget and her son James McGuire also were there; Bridget had been divorced from Terrance McGuire prior to that date.[3] The elder Bridget died in 1879 and is buried in the cemetery at Utica, Illinois, but her husband's final resting place has not been identified. Only the census document that showed him in Rutland told his descendants that, indeed, he had come out of Ireland along with his family.[4]

THE CAROLANS

A number of Carolans (Carlons) had made their way to Rutland by 1860. Several of them were the sons of the Owen Carolan, who leased land in Ballykilcline in the 1830s and who, with his wife Margaret Connor and "her son John," is buried in Kilglass Cemetery (Kilglass Cemetery gravestone inscriptions). Owen appeared on the 1840 tenants' list with three children: John, 22, Bernard, 18, and Mary, 20. For a time, a John Carolan, probably his brother, joined Owen as a leaseholder in Ballykilcline. While John remained on the land and was evicted in 1847, Owen apparently left the townland before the rent strike ended. The senior John Carolan, age 50, his wife Honora, and three daughters took the Crown's passage from Liverpool and settled in LaSalle County, Illinois (Ballykilcline website).

Other Carolans lived in Kilglass in the 1830s: for instance, Pat in Tully townland, and William and John who farmed a single plot in Ballyfeeny, on the Marquis of Westmeath's estate (Tithe Applotment Books). But about two decades later, at the time of Griffith's Valuation [of land], not a single Carolan was recorded in the parish (Coyle 1994, pp. 42–73).

After 1850, Carlons could be found in Rutland and Dorset. Those for whom documentation was available all came from Kilglass except for one of two men named Thomas, whose roots were in adjacent Kilmore Parish. Three of them, or perhaps four of these Carlons, were the sons of Owen of Ballykilcline: their names were Owen, Thomas, Bernard, and possibly Patrick. At least two of these men worked in the quarries.

The conclusive evidence of the Ballykilcline connection comes from the November 10, 1871, marriage in Rutland of Bridget Murray and Owen Carolan, 31, who was a blacksmith. The record named the groom's father as Owen and his mother as Margaret Connor, matching the names in Kilglass Cemetery (Middlesex, Vt., vital records). The immigrant Owen's 1874 naturalization record also established his home place as Roscommon (Rutland Courts). Another immigrant son of an Owen Carlon farmed in Dorset: Thomas Carlon married Elizabeth McGuire in February 1865 (Middlesex, Vt., vital records). Thomas died three years later at age 32 of a lung disease, leaving his wife, two daughters, and a young son. While his gravestone inscription says he was from the parish of Kilmore, he may nevertheless have been part of the Ballykilcline family, given his father's name and the Kilglass cluster there. Kilmore is adjacent to Kilglass, and the family may have moved back and forth across the parish line as others had done then.[5] A Patrick Carlin in the Dorset records may have been their brother; he married Sarah McGuire in September 1865 (Middlesex, Vt., vital records). It was Patrick's second marriage; he and Bridget Cunningham had had a child in Rutland in 1861. Bridget died in April of the following year and was buried in Dorset; her gravestone attests to her Kilglass roots. A second Thomas Carlon, born in 1806 and also buried in Dorset, may have been related as well; his native place was Roscommon (Murphy and Murphy 2000, pp. 210, 211).

The Bernard Carolan to whom Michael Hanley lent money in 1847 likely was the 18-year-old son of Owen Carolan named on the 1840 tenants' list; he stayed only a few years in Rutland. He had immigrated after 1846 with his wife (name unknown) and a daughter, Bridget. His second child, Ellen, was born in Vermont in 1851. Then the family headed to Illinois, where in 1860 he had a farm valued at $2,000 [$48,462] in Waltham, LaSalle County, next to that of evictees James and Susan Carrington Hanley, for whom Rutland also had been only a stopover on the way west. Bernard had $240 [$5,815] in personal assets in 1860. By then his wife apparently had died, leaving him with four children to raise. The youngest two were John, 8, and Mary, 5. Working on the Carolan farm then was a 17-year-old Francis Fox. Could he have been the child of that name who was evicted from Ballykilcline?

In Rutland, two John Carlons shared a two-family house in 1860. The older man was born between 1780 and 1796, the younger in 1838 (U.S. Census, Vermont, 1860). Surely they were related but were not father and son, since the younger man's father was Patrick (Offutt communication, 2003).[6] Living with the younger John was an Ann Carlon, probably his sister. The younger John was an apprentice printer at Tuttle's, a Rutland book dealer. When a Fenian circle formed in West Rutland in 1864, its members chose John Carlon as its secretary (*Rutland Courier*, Dec. 30, 1864); that man must have been the younger John Carlon, since the senior of the two then was quite elderly and could neither read nor write.

Their living arrangements support the Ballykilcline and Kilglass connections of both John Carlons because in 1870 the immigrant Owen Carlon, whose father had farmed in Ballykilcline and had a gravesite in Kilglass, had replaced the younger John Carlon in the house. The fact that the three Carlon men all shared living quarters over time testifies to a family relationship, but the precise connection—grandfather and grandsons, uncle and nephews, other—is unclear and undocumented.

Significantly, however, this evidence shows a Kilglass and/or a Ballykilcline involvement in Irish nationalist activity in Rutland.

The elder John Carlon died in 1874 (Middlesex, Vt., vital records). At the time, he was identified as a farmer, though earlier he had worked as a tailor. He was the son of John and Bridget McDonell Carlon; eight McDonnells had been evicted from Ballykilcline in 1847–48.

In 1865 the younger John Carlon married Fannie Reilly, daughter of Thomas and Rosanna of nearby Castleton, who had immigrated before 1838. John and Fannie soon moved to Indiana so that he could work with printer James Downey. Downeys had resided in Ballykilcline as well; the townland's John Downey had emigrated early and was reported in Boston in the middle 1840s (Harris et al. 1989–); a potential connection between these Downeys, however, remains undocumented.

In Indiana, John Carlon prospered as a businessman, starting as a foreman at the Indianapolis Printing and Publishing House. With a partner, he owned the company a few years later. The partner had sold out by 1881, and the firm's name changed to Carlon-Hollenbeck (Offutt communication, 2002). In Indiana, John was seen as "a thorough, practical printer, and well qualified for the position he now holds, being of a generous and accommodating disposition" (Nowland 1877, p. 547). John was also active in Democratic politics. The couple had five sons—Charles, John, George, Joseph, and Frederick—most of them born in Rutland when Fannie went east for the summers to visit family and friends.

A Civil War veteran named Charles B. Carlon, born in 1841, is buried in Calvary Cemetery in Rutland (Murphy and Murphy, 2000). The common locale, their ages, and the fact that John and Fannie named a son Charles suggest that he and John were either brothers or cousins. The veteran's tombstone gives no death date but identifies his wife as Mary A. Kelley.

Beginning in the 1930s, a granddaughter of John and Fannie Carlon built a career in the theater, radio, television, and films in New York and Hollywood. Fran Carlon's credits mounted: she had roles on Broadway in *Sunrise at Campobello* and in TV's daytime drama *As the World Turns*. In films, she performed alongside such luminaries as Loretta Young and Douglas Montgomery.

THE BRISLINS

An unknown number of famine and prefamine immigrants fled Ireland after trouble with the law at a time when that might mean transportation to Australia—effectively, forever—for petty offenses or membership in a secret society. Patrick Brislin of Strokestown was one of them. He re-settled in Rutland in the 1840s because dozens of people from his native place already had gone there. But since he was a fugitive from the law, the less costly passage across the Atlantic to Canada rather than to the United States may have been his route; from Quebec, he could even have walked across the border into Vermont.

Patrick, born about 1822 to John and Bridget Brislin of Strokestown, arrived in Rutland as a fugitive and an alleged perpetrator of outrage. He had been arrested in Roscommon in May 1843 after a raid for firearms at the home of John Dignan in Ballyrahan, near Strokestown. Brislin was said to be one of a party of six men armed with pistols and swords who broke into Dignan's house, according to a police report. Later, Dignan's wife and daughter singled Patrick out of a police lineup of suspects (Hogg deposition, Oct. 17, 1843; *Armagh Guardian*, April 15, 1845).

Godfrey Hogg, a justice of the peace who had an official role in the events in Ballykilcline, helped to arrest Brislin and provided the details of his legal case in letters to government officials. Brislin and a code-fendant named Gillooly, Hogg said, were let out on bail after jurors in their trial could not reach agreement. The presiding judge, Baron Lefroy, remarked on the jurors' hesitation and warned, "Gentlemen[,] if the evidence in this case is not sufficient to procure conviction, farewell to the peace of your County which before many months will be in as bad a state as Tipperary" (Hogg deposition, Oct. 17, 1843). The case was put over to the 1844 spring session. During his appearance then, Brislin "feigned illness," and the prisoners again were bailed. Familiar with British justice and evidently wanting to avoid a sentence to Australia, Brislin fled to America before his next date in court (Hogg letter, July 23, 1844).

Hogg's deposition alleged that Brislin belonged to a secret society and that his raiding party had forced Dignan to take an unlawful oath. Hogg also charged that Brislin had "set a conspiracy on foot to assassinate this Deponent. . . . Brislawn [*sic*] declare[d] he would die easy if he had Hogg . . . and Major [Denis] Mahon shot" (Hogg letter, July 23, 1844; Outrage Papers Coleman 1999, p. 34). That claim was made three years before Denis Mahon was ambushed and killed. Unfortunately, the record does not explain Brislin's grudge against Mahon, which had apparently developed even before Mahon became the landlord at Strokestown.

In a separate but telling incident, the Dignan family was targeted again in 1845 in another raid for arms, during which John Dignan's brother was killed. In reporting his murder, a newspaper remarked, "Such is the state of society in this unfortunate country that no one would venture to identify the prisoner" (*Armagh Guardian*, April 15, 1845). The facts suggest that the Dignans somehow had violated traditional norms of behavior—they may have taken over the home of an evicted family or purchased distrained goods (that is, property seized in lieu of payment for rent or tithes), for instance—and thus became repeated targets of the Irish people's "midnight justice."

Once safe in Rutland, Brislin filed papers to become a U.S. citizen in 1853, and over the next five years he witnessed citizenship actions in local courts for other Kilglass men. Evictee Patrick Kelly was one for whom Brislin performed that service in 1856. Brislin also witnessed evictee and quarry man William Neary's bid for citizenship two years later (Rutland Courts).

In 1860, Brislin was a forty-year-old day laborer who lived with his wife, Bridget Waters, their four children, and his mother. His oldest child, then 10 years old, had been born in Vermont. None of the adults in the family was literate. Patrick had sizable assets of $925 [$22,413], and it appeared that his sister-in-law lived next door with three children (U.S. Census, Vermont, 1860). What kind of life Brislin led in Rutland and what other ties he had with the former tenants of Ballykilcline are issues worth exploring. Did he live up to Hogg's warning to Irish officials that "there cannot be at large [a] more dangerous character" (Hogg deposition, Oct. 17, 1843)? It does not appear so from the available record. Brislin is buried in Rutland's Calvary cemetery alongside his wife (Murphy and Murphy, 2000). They died weeks apart in 1868, he of heart disease and she of consumption. He was then about 48. His mother died ten years later at age 100.

Other Brislins in Rutland records include one named John, who probably was Patrick's brother, and his wife, Mary Haley Neary Brislin (Rutland RootsWeb Listserv).[7] In fact, Mary was the widow of Patrick Neary of Ballykilcline, one of the townland's strike leaders, when she married John Brislin. Patrick and Mary Neary and their year-old daughter, Bridget, had been among those evicted and sent to New York by Crown authorities. Patrick, according to descendants, died about 1855 in Rutland, and thereafter, his widow married Brislin.[8] By the mid-1850s, no Brislins appeared in Strokestown-area records; perhaps the entire family quit Ireland after Patrick's run-in with the law (Leitrim-Roscommon website; Griffith's Valuation).

Patrick and Mary Neary's daughter Bridget later married John Considine and their daughter Mary Josephine married the son of Terrance McGuire, whose parents were Daniel and Nancy Winters Maguire. The tendency to marry within the group was strong. Years later, before World

War I, a man named Henry C. Brislin became the mayor of Rutland, but any connection with Patrick's family remains uninvestigated (Kelly communication, 2002).

What of Brislin's codefendant in the legal action over the raid at Dignan's house? An Owen Gilluly who was born in Roscommon eventually settled with his family in Randolph County, West Virginia. A descendant recently started building a case that he was the Gilluly who had sought firearms from the Dignans and faced the court alongside Patrick Brislin.[9]

Owen Gilluly's family came from Roscommon town in the parish of Kilbride, which is west of Strokestown. Owen's wife, born about 1833, was named Mary White; she may have been one of two orphaned White sisters in the Ballykilcline home of Bridget Fallon, their grandmother, in the 1840s (List of Tenants). Young Mary White did not receive a Crown-paid passage across the Atlantic. Owen's wife came to the United States in 1849 and may have arrived through the port of Boston, along with sisters named Catherine and Ellen (U.S. Census 1900; John Patrick Gillooly). Among Owen and Mary's seventeen children—the first was born in Wisconsin—were daughters given those same names, though they were commonly used by the Irish. These leads warrant more investigation.

Like Rutland, through the 1840s the area in West Virginia where the Gillulys settled saw a large influx of families—Fallons, Coxes, Murrays, Hanleys, Morans, Farrells, and others—from around Strokestown. Local gravestones attest to it, naming their owners' native places. Many of the local families sold out in the 1890s, however, and moved on after oil and gas were found on their land.[10]

THE PADIANS

Some time after stepping off the *Roscius* in New York in October 1847, Richard and Mary Carlos Padian headed for Texas with their four young children.[11] But the former Ballykilcline strike leader's money took them only as far south as Maryland, according to family lore, where they, or perhaps some predecessors, named the place where they settled after the state that had been their destination. That is one theory at least. The family's oral history about Texas confused family researchers for a long time until they learned about Texas, Maryland—in Baltimore County near Towson—and found 1850s records of the Padians there. Texas had a cluster of Roscommon and other Irish immigrants, so many of the local names were the same as those in Kilglass Parish and, through immigration, in Rutland. And, much like Rutland, it was a quarrying district.

The descendants had another surprise as well: Richard and Mary, like the Winters family in Rutland, apparently had left behind in Ireland a son named John, then about 17 years old, when they joined the Crown's emigration. Young John Padian followed them out of Ireland in 1854.

In Texas, Maryland, Richard Padian soon rented a farm—the Priscilla Owings estate—and by 1860 his own real estate was valued at $5,000 [$121,154] and his personal assets at $600 [$14,538]. Other reports suggest that before the Civil War, Richard either owned or managed a 750-acre farm that had belonged to a John Price. Richard and Mary had four more children. Their offspring were John, William, Bridget, James, Maria, Michael, Peter, Catherine, and Annie.

One descendant, writing about his Padian forebears and cognizant of his ancestor's leadership role in Ballykilcline's strike, said, "Richard Padian's subsequent actions in America give clues that he possessed a strong personality and was passionate about other causes, including the U.S. Civil War" and, it might be added, the Catholic Church and the Democratic Party. The Padians belonged to St. Joseph's Parish, and its written history (Jubilee Book), describes the family's war experiences: "In 1861 when the [Civil] war broke out, he [Richard] sent his three sons off, fearing they would be drafted into the Union Army. He was an ardent Southerner." Federal forces had occupied Baltimore after rioting there in 1861 and needed men to help police the city. The three sons who had evaded conscription, William, James, and Peter, all went to New York (Padian communication).

William's escape from service had its dramatic moments. "It appears that he was drafted," according to a 1933 newspaper account, "and the officers were looking for him. Getting wind of the fact, however, he and one of his sisters left the home in an old carriage with the idea of making some port from which William could sail away from these parts and eventually arrive in New York. But the officers were so hot on their trail that they had to drive through the woods around Baltimore County three days and nights before they were able to throw their pursuers off and strike out for the boat landing. William got away, however, and reached New York [where he] later made a fortune in the liquor business." (The descendants have noted the contradictions in these tales that reported Richard Padian to be a southerner whose sons headed north during the war.)

In Texas, the Catholic church earned Richard's time and attention, and the family occupied a prominent pew on Sundays for decades. They donated to the building of both the school and the rectory and kept an open door in their home for the clergy, as they had done in Ballykilcline, where the only resident priest had lived in their house. Daughter Maria Padian helped care for St. Joseph's altar for years. When James Cardinal Gibbons of Baltimore visited the parish, the Padians offered a "choice cardinal-colored velvet chair" for his use. The Padians also had some black servants; a church publication called Richard "a friend to the colored race," but his legal relationship with the servants is not clear (qtd. in *Bonfire*, Fall 2006).

After the late 1860s, although there are conflicting records about who owned it, Richard Padian lived on an estate called Taylor's Hall in an imposing home. What seems likeliest is that William Padian, the liquor dealer in New York, bought the property in 1866 for about $21,000 [$266,491] and rented or sold part of it to his father or simply opened it to him as his home. By 1870 the census valued Richard's property at $25,000 [$386,000]. William not only became active in politics in New York but also headed the central Liquor Dealers' Association there. He lived at 323 East 19th Street in Manhattan, owned saloons and boardinghouses, and in 1884 helped organize a political party known as the Independent Democracy (*Bonfire*, Fall 2006). William's wife and four children all died young (Padian communication).

The oldest and youngest Padian sons, John and Michael, remained near Texas. John married Catherine Kelly and had seven children; he eventually settled his family in Towson, Maryland, where he strongly supported the Catholic parish. Michael inherited Taylor's Hall from William in 1894, and it remained in the family until his death in 1926 (*Bonfire*, Fall 2006).

Richard Padian, then a widower for eight years, passed away in 1882 and is buried in the family mausoleum in New York. Since the farming work that had attracted him in Maryland was unlikely to produce the occasions for collective action that confronted the Ballykilcline immigrants in Rutland's quarries, Padian had channeled his efforts in his new home place into family, church, and politics. A local railroad station bears the name Padonia after the family.

THE McCORMICKS

John and Catherine McDonnell McCormick survived difficult years around Strokestown during and after the famine before uprooting themselves and relocating in industrial Lancashire County, England. It is not apparent that they received any "assistance" out of Ireland. And it was years later when the family made the greater leap to the United States, following relatives to Albany, New York.

Although there were several McCormick families in Ballykilcline and at least one of them went to Rutland, no direct connection so far has been established between them and John McCormick's family line. Nevertheless, John's story captures the shared hardships experienced by many of the Irish whose lives began in the Strokestown-Kilglass area during the early nineteenth century.

John and Catherine married on January 23, 1845, in the Catholic church in Strokestown, which custom says was Catherine's home parish; no record tells where John lived then. On their wedding day, of course, John and Catherine had no foreknowledge of the catastrophe that would break over them and all they knew only a few months later because of the fungus that destroyed that season's potato crops and subsequent ones year after stricken year.

Descendants have found that seven sons were born to the couple; the first was Michael, in 1851 (they apparently had no children, or none who survived, during and immediately after the famine). Michael was followed by James in 1853, Patrick in 1855, Thomas in 1859, John in the following year, William in 1861, and finally Francis in 1864.

That year of Francis's birth was one of sorrows too for the young family. Francis was born in October in the Strokestown workhouse (which had opened in 1852 and could accommodate six hundred persons; it was not uncommon for women to go to the workhouse for childbirth, though the birth record listed the McCormicks' home then as in Corboghil, a short distance south from Strokestown). Three weeks after Francis was born, little Thomas McCormick succumbed to scarletina, followed by William only weeks later. Those deaths have led descendants to ask whether Catherine had brought the disease home with her from the workhouse.

Some time during the seven years of Francis's early childhood, John McCormick moved his family to industrial Bolton, about fifteen miles from Manchester in Lancashire County, on the northwestern British coast. Textile manufacture had been based in Bolton since the 1300s, and cotton fabric was made there on hand looms as early as 1640. In 1779, Bolton saw the invention of the spinning mule, which galvanized cotton production. The city was home to the first spinning mill a year later (Bolton website). Bolton had grown to 11,000 citizens by 1789, and in the early 1800s its sizable laboring class joined in public protests over inadequate working and social conditions. As E. P. Thompson noted, "In the 1790s only Norwich and Sheffield were regarded as incurably Jacobin centres by the authorities; by the early years of the nineteenth century, Nottingham, Coventry, Bolton were added to the list" (1966, p. 605).

The McCormicks first show up in Bolton records, in an 1871 census, as living on Andrew Street in Irish Newtown in the city's central district. Other McCormicks and McDonnells lived nearby, though any relationship is unproved so far.

Bolton had numerous iron foundries as well as cotton mills and at least one paper mill. They attracted a large working class that lived, as in many of England's factory towns then, in central housing which was not only poor but also unhealthful. The Bolton Sanitary Committee's words for it were "substandard" and "unsanitary." John McCormick and son James worked in the Bolton paper mill, as did a lodger in their home—who likely was related to Catherine—named James McDonnell. Michael and a second lodger were laborers at the ironworks. The McCormicks' third son, Patrick, then sixteen, was a piecer in a textile mill. The two youngest children were still in school, and Catherine had no outside job. But Michael McCormick, 20, did not survive long in the city environment; he contracted smallpox and died on March 8, 1872, even though his death certificate said that he had been vaccinated against the disease.

In 1877, Patrick McCormick married Catherine Finneran from the same block of Irish Newtown; her family, also natives of Roscommon, had arrived in Bolton only a few years earlier. The path to Bolton's mills and factories was well trodden by Roscommoners. A year later the couple had a son they named Michael. As an adult, that Michael McCormick never acknowledged that he had been born in England, according to a granddaughter, but claimed that he had first opened his eyes to the world aboard ship on the high seas. Patrick's father had only a few months to enjoy this new grandchild, since he died of pneumonia in January 1879.

Patrick McCormick and his brother-in-law Patrick Finneran emigrated to the United States in April 1881 and went to Albany, where two Finneran siblings had lived for a decade. In doing so, the two Patricks left their families behind in Bolton for two years, probably to earn the money to bring them across the Atlantic. During that time, Catherine Finneran McCormick took a job in a cotton warehouse in Bolton. Patrick McCormick's mother followed him to New York later that same year but then dropped out of sight in Albany's records; brothers John and James arrived in 1883, and Francis in 1886.

The family's travel pattern in coming to America was not uncommon for the Irish who lacked means: moving in stages from their home county to jobs in industrial Britain in order to save the funds to cross the Atlantic to join family or friends who had preceded them. The immediate immigrant in the migration chain that ended with the McCormicks apparently was Patrick's wife's sister Mary, whose husband was Terrence Riley. They were still single when they emigrated a week apart in 1869 but must have married soon after settling. They had chosen Albany because Riley had relatives there. Mary's siblings followed her over a span of years, and in time, Patrick's family followed him.

If life in Strokestown and Bolton had been hard, the McCormicks struggled in Albany, too, though the family lived in a neighborhood where many people around them bore Roscommon names. Patrick supported his family as a laborer. By 1892, he and Catherine had six children, but they lost three of them within ten months to scarlet fever and croup. Two more children—Josephine and Francis—were born by 1897. Tragedy struck again on Christmas Day 1902, when Patrick died of heart disease at 47. The older children married in the following few years, and two of them each took a younger sibling into his home. The widowed Catherine Finneran McCormick lived until 1924. In her last few years, she worked as a housekeeper. Patrick and Catherine's son Michael had married a daughter of German immigrants whose name was Anna Gaertner, and they had six children. But Michael was widowed after Anna contracted the flu during the great epidemic of 1918.

From famine to flu epidemic, the McCormicks' story captures the hardships confronting the Irish, the emigration difficulties, the risks to health, the operation of chain migration, and the burdens of immigrant laborers in the United States.[12] The last of Michael and Anna McCormick's children, living near Albany, turned 100 on Christmas Day 2006.

THE RILEYS

John, Hugh, and Michael Riley were the sons of Michael and Ann Colligan Riley of Kilglass Parish.[13] People bearing their parents' surnames were present in Ballykilcline, but so far no direct relationship has been established. The Rileys, though, had proven links to nearby townlands of Legan and Knockhall, across a roadway from Ballykilcline, as well as nearby Dooslattagh, and thus probably had extended connections with one or more families in Ballykilcline. John, born in 1822, was the oldest of the seven siblings who by 1850 had gone to Rhode Island, where they started their American lives in Providence. The city ranked ninth in the country in 1870 for number of Irish residents (Kenny 2000, p. 105).

By the middle 1850s, several of the Riley immigrants—the sisters were Bridget Riley O'Reilly, Mary Riley Henry, Ann Riley Featherstone (and, by second marriage, Henry), and Alice Riley Smith—had moved north to Burrillville, a textile mill and farming community near the Connecticut border. John had married Catherine (Kate) McNally who had come from County Monaghan; Hugh married Ann Sweeney; and Michael's wife was Catherine Elwood, also a Roscommon native. John and Michael could both read and write; Hugh could not. For a time, gregarious Michael kept a saloon in Burrillville. A few years and several children later, John and Kate crossed the state border and bought a farm in Hampton, Connecticut. Joining them were Hugh and the Henrys, Featherstones, Smiths, and their families. Michael's family did cross briefly into Connecticut, but two of his young children died there, and afterward the family resettled in Warwick, Rhode Island, where they remained. Bridget O'Reilly and her family arrived in Burrillville later than the others, but she died young of heart disease, and eventually her family returned to Providence. For decades, members of the family crossed and recrossed the fluid state border to visit and help one another, to celebrate and to mourn.

Among them, the seven Riley siblings had about fifty-five children, including several sets of twins. John and Kate Riley had ten children, but of their two sons, both named Thomas, only the second survived infancy. The siblings' families farmed for decades in Hampton, and for a time, at least, John's biggest crop was potatoes. John and Kate did well—well enough to send their only son off to college in Ohio about 1880. That experience apparently led Thomas later to forsake farming in Hampton for a city job in Boston, where he landed work in a hotel and a home in Dorchester—apparently a decision his father struggled to understand. John and Kate's second daughter entered a religious order, the Sisters of St. Joseph of Chambery, and studied in France. When she returned in a black habit with a new name, Sister John Theresa, she taught school in Lee, Massachusetts, and then was assigned to Hartford, Connecticut, where, with several others, she helped found St. Francis Hospital in 1897 and was the head of its nursing school for decades. The facility is now the largest Catholic hospital in New England, licensed for more than six hundred beds. Her sister, a niece, and a grandniece, in their time, followed her to classes at the nursing school or careers at the hospital. The Rileys' oldest daughter tutored children in a Yankee household and taught in a Hampton schoolhouse for several years. Another, like Maria Padian in Maryland, helped out for years at the local Catholic church.

By the 1870s and 1880s the Irish had moved to Hampton in numbers, and many of them had Roscommon roots. As early as 1860, they thought about establishing their own church, and John Riley committed to that effort. As a historian of the town continued the story:

> The established Protestants greeted this idea with no little resentment, and the church was sited, not on the main street, the usual location of village churches, but around the corner. The building site, donated by Governor Chauncey Cleveland, was on Cedar Swamp Road, a lot bordered by a thick row of pines that blocked the view of the church. . . . This pretty church is now clearly visible from Old Route 6, thanks to the destruction of the pines in the hurricane of 1938, but its position off the Main Street of town is a reminder of the religious, social, and political divisions of the nineteenth century. (Trecker 2000, p. 68)

The Irish were used to it. The account of how Hampton's town fathers positioned the new church echoed the treatment of Catholics by local elites in the town of Cloone in County Leitrim, not far from Kilglass, as described by a local historian: "The Protestant church and yard [was] on an elevated one-acre site at the northern end of the village. . . . The Catholic church and yard . . . occupied a very different position . . . off the main street and behind a row of private dwelling houses. According to [Historian Kevin] Whelan, such an inferior location is indicative of the attitude of landlords to Catholicism; 'Where the landlord was hostile, the chapel was consigned to the outer fringes of the estate, or to very marginal back street locations in the town'" (Heslin 2004, p. 84).

When the Civil War came, the Riley men had young children, and none of the three brothers served. It was said that John had broken his trigger finger and that Michael had bought his way out of military action. The record is silent on Hugh.

The youngest daughter of John and Kate, years later, recalled that her father wrote to a brother in Kilglass Parish, a fact that was passed down in the family; in seeming defiance of Irish naming customs, all but one of the Riley immigrants had called their oldest son Thomas, even though their father's name was Michael. The speculation is that perhaps an older brother by that name had remained in Ireland and was remembered in this way by his emigrant siblings.

After Hugh Riley died in the 1880s and his wife several years later, John became the guardian of their youngest children. Hugh and Ann Sweeney Riley had a set of twins, a son who was mentally retarded, and a son who later lost his life in a construction accident near Willimantic, Connecticut, around 1900. Their oldest son later became the town's sheriff. Ann, their only daughter, evidently crossed into Massachusetts after her parents' deaths; nothing more about her is known to current family researchers.

From Hampton, John eventually saw his sister Mary and her husband James Henry move their family farther west to the mill town of Willimantic. Daniel and Alice Riley Smith remained nearby in Brooklyn, Connecticut, but after Ann Riley Featherstone Henry had outlived two husbands, she took her family back to Burrillville, where she had buried children and a husband, her sister had died, and her stepdaughter and family still lived. Her first husband Peter Featherstone's gravestone in Burrillville noted that he came from Dooslattagh in Kilglass Parish where, other sources said, his father, Thomas, had been a hedge schoolmaster who educated Irish children despite British laws that banned doing so. Ann's granddaughter Mary Featherstone became the second wife of prominent Pascoag textile manufacturer William H. Prendergast and took public roles, such as state regent of the Daughters of Isabella, in the Rhode Island church. In 1932, seven years after her husband's death, she ran for public office in Providence. As the Democratic candidate in the second ward, she was the first woman to seek a city alderman's position (*Providence Journal*, Dec. 30, 1943), but her grandmother Ann did not live to see it happen.

By 1890, two of the Riley immigrants had died, and the other five lived in five different communities—Hampton, Brooklyn, and Willimantic in Connecticut; Burrillville and Warwick in Rhode Island—on both sides of the state line. Many of their children by then had families of their own.

At least two other couples who lived locally apparently had close connections with the Rileys of Hampton: Thomas and Ann Colligan Riley of Hampton and James and Mary Foley Dockery of Brooklyn. The couple named Riley, both of them born in the early 1840s, arrived in Hampton in the late 1860s and had twelve children. John and Kate were godparents for some of them; they reciprocated for John's and Kate's children. Thomas had two brothers in Rhode Island, and after some years in Hampton he moved his family there. The brothers were the sons of Luke and Elizabeth McDermott Riley, probably of Knockhall in Kilglass, but the precise relationship between them and the seven Riley siblings in Rhode Island and Connecticut remains a mystery. As for the other couple, James Dockery came from Legan, and his wife, Mary ("Aunt Mary" to John's children) Foley, was from Killeegan, both Kilglass townlands. The childless couple died of flu on the same day in the mid-1890s, and their will named a son of Mary Riley Henry as their executor, citing a cousin relationship that remains a mystery.

In February 1903 a grand occasion was celebrated on the Rileys' Hampton farm: John's and Kate's fiftieth wedding anniversary. It was a large gathering with a turkey dinner, recitations, a group photograph, and lively music. The local newspaper recorded it in detail and preserved some information for history, naming Catherine McNally Riley's birthplace as Latton in Aughnamullen West Parish in southern County Monaghan. The couple's gravestone in Danielson identified the Rileys' home place as Kilglass Parish in Roscommon.

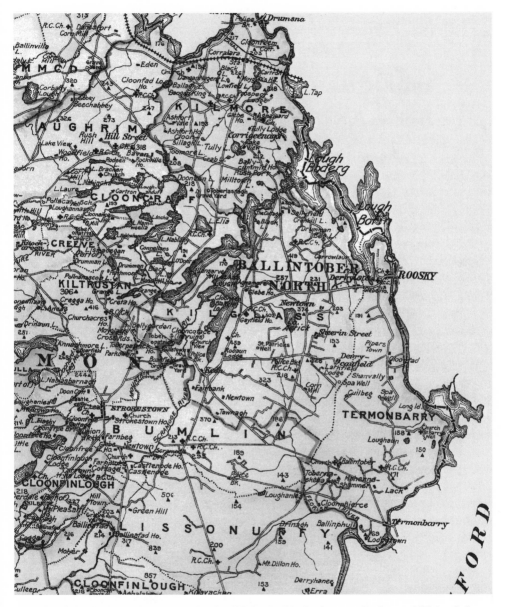

Detail of a map of County Roscommon showing Kilglass Parish, Strokestown, Ruskey, and Kilglass Lake. Ballykilcline is to the east of the northern part of the lake. Aghamore, a neighborhood in the townland, is marked. From *A Memorial Atlas of Ireland* (L. J. Richards & Co., Philadelphia, 1901).

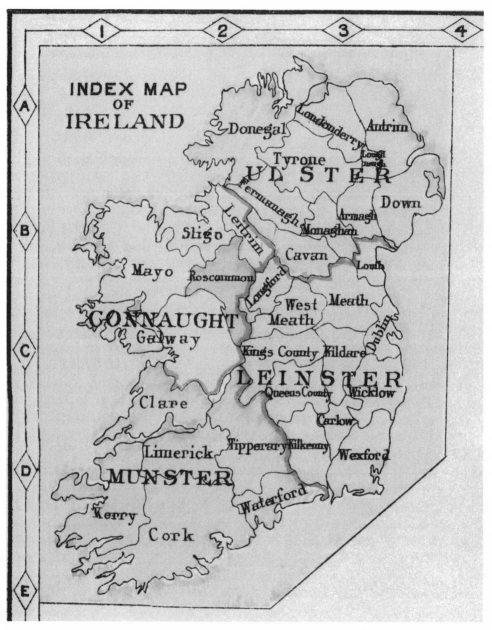

Map of Ireland situating County Roscommon on the eastern border of Connaught in "the heart of Ireland." Detail from Roscommon map in *A Memorial Atlas of Ireland* (L. J. Richards & Co., Philadelphia, 1901).

Bridget Mullera, who with her family was evicted and sent to the United States by Crown authorities. They resettled in Rutland, where they lived for about ten years; one son died there. The family later moved to LaSalle County, Illinois. Photo courtesy of the Mullera Family.

Terrance McGuire, son of Nancy Winters and Daniel McGuire, prefamine immigrants to Rutland. Terrance was the father of James McGuire, whose family is pictured in this gallery. Photo courtesy of William Vinehout.

The James McGuire family in a photo from the 1890s. Both husband and wife descend from Ballykilcline evictees: he from Honora Winters and she (Mary Josephine Considine) from Bridget Neary, who was evicted at the age of one with her parents, Patrick and Mary Haley Neary. Photo courtesy of William Vinehout.

Patrick McCormick, whose family moved from Strokestown to Bolton, Lancashire, England, and then to Albany, New York. He was the husband of Catherine Finneran. Photo courtesy of Madeline Sisk.

Catherine Finneran McCormick, wife of Patrick, who was born in Roscommon, lived in Bolton, Lancashire, England, and went to Albany, New York, in 1883. Photo courtesy of Madeline Sisk.

John Riley of Kilglass Parish (seated right) who arrived in New York City in April 1848 at the same time as some Ballykilcline evictees. He went to Providence, Rhode Island, where he married Catherine McNally (left), who came from Latton in County Monaghan. Standing behind them in this photo, about 1880, is their only surviving son, Thomas. The Rileys, who also had eight daughters, settled and farmed in Hampton, Connecticut. Six of his siblings stayed in Rhode Island and Connecticut. Their mother was a Colligan. From the collection of Mary Lee Dunn.

Sister John (aka Jeanne) Teresa, the second daughter of John and Catherine Riley, who entered a Catholic order of nuns, studied in France, and briefly taught in Lee, Massachusetts, before helping to found St. Francis Hospital in Hartford, Connecticut. She led its nursing school for decades. From the collection of Mary Lee Dunn.

The grave site of Michael Hanley and Catherine, a young daughter of John and Sabina Brennan Hanley, at the Pleasant Street Cemetery in West Rutland. Michael and the child both died during the 1840s. The stone is broken and lies on the ground. Photo by Rosemary Vandenburg.

Stone marking the graves of Thomas and Margaret Carroll Winters in Calvary Cemetery, Rutland. Thomas was a Ballykilcline evictee. Photo by Rosemary Vandenburg.

The Mahon manor house in Strokestown as it looks in modern times. The property is home to Ireland's Famine Museum. Photo by Mary Lee Dunn.

1847 : LE DRAME IMMIGRANTS IRLANDAIS

1847: THE ORDEAL OF THE IRISH IMMIGRANTS

Entre 1845 et 1849, une grave famine décime l'Irlande. Plusieurs dizaines de milliers d'Irlandais s'embarquent alors pour l'Amérique du Nord sur des voiliers souvent conçus pour le transport des marchandises. L'entassement est tel à bord des navires qu'il favorise la propagation du typhus, une grave maladie contagieuse.

Ainsi, en 1847, environ 85 % des 100 000 immigrants qui se dirigent vers Québec par le Saint-Laurent sont des Irlandais, souvent affaiblis et malades. La station de quarantaine de Grosse-Île est débordée et le bilan de l'été est très lourd : plus de 5 000 immigrants sont inhumés dans le cimetière de l'ouest. Les décès se comptent par milliers à Québec, à Montréal et dans plusieurs autres villes.

Pour les Canadiens de descendance irlandaise, Grosse-Île incarne le souvenir douloureux d'un épisode marquant de l'histoire du pays.

Between 1845 and 1849, famine wreaked havoc in Ireland. As a result, tens of thousands of Irish men and women embarked for North America on sailing ships which often had been designed for transporting cargo. Quarters on board the ships were so cramped that typhus, a serious contagious disease, was able to spread unchecked.

Thus, in 1847, approximately 85% of the 100,000 immigrants on their way to Québec City via the St. Lawrence were Irish; all too often, they arrived sick and weak. The Grosse Île quarantine station was overwhelmed. By summer's end, the death toll was very high: more than 5,000 immigrants were buried in the island's western cemetery. In Québec City, Montréal and several other cities, disease victims numbered in the thousands.

For Canadians of Irish ancestry, Grosse Île is a painful reminder of a tragic chapter in our country's history.

Vue du cimetière de l'ouest au début du XXᵉ siècle.

View of the western cemetery at the turn of the 20th Century.

An exhibit at Canada's National Park at Grosse Ile, near Quebec. The island was a quarantine station for arriving European immigrants as early as 1832. Nearly a thousand of Denis Mahon's evicted tenants were sent to Quebec in 1847. Approximately half of them died crossing the Atlantic, in quarantine on the St. Lawrence River, or in the island's hospitals. Photo by Mary Lee Dunn.

Postcard showing a Rutland quarry, mailed from Rutland to Dublin in 1908. Postcard courtesy of Des Norton.

The marble facade of St. Bridget's Church in West Rutland, built by Irish quarry workers. Photo by Rosemary Vandenburg.

6

Quarry Actions—Striking Again

[Ralph Waldo Emerson] offered a biting commentary on the relationship between the two slaveries cited by North and South alike, that of the black, or chattel, slave, and that of the wage-slave selling his or her time to the industrialist without a share in the product. His resentment of the idea that some need not labor, that their triumph was defined as progress, expresses a strong opposition to the beliefs and propaganda of the capitalists.

—Lawrence Gross, *The Course of Industrial Decline: The Boott Cotton Mills of Lowell, Massachusetts, 1835–1955*

The first tragedy of mortality is that nothing lasts, but the first glory of human consciousness is the capacity to regain, by simple thought, what is lost to time. The merely chronological becomes personal. Memory is half of how you do this. . . . The other half . . . is by anticipating the future. Worry is the most obvious mode of doing this.

—James Carroll, *Boston Globe,* January 1, 2007

THEIR EXPERIENCE breaking rocks on the public works in famine Ireland equipped the Irish for marble quarrying, it has been said (Healy communication, July 2002). More likely, though, it was the Kilglass men's experience in the stone quarries of their home parish or the limestone ones in adjacent Kilmore, whose product was used both for construction and for agriculture (Lewis 1837). Some of Rutland's Irish quarry men may also have worked for a time building canals in the United States or Canada. In any case, the Irish in Rutland went into the quarries in great number in the early and middle 1850s, almost as soon as the railroad tracks they had laid connected Rutland with marble markets. As their jobs on Rutland's many rail lines ended, work in rail operations and quarrying opened up. Marble expanded rapidly.

Rail lines marked a critical turning point for Rutland because they enabled the growing marble extraction industry to move its massive product more easily to market. The industry at Rutland had been crippled by the difficulty and expense of hauling huge blocks of marble overland by oxcart to Whitehall on the New York border. Starting in the 1850s, however, such inhibitions on the industry faded away, and the Irish moved into the quarries in large numbers to cut the stone from its solid beds.

Even before the industry's enormous growth spurt in the 1850s, two local figures apparently had made fortunes, by then-current standards, in marble. William F. Barnes quarried marble, and in 1850 his personal real estate was valued at $12,000 [$309,590], plus he had $40,000 [$1 million] of capital in his quarry operation; William Ripley was a Rutland marble dealer with $19,600 [$506,000] in personal real estate. The 1850 census documented only twenty other people in the marble business: fourteen of them were stonecutters, mostly native-born Americans but three from Ireland and one each from Canada, England, and Scotland. Three other marble dealers and several marble supervisors lived in the town, but none had real estate exceeding $1,000 in value [$25,799]. The 1850 census, however, must mask quarry workers who were listed simply as laborers or blacksmiths but who performed those jobs for quarry operations. Local historian Dawn Hance said that three hundred men were working in four local quarries as early as 1848, most of them "Irish immigrants who had come to work either in railroad construction or in the quarries. The next year another hundred workers had been hired" (1991, p. 542). Evidently, the quarry workers were camouflaged as general laborers in that census. A few years later, census data—both St. Bridget's Parish Census in 1857 and the federal census in 1860—specified when a man worked in the quarries; by then, the workforce was almost exclusively Irish.

MOVING INTO THE QUARRIES

William Colligan was one of the first Kilglass men to go into quarry work in the 1830s, at Slason and Barnes (Butler letter, March 12, 1969), and he undoubtedly helped friends and relatives to obtain quarry jobs. But then Colligan uprooted his family and briefly went west (Madden communication, 2002). By the early 1850s, however, the Colligans had returned to Rutland, and William probably worked for William Barnes's operation, which, Michael Austin found, had thirty-five employees in 1845, eighty in 1854, and an equal number from St. Bridget's Parish alone in 1857 (St. Bridget's Parish Census). The marble industry employed some 1,300 throughout the state that year, and nearly a thousand of them worked in Rutland's quarries (Austin 2002, pp. 30–32).

Local historians view Barnes as an important industry pioneer, and he has been lauded for developing the tactic of hand "channeling" (i.e., drilling) to free a block of marble from its encasing rock, a process that took the place of laborious and slow mallets and dangerous, damaging, and imprecise explosives. It came about, the story goes, when Barnes found a vein that had seams on three sides; his men drilled on the fourth side to create a channel by which the whole block could then be pried free (Hance 1991, p. 527). Although Barnes has been credited for the technique, it actually may have been developed by his employee William Colligan, as the oral history of his family contends (Madden communication, 2002).

"People at first laughed at this slow process [channeling]," Barnes said, "accomplishing not more than a foot a day, but after a lapse of some days or weeks, they saw that I got something for my labor and it was not long before all who were engaged in the business adopted the same method." The work was tedious: "Thirty men working side by side can liberate a layer of marble six feet wide, four feet thick, and about eighty feet long in six days" (Hannon 1986, pp. 60, 68). Indeed, channeling was a breakthrough, and it was relied on until 1863, when Rutlander George Wardwell devised and built a steam-operated machine to cut channels: "It performed the work previously done by twenty-five men per day" (Hance 1991, p. 527).

William Colligan was injured in a workplace drill accident in 1854. The wound became infected, and he died a short time later (Madden communication, 2002), an early casualty among the numerous accident victims in Rutland's quarries and on its rail lines over the decades. Danger was inescapable in marble jobs.

Marble quarrying had begun in 1785 in Dorset, part of the valley that also ran through Rutland and north (Austin 2002, p. 21), when Isaac Underhill opened a quarry near Mount Aeolus. Over the next 130 years, twenty-five quarries at Dorset, employing at peak production some four hundred workers, produced more than fifteen million cubic feet of product. From the 1830s, Dorset's marble works offered jobs to the Irish and thus brought about "the only real ethnic diversity Dorset has known" (Resch 1989, p. 127).

Rutland started to tap its deposits in the 1790s, but five decades later the value of what the industry produced at West Rutland was only $10,000 [$233,000], giving little sign of what was to come. Nevertheless, a handful of men worked hard to commercialize it and were poised to do so when Rutland became a rail hub. By 1850 the value of the industry's product had multiplied nearly thirty times, to $297,000 [$7.7 million], and the next decade brought the boom to both the industry and the town (Austin 2002, p. 17).

Barnes helped it to happen when he followed his father into quarrying. The elder Barnes had begun in Pittsford, just to the north, and then moved to Rutland. He subsequently migrated west with his family, but his son stayed in Rutland and founded a quarry operation of his own about 1842 when he bought land where he had found marble near the cedar swamp in West Rutland. The site was close to John and Sabina Brennan Hanley's property. Local lore says that Barnes bought the tract from an elderly man and paid him with an old horse worth $75. To develop the property and reach the higher-grade marble underground, though, Barnes had to take on debt (Austin 2002, pp. 26, 27; Hannon 1986, p. 62; Hance 1991, pp. 526–534).

During the 1840s, wrote Austin, "the industry slowly shifted from individuals and small firms that dealt with one or two aspects of the business, to marble companies that integrated the mineral's quarrying, cutting, polishing, distribution, and promotion." By 1850, Rutland probably quarried more marble than anyplace else in the world, and its marble was considered superior in grain and strength to the Italian product. By 1857, hundreds of workers had catapulted it to the status of largest nonagricultural industry in the state (Hance 1991, p. 542; Austin 2002, pp. 26, 30, 31). The *Rutland Herald* gave this picture of quarry operations: "The magnitude of the works, and the novelty and beauty of their appearance; the marble floor, walls and roofing, on, around, and under which hundreds of men were busily engaged in getting out the huge blocks; the tumultuous din of innumerable [*sic*] drills; the removal and raising, from a depth, at places, of eighty feet, of immense masses, four to ten tons in weight; and the singularly soft and down appearance given to the atmosphere by the fine vapory dust, which, rising from working, is suspended in it, all unite to render a visit one of novelty, excitement and interest" (qtd. in Hance 1991, pp. 527, 528).

STRENGTHENING CLASS IDENTITY

The fact that the quarry workforce in Rutland was for some years predominantly Irish, that the men lived and worked closely together in jobs dangerous to life and limb and shared family relationships, workplace risks and grievances, and world experience nurtured a strong sense of camaraderie, a sense of class identity. James Patrick Carney captured it in his poem "The West Rutland Marble Bawn." *Bawn* is rooted in the Irish word for cattle fort and is the basis for the word *barn*. It was a tower house's wall to protect livestock during attacks (Wikipedia).

> The Irish boys that fear no noise, they will stand on the rock so brave . . .
> They are the very best boys that ever wore frieze for chipping on the
>   Marble Bawn. . . .

There's nothing can compare, but the snow from the air, to that beautiful
  marble stone . . .
So now my song I'll end, and success to every friend that ever left the
  Shamrock Shore;
May they live in peace with the Yankee race, and each other dearly adore.
So now as we are free in the land of liberty, where no tyranny over us will
  be drawn;
We will sit down at ease and sing the praise of West Rutland Marble Bawn.
(Carney, *Violet Book*, p. 17)

But Carney's experience of quarry work came between 1855 and '61, mostly before continued low wages, tough work conditions, mounting deaths and injuries, and repeated strikes had chastened the Irish work crews and cast a shadow over Carney's hope that they might "live in peace with the Yankee race." Carney himself exchanged work on rocks for work in soil when he left the quarries to become a gardener in Castleton (Healy communication), but his words about the "Marble Bawn" illustrated the willingness of the Irish in "the land of liberty," where they felt protected from the tyranny they had known in Ireland, to get along with the local Yankees. Carney made the case for peaceful coexistence in Rutland before business practices and quarry conditions undermined that notion.

Barnes partnered with marble magnate William Y. Ripley for five years, beginning in 1845; then, under a new arrangement between them, Barnes supplied marble to Ripley without charge, and Ripley got it to market and split the profits with Barnes. In August 1850, Barnes acquired land and water privileges in Center Rutland and planned two sawmills, one using water power and the other steam. By 1854, his work force was producing 300,000 feet of product a year (Hance 1991, pp. 539, 354). Barnes also was the first owner to use a derrick and horses or oxen to move the bulky blocks of marble to the "stone boats" that carried them to the sawyers in the mill.

Other marble men through the 1850s included Pitt W. Hyde and Lorenzo Sheldon. An operation that had been run by brothers named Ormsbee and others named Humphrey changed hands several times through the late 1830s and '40s, and in 1852 the North River Mining Company purchased it. Two years later, Edwin Hamilton took it over and, with partners, formed the American Marble Company. In 1855 it acquired the Sutherland Falls (later Proctor) and Sudbury quarries. A mill at the falls was to be enlarged to accommodate twenty gangs of sawyers. A reorganization took place, and the outfit was renamed the Sutherland Falls Marble Co. In the early 1850s, Charles H. Slason joined a firm begun by

Sheldon and David Morgan. By 1855, their company had 250 employees. William Barnes sold a portion of his quarry and a boardinghouse in 1854 to three men for $125,000 [$2.9 million]; they turned it over immediately to the Rutland Marble Co., headed by H. H. Baxter, whose 150 employees produced 400,000 feet of product in 1855. In addition, Clement and Gilmore ran a sawing operation at Center Rutland. These men were the major players. In the 1860s, Rutland Marble was the largest operation and even had gangs of saws at Salem, New York. West Rutland firms shipped out 37 million pounds of product, worth nearly $500,000 [$10 million] in 1862, during the Civil War (Austin 2002, pp. 31–32; Hance 1991, pp. 528–538; Hannon 1986, pp. 63, 65).

High Returns for Owners

Michael Austin has pointed out the high returns for owners and investors in marble: "Based on the 1850 Industrial Census, and looking on the rate of return after subtracting labor costs and start-up costs, lucrative returns were possible. . . . Sheldon, Morgan, and Slason led producers in 1850 with a 308% investment return. The Hydeville Company, just to the west of Rutland, near Castleton, was a close second with a 307% return. Some of the marble leaders more than recouped their investments in one year. And it was this financial return that attracted the emerging social and political leaders." In Austin's calculation, for example, Sheldon, Morgan and Slason, with $3,000 in capital invested, produced $105,000 [$2.7 million] worth of product a year on a payroll totaling $9,600 [$247,672]. Each quarry laborer received an average of $20 [$516] a month. In 1867, Rutland Marble Co. had more than $41,000 [$558,389] in assets, and its investors that year earned dividends of $75,000 [$1.02 million] (Austin 2002, pp. 33–42).

Vermont counted fifty quarries by 1860, mostly around Rutland (Austin 2002, p. 37). During the Civil War, some of them won significant government contracts for producing soldiers' tombstones (Hance 1991, p. 536). As the scale of their operations grew, so did their workforces. Whereas West Rutland had only twenty houses in 1847, when the priest conducted St. Bridget's census ten years later, the parish had about 1,300 people, all of whom except a handful of French-Canadians were Irish. St. Peter's Parish in Center Rutland also was mostly Irish. By 1860, when the town's population was 7,500, more than 460 Irish worked in Rutland's quarries, and another 37 Irish in Dorset were marble men. Many of them lived in company housing and shopped in the company store, where goods cost significantly more than elsewhere but could be obtained on credit, a costly but often necessary option for the work crews. Their store

bill was deducted before their pay was issued. By the late 1850s, the immigrants' satisfaction at having any job at all had splintered like so many
of the marble chips they generated each day under harsh working conditions and low pay.

The Conditions of Work

The work day was long—twelve hours—and the men made ninety cents
a day for summer hours and fifty cents in winter, hardly more than a laborer had made in the 1840s. Layoffs were common in early December and
lasted until spring (Hannon 1986, p. 74). The work was dangerous and de-
bilitating, as shown by the death of William Colligan after a drill accident
and the deaths of and injuries to so many others. The operations were not
regulated; the state did not step in to protect workers when it came to either unfair or unsafe working conditions or wages (Hancock 2001, p. 3). By
1859 the quarry men—some of whom may have been veterans of the 1846
Central Vermont railroad strike, during which the state had called the militia out against them—were so aggrieved that like Irish mill workers in
Lowell, Massachusetts (Dunn 2000), and iron workers in Troy, New York,
that year (Albany History website), they organized their first strike. Some
four hundred men at four companies quit work on April 1. A frustrated and
worried quarry man wrote to the newspaper to explain their grievances:

> How can an employer expect to find people to work for such small wages?
> How could a man of a family support himself, his wife and children, out
> of fifty cents a day, during the cold winter, when he had to pay thirty or
> thirty-six dollars for a house (if houses can be called the kind of build-
> ings they have for the poor man), when he has to pay four dollars a cord
> for the worst kind of wood, to pay fifty cents for a bushel of potatoes, and
> to pay for everything else in the same proportion? . . . What would this
> country be without the foreigners? And yes is there any hope that justice
> will ever be done to them? When will they be treated as free citizens of a
> free country, as they should, according to the general laws of the Union.
> (*Rutland Courier*, April 29, 1859, p. 2)

Justice, free men, a free country—he must have wondered about the
"fruit" in the land of liberty that Jimmy Carney wrote about. The letter
writer had concluded that the quarry man—who, Carney said, was "working hard from morning till night, and he never stands at ease" (*Violet-Book*,
p. 17)—deserved more than he was getting and that a just system should
give it to him. The Irish immigrant's idea of freedom was linked to fair
play, as Carney so clearly asserted in describing Ireland's plight—"Fair
play and liberty we must have" (*Violet-Book*, p. 15)—and the tyranny of

money and ownership that deprived them in new laboring relationships was only a camouflaged form of what they had known at home in the old country. At issue in the strike were wages, and credit at the store, which charged one-third more than prices elsewhere. Yet as Hancock found in his study of the nearby slate operations, the threat of losing their jobs may have hung over men who did not patronize the company store (2001, p. 5). The marble men also complained that the owners had not kept the bargain they had made the previous fall to pay the work crews an additional fifteen cents a day for winter work.

Though he had not been informed in advance of their intention to strike, Father Picart at St. Bridget's helped the striking workers maintain unity, and he was castigated in some quarters for it. "The companies are complaining bitterly of the priest, saying he excited the men to rebellion, although that is a well-known falsehood," a quarry man wrote to the newspaper under the name of "Hibernicus." He also credited Picart with "sacrificing a good deal of comforts" to help the poor strikers and said that the priest had urged them "not to go against each other." The priest even approached a marble company owner on behalf of the workers; the owner called him a fool (Austin 2002, p. 130).

After marble owners took the strikers to court to evict them from company housing, quarry owner William Barnes—whose employees already made a dollar a day and therefore had not walked off their jobs—lent housing to those strikers who were made homeless. "All honor to Mr. Barnes," Hibernicus commented (qtd. in Hannon 1986, pp. 70–71). One also can imagine the Irish in their housing enclave supporting one another both morally and with food and other help as needed. Shared distress bred solidarity.

The four companies capitulated weeks later and agreed to pay a dollar a day in the summer and seventy-five cents in winter. Accordingly, the men returned to work on June 1. They had won.

THE STRIKES OF 1864 AND BEYOND

But their contentment was short-lived. Another marble strike in 1864 shut down all operations except Sheldon and Slason's, and it took a dramatic turn. Wages again were at issue, as were long hours, when the men walked off their jobs in early April, just as work was set to resume after the winter layoffs. The owners offered strikers $1.50 for an eleven-hour day, but the workers countered, seeking that amount for ten hours of cutting and hoisting the blocks. Management told them to quit the company houses if they did not accept the company's offer. The men set a deadline for the owners: if *their* offer was not accepted by April 11, it would take $1.75 a day to bring them back to work again. (Hannon 1986, pp. 74, 71). John Cain's *Rutland Courier* supported their call for a shorter workday (May 20, 1864). Nevertheless, the order came down from the owners that the men should vacate their homes by April 15. When the men did not move their families out, Rutland Marble took sixty-nine of them to court in an eviction action. "It is the intention of the company to clear the tenements of their present occupants," the *Rutland Herald* reported, "and to employ new hands and resume work as soon as possible" (May 5 and 12, 1864). The first quarry man's eviction case heard by the court was John Teelon's, and when he lost, the other workers gave up and moved (Hannon 1986, p. 72). Teelon may have had Ballykilcline roots.[1]

Courier editor Cain reminded his readers that the $1.50 demand "is in a depreciated currency, and that all they actually demand in the old Democratic national gold currency of the country is eighty-four cents per day. The laborer is worthy of his hire, and while the owners of the quarries are amassing large fortunes, we are astonished that the 'loyal' leaguer who writes the editorials for the *Herald* should even insinuate that the quarrymen are unreasonable in demanding *eighty-four cents* per day" (*Rutland Courier*, April 15, 1864; original emphasis).

A compromise was worked out in this strike whereby the West Rutland quarry owners paid the higher rate of $1.75 a day, but the men continued working eleven hours daily, one hour longer than they had demanded. Cain reported:

> We are glad to learn that the proprietors of the West Rutland marble quarries have consented to comply with the demand of the workmen for higher wages, and that the latter have gone to work for one dollar and seventy-five cents per day of eleven hours. The depreciation of our paper currency, and the advanced price of all the necessaries of life, entitled the workmen to this advanced compensation for their laborious services, while by the advance of marble from the demand for tombstones for the thousands slain in this bloody war, the proprietors can well afford to pay these men the advanced wages, if we can call it such as with gold quoted at 1.82 it is only equal to about ninety-six cents in the hard money currency that the people were allowed to have when Democracy ruled the land of Washington. (*Rutland Courier*, May 20, 1864)

In 1868, when the men at several West Rutland quarries once more walked off their jobs for higher wages, the owners resorted again to evictions and the replacement hiring that had worked well earlier: the Rutland

Marble Co. brought in sixty French Canadians as well as Germans from New York. The French Canadians arrived by rail from Montreal on May 21, but word that the Irish planned to stop the train and send the newcomers packing got back to the owners, so they halted the train outside of town to allow their new employees to walk safely the rest of the way to Rutland. That precautionary move, however, did not avert trouble, and a riot was reported that night. A few days later, the newspaper noted that all was quiet, since "there are not enough of the original strikers left to raise much of a disturbance" (qtd. in Hannon 1986, p. 73). The newspaper's judgment seemed premature when trouble broke out again on June 11: two groups squared off, and a number of men suffered minor injuries before police broke up the ruckus: "Yesterday being observed as a holiday by the quarrymen at West Rutland, and many of them indulging in too frequent potations of intoxicating liquors, a melee ensued between a number of Frenchmen and Irishmen, and resulted in the dispensation of various black eyes, cut heads and bloody countenances. Upon the arrival of the officers quiet was restored. But one arrest was made" (*Rutland Herald*, June 12, 1868).

St. Bridget's Parish Census that year showed the changes wrought by these events: two hundred Irish families, 150 fewer households than the year before. There also were seventy-five French-Canadian families. "Stories handed down from those days tell of families walking, with the family cow, to East Dorset and other places in search of homes and the means to support their families." The parish priest wrote, "So many people were left destitute of even the means of removing from this place that the pastor was obliged to assist them in doing so" (qtd. in Hannon 1986, p. 74). By 1870, there were scores of French Canadians and Swedes working as quarry men in Rutland, and the Irish workforce in marble had dropped to 275 men.[2] By then, Wardwell's steam channeling machine, used to liberate the blocks of marble, had eliminated many jobs.

The owners had successfully used the "wedge" of French Canadians and other European laborers against the Irish quarry men, just as the mill owners in industrial Lowell, Massachusetts, had used the Irish after 1850 against their Yankee female workforce to keep the costs of labor low. Soon after that 1868 strike in Rutland, a labor experiment to the south across the Massachusetts border drew extensive national attention. Like Rutland, North Adams had boomed after the railroads arrived and was then a town with some thirty-eight factories. Its population had doubled since 1860, and one-third of the inhabitants were Irish; textile and paper mills and shoe factories had drawn the immigrants there for jobs. Calvin

Sampson ran a "model" shoe factory and had capitalized on mechanization and cheap labor.

The Massachusetts shoe workers had organized under the banner of the Knights of St. Crispin, which quickly became a large and powerful organization. In 1870 the Knights at Sampsons' factory struck over a series of demands, including higher wages, shorter hours, and a union funding matter. Interestingly, they also sought to have their pay set in tandem with profits and wanted access to company records.

In an attention-getting experiment, Sampson brought in Chinese workers from San Francisco as strikebreakers, and several months later his new workforce was making more shoes of high quality at a lower cost and saving him money at the rate of $40,000 [$617,549] a year. Other manufacturers watched and followed his well-publicized example. Fearful local workers also eyed his experiment; days after the Chinese arrived, the workforces at neighboring plants returned to their job stations with wage cuts of 10 percent. In print, owners crowed about their new tactic to deal with strikes by European immigrants and other white workers but simultaneously puzzled about how to deal socially and politically with a "yellow proletariat" (Takaki 1990, pp. 232–240). A few years later, Rutland newspapers reported that some unhappy quarry men had left Vermont for North Adams and elsewhere in search of better jobs (Hannon 1986, p. 77). Consolidations of strength by industrial owners were widespread, abetted by judicial decision making and large immigrant labor pools. Better jobs were a scarce commodity for workers during that season.

The 1860 federal census, conducted one year after the Rutland marble workers' first strike, told just how well the company owners, who had balked at ten cents more a day for workers, had been doing: William Ripley, marble owner and by then also a banker, showed property and cash assets of $300,000 [$7.27 million]; William Barnes reported $90,000 [$2.18 million] in real estate and savings; Lorenzo Sheldon had $99,000 [$2.4 million]; and Henry Sheldon had nearly $80,000 [$1.94 million]. Neither strained resources nor economic constraints seemed to be the reason why they resisted workers' pressures for small raises.

The manufacturing supplement to the 1860 census shows even more plainly and in detail the profitability of Rutland's marble operations. Ripley and Son Marble Mill, for instance, had $100,000 of capital invested, spent $35,000 on raw material, employed fifteen workers at a total of $450 [$10.900] a month, and produced product valued at $75,000 [$1.82 million] a year. Rutland Marble Co., the largest firm, had $185,000 [$4.43

million] invested in its operations, bought kegs of powder—its raw material—for $600, and paid 150 workers a total of $3,800 a month to generate $300,000 [$7.27 million] worth of product a year.

While 461 quarry men, many of them with five or six dependents each, earned a total of $131,640 [$3.2 million] that year, or an average of $286 [$6,930] each, the handful of owners were producing a product valued at three-quarters of a million dollars [$18.2 million]. It must be borne in mind too that the capital invested, for the most part, was not a recurring expense, whereas the profit was produced *annually*. Thus, in some cases, the product value generated in one year's operation far exceeded the total capital invested in the firms; in others, it might take another year or two to recoup the investment, as Austin found. Meanwhile, scores of quarry workers in 1860 had a mere $50 [$1,212] or $100 put by as their total reserves, and many quarry men with families had nothing at all to show for years of labor (U.S. Census, Vermont, 1860).

Quarry workers from Ballykilcline and Kilglass Parish certainly joined in Rutland's marble strikes. Records show that at least twenty-three men who came from Ballykilcline or had married Ballykilcline women were employed in quarries in Rutland or Dorset up to 1870. If average family size continued the same as in Kilglass, then these jobs supported immigrant families totaling nearly 150 people. At least sixty-two immigrants from Kilglass Parish were quarry workers.

The counts surely are underestimates, given that a number of immigrants—for instance, James Mullera, Patrick and Bartley Neary, and William Colligan—died early and thus are not captured in the records generated after 1857, when such links were made explicit. Several of the twenty-three worked in Dorset, including Patrick and Thomas Carlon and sons of Pat and Eliza Cline Kelly, but most labored in Rutland's pits. James Foley was a quarry blacksmith; Patrick Colligan was a quarry man before the Civil War and a blacksmith during and after the war, but the record does not say whether his postwar work was in a quarry setting.

WORKERS' ASSETS

By 1870, Foley and Michael Igo, both then nearing fifty years of age, each reported $2,500 [$38,597] in assets, the highest in the group; Foley was still in the quarries, but Igo had become a farmer in Poultney. And the next highest, Civil War veteran John Winters, listed assets of $800 [$12,351] in 1870. Years after his arrival in Rutland, he remained in the quarries, as did a number of the men.

Quarry workers with assets that high were exceptions, though; indeed, more than twenty years after their arrival in the United States, eight of the twenty-three men reported no assets at all. Twelve of them had started quarrying by 1857, when they appeared in St. Bridget's Parish Census. In two cases, their assets had declined rather than increased during the profitable war decade: Michael Foley had $50 [$1,212] in 1860 and nothing in 1870; Edward McCormick had $100 [$2,423] in 1860 and nothing in 1870. Two men who had arrived years before the evictees, Gilbert Hanley and Daniel McGuire, reported no assets. McGuire, however, was a Dorset farmer in 1870, and earlier assets likely had helped him to reach that station; Hanley, the son of John and Sabina Brennan Hanley, may have been constrained in accruing assets by having suffered a battle injury during his service as a Civil War soldier. At least a couple of the men had died by 1870, and no information was found in that census for ten of the others (see table 3 in the Appendix).

Although the information generated during my study showed several Ballykilcline immigrants doing very well, those who did so had generally built their assets by farming. In 1870 they included John and Sabina Brennan Hanley, with $4,000 [$61,755] in assets, and Sabina's siblings, who all lived in Poultney: William Brennan and his wife Bridget Geelan, $4,000; Daniel and his wife Maria Kelly, $6,400 [$98,808]; and Jane and her husband John Driscoll, $3,200 [$49,404]. Evictees Patrick and Eliza Cline Kelly, who farmed in Dorset and who were Daniel Brennan's in-laws, listed $3,900 [$60,211] in their "estate" as well (see Table 3 in the Appendix).

Only a handful (fewer than ten) of the study's Ballykilcline subjects in Rutland town, including John Hanley and his son and namesake, were farmers in 1870. Several of them (Hanleys, Igos, and McGuires) had left early from Ballykilcline and thereby had a chance to start building assets before the market influx of famine-immigrant labor, which suppressed wages. Either the Irish could not acquire the capital to purchase land in Vermont or when they did acquire the means, they went elsewhere, probably due to cost. A dozen randomly selected Rutland farm properties, half owned by Vermont natives and half by Irish immigrants, ranged in value in the 1860 census from nothing to $28,000 and averaged $6,430 [$155,804], which made cost seem a likely major deterrent for the Irish who wanted a farm of their own. In 1870, more than two decades after many of them arrived in the U.S., large numbers of Rutland's Irish still worked as laborers, railroad employees, or quarrymen at low wages.

Building assets was easier in the West, where some of the Ballykilcline evictees who farmed generally accrued wealth at a higher level. James and

Susan Carrington Hanley, who spent a couple of years in Rutland before heading west, farmed in LaSalle County, Illinois, alongside earlier emigrants from Ballykilcline. In 1870 their real estate and personal property were valued at $21,300 [$328,845], $19,000 of which was in the land itself. Edward Neary, who identified himself in the census as a laborer at age seventy, nevertheless had $4,000 [$61,755] in real estate there and $600 [$9,263] in his personal estate. In Iowa, Patrick Malary (Mullera) had a farm in Highland, Clayton County, that was worth $4,000 and he had put aside $1,200 [$18,526] by 1870. Without knowing more details of their individual stories, though, it is hard to account for disparities in asset-building experience.

Historian Joseph Ferrie (1999) has studied immigrants' economic achievement and mobility. He found that the immigrant Irish ownership of wealth matched that of German and British immigrants by 1860, once his data were controlled for place and occupational changes. The immigrants' wealth averaged half the wealth of those born in the United States, up from 20 percent ten years earlier. Some 60 percent of the Irish in his study, significantly higher than either of his other immigrant groups, remained in the cities and towns of the Northeast (Steckel 1999, p. 2). In general, these findings seem to be at variance with the data for the Ballykilcline workers in Rutland, many of whom had difficulty establishing economic security, perhaps because the town's economy was so largely based on a single industry (along with farming and railroad operations) and because of its easy access to significant other immigrant labor pools from Canada and Europe, who were played against each other. It is also worth noting that Rutland's marble sales were aimed primarily at a national and international market, and a number of the investors who profited lived elsewhere and spent their profits elsewhere.

Marble wages continued low for years and, though unions of quarry men and stonecutters existed in New York, and were even run by the Irish (Ignatiev 1995, p. 116), there is no sign that they gained an early foothold in Rutland. In 1867 a union of stone carvers in Chicago was the first in the country to win an eight-hour work day (Austin 2002, p. 80), only a few years after Rutland workers battled for a ten-hour day and then caved for more money and continued to work eleven hours. It was not until the mid-1880s, when the Knights of Labor came to town, that Rutland's marble workers unionized.

Still, they did take collective action to protect themselves. For instance, they formed their own Benevolent Society in 1859—the year of their first strike—to help members through illness and disability and to aid the

families when a worker died (members were obligated to attend the fu-
nerals of fellow members). Father Picart was selected as the organization's first president, and members paid dues of twenty-five cents a month
(*Rutland Courier*, July 29, 1859). Eighteen years later the organization employed a physician and was still caring for quarry workers; by then, two
Kilglass men—Patrick Madden and Michael Duffy—and Roscommoner
Peter Gaffney were among its elected officers (*Rutland Globe*, April 13,
1877). The association aspired to be a force for social good in another
way as well: members who became intoxicated or who quarreled were
subject to fines. These group actions had precedents in Ireland, where
working men had organized in a similar way: Dublin printers in 1838 had
had nearly 450 members and apprentices who met weekly, and the union
had "a fund from which contributions were made towards unemployment
or sickness benefits and towards the funeral expenses of deceased members" (Ó Tuathaigh 1972, p. 154).

THE PASSING OF A BENEFACTOR

In May 1871, quarry owner William Barnes was killed in a dreadful quarry
accident when a hundred-pound block of marble, its ground undermined
by rain, fell sixty feet and hit Barnes on the head (Austin 2002, p. 31).
One can imagine that the workers, certainly including many from Kilglass who had worked for Barnes over a span of years, turned out in force
for his funeral. Barnes had earned their respect as a savvy and successful
owner who also was kindhearted, who kept even failing elderly men on
in his business because they had aged in service to him (Marble History website), who offered company housing to needy strikers and their
families, and who paid a higher wage rate in the late 1850s than other
local marble men offered. A former Rutland selectman and state legisla-
tor, Barnes had been a land developer as well; he recycled quarry wastes,
used them as landfill, and sold the lots; he also "permitted his workers to
construct their own housing near the quarry" (Austin 2002, pp. 84, 131).
Thus, Barnes had distinguished himself in humanitarian ways from the
other marble owners in Rutland.

The local newspaper noted his singular relationship with the local
immigrants: "Mr. Barnes, in his lifelong relation with the Irish laborers
here, was deservedly respected and popular, and had become, as it were,
the acknowledged champion of their rights. His death is indeed a public
calamity. . . . We cannot wonder then that his loss is keenly felt by thousands who live to eulogize and bless the name of their best benefactor"

(*Rutland Weekly Herald*, May 18 1871, p. 4). In some other owners' operations, by contrast, the workers sometimes must have felt, in a magazine
writer's words as he looked deep into the pit of a sparkling white quarry
in Rutland, "like ants toiling in their cells, hundreds of feet below the
surface" (Robinson 1890).

Some Roscommon marble workers eventually did move out of the
quarries. Kilglass native Patrick McLaughlin, the husband of Bridget
Wynne of Ballykilcline, was one wage laborer who somehow was able to
acquire his own land, and by 1877 he and his family were farming in
nearby Mendon. For whatever reason, though, the McLaughlins returned
to Rutland in the 1880s. Michael Igo was a farmer as well; he was working
in Rutland's quarries in 1857, but by 1870 he had his own farm and assets
of $2,500 [$38,597]. Thomas Winters was a quarry boss in 1857 and a day
laborer in 1860, but when his widow died in 1893, two years after Thomas
passed on, her estate included a house and a five-acre farm (Vandenburg
communication, 2002). Apparently neither Igo nor Winters had children,
which may have facilitated their accumulation of assets. If McLaughlin,
Igo, and Winters represent one extreme—quarry men who were able to
pull together enough assets to farm, at least for a time—William Neary
may illustrate the other. Brother of the Ballykilcline rent strike leaders
Bartley and Patrick Neary, William worked for years as a Rutland quarry
man, but none of the federal censuses showed that he ever was able to save
any money at all. By the late 1870s he was an inmate at the Rutland Poor
Farm, where he remained for approximately twenty-five years. In fact,
many of the annual Poor Farm reports, which listed not only residents
of the farm but those who received "outside" help in their own homes as
well, included some people who, their names suggested, had come from
Kilglass Parish (Rutland Poor Farm reports).

Quarrying was not a worker's route to a life of ease and comfort. The
immigrants may have secured citizenship and the vote; they may have built
a civic life of some satisfaction, kept alive the flame to liberate Ireland, and
even acted on behalf of that sacred cause; they may have brought family
out of Ireland—but they did not acquire freedom from the tyranny of
unfettered markets and elite power, the same forces they had opposed so
vehemently at home. Importantly to them though, they had escaped British rule, and if others shared Civil War soldier Peter Welsh's views, some of
them saw even their jobs as American wage earners as part of a continuing
battle to overturn British might; if they could help the United States "to
surpass her as a manufacturing nation," then "Englands star of asendency
[*sic*] will have set to rise no more" (qtd. in O'Neill 2001, p. 129).

7

Still Standing in the Gale

❧

> If there is any central theme in the story of the Irish in America, it is . . .
> how they stayed Irish: how an immigrant group already under punishing
> cultural and economic pressures, reeling in the wake of the worst catas-
> trophe in western Europe in the nineteenth century, and plunged into
> the fastest industrializing society in the world, regrouped as quickly as it
> did; built its own far-flung network of charitable and educational institu-
> tions; preserved its own identity; and had a profound influence on the
> future of both the country it left and the one it came to.
>
> —Peter Quinn, *Looking for Jimmy: A Search for Irish America*

> Irish-American ethnic identity needs to be understood as historical, con-
> tingent, and contested, rather than essential, fixed, and agreed upon. . . .
> [D]efinitions of Irish-American ethnicity, moreover, were caught up in a
> larger social conflict whose outlines are best described in terms of social
> class.
>
> —Kevin Kenny, *Making Sense of the Molly Maguires*

MANY OF THE BALLYKILCLINE immigrants in the United States avoided
the worst fears envisioned for them by their primary storyteller, Robert
Scally, who worried darkly after resurrecting their history that they might
have ended up as skid row charity cases (Scally 1995, pp. 226, 227). In fact,
many of them did far better than Scally envisioned, though unsurpris-
ingly, it took some time, tremendous obstacles confronted them, and not
all of them made it. In Rutland though, a sizable and helpful community
from Ballykilcline and surrounding Kilglass Parish had taken root before
the arrival of the immigrating evictees and mentored them in settling in.
It was enormously helpful to the distraught people who, forced from their
homes, were wearied by their ordeals and still grieving their losses.

The Ballykilcline immigrants came out of a long, bitter strike experience that pitted them against elites at home, and they had seen their
ground dissolve into chaos by reason of famine and death, a hostile government, interclass conflict, widespread eviction, and forced emigration.

151

They stood up against the Crown's agents, the highest British administrators in Ireland, the property owners, a biased judicial system, massive police forces (especially in the wake of the landlord murders in Roscommon), and incursions into their townland. During the famine, many of them witnessed the deaths of family and friends in politically frustrating circumstances beyond their control. Of course, the farmers of Ballykilcline lost to towering opposition, oppressive power, and catastrophe. In the end, those who lived were forced to surrender their homes, their grip on the life-giving land, their place in Irish society, and their cherished homeland. They were forced out to a new world, forced into risk—though risk was hardly foreign to them. In the United States it took them a decade or so to regroup while they recuperated from their wounds and their harsh memories, found themselves and family members again or made new families, and adjusted to and remade their place in the world—that is, built those "useful and coherent bridges to membership in the American community" that Kevin O'Neill cited (2001, pp. 121, 122).

The strikers arrived in America with both certain liabilities and some distinct advantages. Among their liabilities were a particularly horror-filled experience of the famine years in hard-hit Kilglass; being forced to leave after many had lost family members to hunger, disease, and emigration chaos; their lack of financial assets and job skills for a demanding industrial economy in flux; and other legacies, mental and physical, of their protracted and contentious strike.

If their liabilities were burdensome, their advantages for life in the United States were nevertheless many and significant. They included, for some, that they had previously worked in England or Scotland; that they had been sent to the United States and their way paid; that friends had preceded them; that they came from a cohesive communal culture; that they were bilingual and mostly literate; and that they had lived alongside Protestants so that they knew something more about interclass relations and getting along with Anglos than did those Irish from more homogeneous western parts of Connacht and Munster. They had devised strategies for dealing with Protestants and their culture. They had a strong and practiced sense of identity politics, of being underlings in a hierarchical social structure, and of collective action on uneven ground. Moreover, the fact that such a large group from Kilglass had settled in one place over a short interval, where many who had arrived before they did—and without their traumatic famine and strike experience—gave them help with jobs, housing, citizenship, loans in hard times, knowledge of conditions elsewhere, and an understanding of the American system. It reinforced their bonds and created solidarity—a consensus about what was important and where to focus their energy and attention. Their numbers and their heritage meant that the Catholic churches moved quickly to serve them and helped to protect and support them. The immigrants' numbers in Rutland gave them the social relations they valued, which augmented and solidified their sense of class. It is possible too that some of the immigrants may have outwitted their British overseers to secretly secure passage for themselves and their families under the government's emigration plan for Ballykilcline or to have worked behind the scenes to ensure that paid emigration was part of the plan after the evictions in the townland. How events worked out may have enabled some to see themselves as winners in the end. Certainly, too, the hegemony of Yankee culture and the nativism they encountered in Vermont only tightened the bonds among them as a form of self-preservation and protection. The Yankee environment that confronted them must have fostered their commitment to Irish nationalism.

It is worth noting that while their immediate opponents in Ireland had been the Anglo landlords who controlled tenancies and access to tillage land—conacre—to grow potatoes, the landlord was the neighborhood face of an entire infrastructure (the government and the Ascendancy— the British Protestant upper class in Ireland) arrayed against the Irish smallholders and cottiers. The land confiscations; the Penal Laws; the Act of Union; the military forces deployed; the unfair judiciary; the tithe laws mandating support for the Church of England and the proselytizing on its behalf; the laws of property, inheritance, guns, and trade; the bars against Catholics holding public office; the substitution of the English language for their own Gaelic—it was a *system* of oppression, not merely a land policy, under which they suffered, though the oppression was felt most acutely on land issues because land meant food and therefore survival. While the lower classes fought for a subsistence living, Daniel O'Connell battled at higher levels of the system and brought the smallholders across the countryside into those fights through his oratory and his associations.

Their Numbers in Rutland

My research found about 260 first- and second-generation individuals in Rutland who had roots in Ballykilcline, though not all of them had been there at the time of the evictions. At least sixty-three of the Crown's evictees in 1847 and '48, or 17 percent, chose to stop for a time or stay permanently in Rutland or surrounding towns—Dorset, Poultney, Castleton, and Fair Haven. Some of those who moved on from Vermont went to La-Salle County, Illinois, where a cluster of Ballykilcline immigrants had early established themselves, and to Massachusetts. Some who went to Illinois then moved again to Hennepin County, Minnesota. At least a few of the families (Nearys, Hanleys, Carolans) remained split between Vermont and Illinois, with branches in both locations. Some second-generation individuals went to Providence (Winters descendants), Boston (Winters and Kelly descendants), and New York City (Hanleys and Brennans): cities that were linked with Rutland by rail and had large communities of Roscommoners. The available clues show that most of these immigrants had settled permanently by the later 1850s. One wonders how those who moved on from Rutland calculated their decisions.

Census records disclose that the immigrants from Ballykilcline had a higher-than-expected literacy rate, and the evidence shows that they were activists in organizing their lives: many of them naturalized early, acting on the political consciousness they had developed in Roscommon and the political lessons of Daniel O'Connell. They maintained large families, reconstituted Irish communal culture, supported their church and were supported by it, apparently preferred to continue farming despite their contentious land history (farming was more remunerative around Rutland than much available other work), and willingly banded collectively in community endeavors, such as the marble workers' Benevolent Society and the building of St. Bridget's church. They also went on strike again when they thought doing so was justified. Although some of them moved several times in the United States before finally settling down, the immigrants established a web of communications, and their mobility was high on the canals and railroad lines they had worked to build in the United States. The Irish sent money home to help family and to bring those who would leave, thereby not only assisting relatives but also enlarging and strengthening their own community in Rutland. They learned how to function and think in order to interact successfully in their new environment. They early planted the seeds for their cultural revival, establishing fraternal and social organizations to lighten their loads and tighten their bonds. And as the senachie James Patrick Carney described, by the late 1850s they had developed pride of both heritage and work: "nothing can compare, but the snow from the air, to that beautiful marble stone."

Of sixty-three documented Kilglass men working in the quarries up to 1870, at least twenty-three were linked with Ballykilcline. Given these numbers, some of the Ballykilcline immigrants, and by extension their families, certainly were involved in the strikes against the marble companies, in the West Rutland draft protests against the Civil War Conscription Act, and in Irish nationalist activity by the Fenians.

Their actions bespeak a sense of agency, a willingness to battle to improve the conditions of their lives, to act in their own interests rather than to be merely passive observers. Michael Huggins, it should be noted, found a shift in agrarian conflicts in Roscommon to radical responses, ones making claims that were new, not merely focused on preserving the old customary order (2000, p. 44). That characteristic of agency must have been present retrospectively as well, implying more intention in their strike in Ireland than perhaps they have received credit for. The finding of high literacy among them operates in the same way, suggesting that in their strike they were not merely pawns between outside power brokers and that they had some capacity to comprehend legal situations. They were not mere witnesses to their own lives; indeed, Daniel O'Connell's Ireland had a complex political organization that relied on commitment by the common people. Further, the lessons of secret society action across the rural Irish landscape showed that force and collective efforts worked to achieve immediate ends, as Joel Mokyr (1983) demonstrated and Huggins found. The secret societies helped, for instance, to hold prices down and to prevent consolidation of some properties. Given those lessons, it is unlikely that they would have abandoned all forms of such tactics in their subsequent conflicts.

Charles Tilly has delineated changes in British state policy and strategy—for example, starting a police force in London—in response to opposition from England's underclasses. Those changes at the top, of course, also affected Ireland. More important, the Irish observed, shared, and to some extent "borrowed" or adapted the experience and tactics of British underclasses to press their own demands. As Tilly said:

> During the eighteenth century, broadly speaking, [British] popular politics proceeded on the basis of the following assumptions:
> 1. that citizens grouped into legally recognized bodies, such as guilds, communities and religious sects, which exercised collective rights;
> 2. that the law protected such collective rights;
> 3. that local authorities had an obligation to enforce and respect the law;
> 4. that the chosen representatives of such recognized bodies had the right and obligation to make public presentations of their demands and grievances;
> 5. that authorities had an obligation to consider those demands and grievances, and to act on them when they were just. (Tilly 1995, p. 142)

He then traced change as it evolved in the early 1800s to something more autonomous, more focused on national issues, and innovative in the forms it employed: the public theater in the streets of Britain was carried too into Ireland.

The underlying assumptions came with the immigrants to Rutland and were put to work in their U.S. actions. The people from Ballykilcline could draw on the expanded claim-making repertoire that Tilly described. A Painite sense of the world had crossed the Shannon as well, and then the Atlantic: "The protests of the rural poor were parochial and filtered through tradition but at the same time demonstrated a consciousness of new egalitarian notions derived in the early nineteenth century from the Tree of Liberty and, as the century wore on, other cosmopolitan developments" (Huggins 2000, p. 20).

Huggins traced the networking, association, and tactics shared by British radicals with the Irish, and vice versa, and showed that many of them were taken up in Roscommon. Moreover, he demonstrated that protests were not based solely in nationalist aspirations or religious conflicts but generated in rural areas by a range of economic and social concerns that included tithes, prices, wages, lack of jobs, scarcity of land, and lack of security in holding it. As Matthew Jacobson explained the phenomenon, alluding to O'Connell's 1840s agitations for Repeal, which drew massive numbers of Irish, "When the potato blight hastened the trans-Atlantic exodus . . . many who fled bore with them a newly acquired political vocabulary for interpreting and discussing the woes of the old country" (p. 25).

These Irish were a social class before they got to the United States with the massive famine influx. The Ballykilcline strike in Ireland was a pragmatic response to their situation, given their communal background and cultural history; the developments in local politics, economics, and collective action by the early 1830s; the ties that bound them tightly to each other within their townland; and the development of mass political agitation in Britain. They were exposed to that agitation in several ways: through seasonal migrant labor, which involved a significant number of adult males in Kilglass parish, including some in Ballykilcline; through newspapers (a survey of one Roscommon newspaper demonstrated as much); through the development of Irish physical infrastructure (e.g., in transportation, mail, and banking systems); and from travelers and in-migration to their county and parish, including the police and military units assigned there.

EARLY MIGRATION FROM BALLYKILCLINE

Multiple instances of emigration from Ballykilcline between 1834 and 1847 can be documented. Gerard Moran pointed out that "the biggest obstacle [to willingness to leave] was an ignorance of the new country they were going to. Such problems were largely overcome when letters came back to Ireland from North America providing detailed information on the type of work that was available, wage levels and the cost of living" (p. 31). Through letters from earlier Kilglass emigrants, later ones learned what they might encounter, and realistic expectations were an important advantage. Moreover, they had connections in the United States from at least the middle 1830s, emigrants whose letters home told about American life, climate, and job markets.

Social class arises in the conflicts between privileged groups and other cohesive units who share contested ground in underprivileged circumstances, according to Ted Gurr. By famine time in Ireland, such factors had been in play for generations and the native Irish had developed a quiver full of responses to act out against the landlords and authorities—despite repudiation of their actions by church and government. It is a strong measure of the people's sense of injustice that they overrode the views of the priestly hierarchy to press their claims through secret society and nationalist activity. For the people, it must have been a highly conflicted stance to retain allegiance to a church that institutionally rejected their major weapon against oppression. John Newsinger has pointed out though that the nationalist Irish Republican Brotherhood's position "did not amount to an anti-clerical assault on the Church as such, but was restricted to the smaller target of 'the priest-in-politics,'" and in the nineteenth century "Catholicism and nationalism were inseparably linked in the consciousness of all classes of the Irish population" (pp. 33, 35).

The native Irish also joined forces despite an extensive authoritarian police, military, and judicial infrastructure that wielded uncommon punitive powers so that a man or woman might be banished to Australia for life, separated from family and homeland, for stealing a handkerchief or a loaf of bread or administering an unlawful oath. Irish people had been sent away for decades for just such infractions. The people viewed the judiciary as unfair. "Those who presided at the Courts were Protestants, often Orangemen; the Sheriff was a protestant and the juries . . . [were] very likely to reflect his political bias." Catholics were excluded from top judicial jobs until 1829 (Ó Tuathaigh, p. 87).

Agency among the townland's tenantry meant that they controlled, to some extent, what happened during the Ballykilcline strike; undoubtedly, some of them had decided by the end of 1846 or soon thereafter that going to the United States was what they wanted to do. This decision, probably arrived at reluctantly and with anxiety, may be why they made no counteroffer to authorities in December 1846 and January 1847, when the government gave them a deadline to respond to its offer. The idea is strengthened by the finding that so many family members and friends had preceded them to Vermont or to Illinois, Kentucky, and elsewhere as many as a dozen years earlier. It is reinforced by testimony about the numbers of Irish who by then were struggling, scheming, and begging to leave their native land.

Most of the Ballykilcline farmers were literate, and a number were letter writers. John and Sabina Brennan Hanley wrote home to tell about their new property; Patrick Kelly had a "foreign letter" awaiting him in Rutland in 1848, almost as he arrived in America. Honora Winters, before the evictions, had a daughter and family in Rutland. There had been a two-way correspondence, facilitated by improvements in the Irish postal system. The strikers in Ireland knew the experience of their children and neighbors in America and could visualize where they themselves might go and how they might live and work outside of Ireland. And 1847 was that point in time when the relentlessness of the famine made the hopelessness of remaining on their ancestral lands all too clear. In securing paid passage to the United States, some of them surely got what they wanted.

Several men who were "outlaws" in Ireland seemingly became upstanding citizens in the United States. Patrick Brislin of Strokestown and Bernard Colligan of Kilglass had faced trouble with police authorities in Ireland, but Brislin apparently settled down as a family man and working-class wage earner in Rutland. Colligan had apparently planned to join an extended family in Rutland but died too early on the western side of the Atlantic to make a record for himself. John McGann, once a suspect in Denis Mahon's murder, moved to Minnesota, where he had six children and farmed for years on land that adjoined the parcel of John and Ann McGinty, who had spent earlier years as immigrants in Rutland. Ann was most likely McGann's sister.

Brislin was a witness for several of the Ballykilcline men's citizenship applications in Rutland, as was John Hanley, who defended his own property from encroachment by a litigious neighbor and initiated a countersuit through the Rutland court system. If at first he and family members confronted Samuel Butler angrily in their Rutland property dispute, ascribe that anger to what O'Neill saw as "less rational responses as well, responses that were likely derived from Irish more than American experience" (2001, p. 123). Ascribe it to that "uneven consciousness" noted by Huggins.

John Hanley bought property early, headed a large family, and for a time was one of Rutland's wealthiest Irish immigrants in property value. Born in Ballykilcline in 1805, Hanley was one of the senior Irish in Rutland. Undoubtedly he was called on by his immigrant friends for help in finding a job or navigating American systems of citizenship, justice, and economics. He was named a contact, for instance, in ads for missing family members that the Irish placed in the *Boston Pilot*. The Brennan brothers, William and Daniel, like Hanley, went into farming early and succeeded at it, amassing assets by 1870 that were worth the equivalent of $62,000 and $99,000 today. William's children included sons who became a doctor and a lawyer and several daughters who were school-teachers—reaching for more, it would seem, than many of their second-generation Ballykilcline counterparts. William's father, who died of ship's fever soon after landing in Rutland, had not been a leader in Ballykilcline's rent strike.

THE FITZWILLIAM AND LANSDOWNE CLEARANCES

Historians have explored to some degree two other assisted emigrations from Ireland to North America that occurred about the same time as Ballykilcline's: one a nine-year phased clearance from the Fitzwilliam estate in County Wicklow to Quebec and New Brunswick, Canada; another from the Marquis of Lansdowne's estate in County Kerry to New York City, also during the famine years (Rees, 2000; Anbinder 2002).

The assisted emigration from the Fitzwilliam estate, called Coolattin, occurred from 1847 to 1856 and moved approximately 5,500 tenants to Canada (Rees, 2000). A number of them crossed paths with Denis Mahon's Strokestown evictees at Grosse Ile in that summer of death in 1847. Fitzwilliam's first ship, the *Dunbrody*, arrived at Grosse Ile on May 25, 1847; the *John Munn*, carrying Mahon's tenants, docked in July. Immigrants from both places may have successively occupied the same beds in the island's hospital sheds or filled neighboring plots in its cemetery.

Like Mahon, Fitzwilliam was consolidating his property. In Jim Rees's account (2000) Fitzwilliam was viewed as a liberal and benevolent landlord who showed concern for his tenants, except when their interests conflicted with his own. When the landlord cleared his estate, his tenants agreed to go voluntarily, in contrast to what happened when the Crown cleared Ballykilcline and when Mahon evicted and then transported his tenants. The cases were not entirely parallel. Rees focused on one hundred Fitzwilliam families sent to St. Andrew's in New Brunswick, where their landlord had arranged railroad construction jobs for the men. The emigrants' ship, named *Star*, met bad weather as it neared its destination, and nine of its 383 passengers had died; another sixty-three were ill or injured. Two more died upon landing, and ninety-eight were detained for medical attention. The ship's food had been poor; overcrowding was apparent; and the railway company had no housing prepared for the arriving Irish, despite their promises to make ready.

Months later, the company sought to end its obligation to the immigrants by declaring that their jobs were over. A rail official said, "A hundred ABLE BODIED MEN were all we had any reason to expect but, to our surprise with the hundred men sent out were 277 old men, women, and children, and the whole afflicted with sickness, death, and poverty. . . . [W]e have employed those men and boys principally out of charity, as their work is not worth six-pence per day, being so enfeebled by the voyage and sickness, that but few of the men were able to do a day's work" (qtd. in Rees 2000, p. 108; original emphasis).

Although the local emigration officer believed that the railroad officials had treated the immigrants unfairly and had misrepresented their dealings with the Irish work crew, hard times had hit the local economy; no jobs existed, and there was no will to give the Irish public charity. Company officials also claimed that the immigrants had "become refractory" on the job. As Rees saw it, "Perhaps their attitude to the company had hardened when they realized that indigenous labourers working with the surveying crews were receiving five shillings a day, more than double what the immigrants were paid" (2000, p. 103). Like Rutland's quarry workers, only much sooner, these immigrants objected to what they considered unfair conditions of work.

In March 1849 the destitute Fitzwilliam immigrants asked officials for fifty acres per family and aid to get through a year, which they pledged to pay back. But they were told to move on to the United States: "It was a repeat," Rees observed, "of what they had faced earlier in Ireland. Then they had been urged to emigrate to Canada or starve in Ireland while now it was move on to the United States or starve in New Brunswick." It was not unlike the choice that confronted the Ballykilcline people in their rent and wage arrangements: accept the Crown's or the U.S. employer's terms on rent or wages or lose their homes. Nevertheless, 25 percent of the County Wicklow people remained in St. Andrew's in 1860 (Rees 2000, p. 112).

These immigrants, too, had demonstrated agency by voluntarily leaving Ireland for Canada and accepting the railroad jobs, by objecting to discriminatory wages in the work, and by proposing a plan for loans to lift themselves out of the plight that their government, landlord, employer, and the markets had created for them.

In the other case of assisted immigrants, Tyler Anbinder showed that some of the hundreds of woeful tenants whom Lord Lansdowne had "helped" out of County Kerry to New York were able to save significant amounts of cash in their first ten years in America, even though they had settled in a city slum and worked in the meanest jobs. Anbinder used the records of the Emigrant Savings Bank to produce a picture that "suggests that the famine immigrants adapted to their surroundings far better and more quickly than we have previously imagined" (2002, par. 68). The size of the savings that so surprised Anbinder ranged from about $100 to $658—that is, up to the modern equivalent of about $15,000. By comparison, some of the Ballykilcline immigrants did far better and some did worse. Given the range of kinds of work, the limitations of the records, and the variability of individual circumstances, commitment, experience, and geography, it is hard to know how to interpret the disparities in their economic performance. But saving money is a forward-looking action that sees beyond present circumstance to anticipate future needs.

Uneven Success in Vermont

In Rutland, the immigrants' acquisition of assets was uneven. Patrick Brislin, for one, was an illiterate laborer in 1860 with several children and about fifteen years of experience in the United States, yet he had $975 in assets [$23,625], whereas Daniel McGuire, who had emigrated years before Brislin, had several children, and was a Dorset farmer in 1870, reported no assets (though it may be that McGuire had invested all his assets in securing his property). In 1870, James Foley was a quarry blacksmith who had $2,500 [$38,597] in assets, yet many quarry workers reported no savings or assets at all. What accounted for such differences? Was it something in the American system, the level of assets they brought with them, personal misfortune or good luck, or that "uneven consciousness" of the Irish? Further inspection of land, bank, and other records may help to answer such questions. In any case, it is obvious that some of the Ballykilcline immigrants did astonishingly well. The success some of them achieved demonstrated agency, hard work, and a level of acuity in their personal affairs. Moreover, they simultaneously remitted money to support and take out family in Ireland, built their churches and communities in the United States, and supported the cause of Irish freedom—all huge financial drains on meager resources.

By 1857, Rutland had its own Democratic newspaper, the *Courier*, run by John Cain, which favored the Irish and reported much political news from both the home country and the new one. It gave the Irish a voice and set up opposition to the sometimes condescending Yankee-owned *Rutland Herald*. It explained citizenship procedures, sided with workers in the quarry strikes, castigated the Lincoln administration during the Civil War, delivered news of the arrests of Young Irelanders in the homeland, and commented on the goals of the Fenians. The *Courier* was a force for class cohesion, individual agency, political partisanship, and activism in Rutland. As a participant in Democratic Party politics nationally, editor Cain extolled the party's views and issues, immersing the local Irish in the potentiality of political solutions to the problems that affected them; in doing so, he echoed the earlier approaches of Daniel O'Connell. Since they advertised for lost relatives in the *Boston Pilot*, apparently some number of Rutland's Irish also read that Catholic newspaper, which was an advocate on behalf of the Irish across the country. Models of activist stances in life were prevalent in Rutland among the Irish—in their priests, the Irish physician, the newspaper editor, and probably some businessmen— such as the printer John Carlon, who retained his links to Rutland even after he left for Indiana, where he became a well-known business man and Democratic Party figure. From a distance, the Ballykilcline people may even have followed the career of liquor dealer William Padian, who was active in New York City politics.

Another factor reinforcing class cohesion was what has been called "clannishness" in the Irish: intermarriage, loyalty to family and neighbors, religious and cultural chauvinism, group action, and political sensitivity. In Ireland, it had been a necessary force; in America too, it proved useful. In both places, it is possible to recognize how it developed as a response to social, economic, and political powers arrayed against displaced people.

The Ballykilcline immigrants came out of a particular background and experience in Ireland and moved into the American context then being developed and expressed in Rutland as the area became a world center for marble production. As Thomas O'Connor has said of Boston, it may have been an unlikely place for the Irish to choose (1995, pp. xv, xvi, 5, 6), steeped as Rutland was in Yankee culture and tradition. Yet Vermont had jobs in railroads and marble, and jobs for women as well as men in the homes of Rutland's elites. The farmers grew potatoes, and the landscape looked like home. That the town was close to ports of arrival at Quebec, New York, and Boston made it easier to reconnect with the family and friends who had preceded or who followed them. All things considered, there were logical reasons to stay—together—in Rutland.

The 1857 census of St. Bridget's Parish in West Rutland documented precisely which immigrants worked for which companies that year; it gave their ages and even the maiden names of the married women. In its specificity, this census went beyond others in occupational data: the early federal censuses and Rutland vital records listed jobs only generically—"quarryman," "marble sawyer," "runs channeling machine," "derrick man," and so forth—but the parish enumeration established the links between the Ballykilcline people and specific quarries in Rutland.

New Muscle but Uneven Ground

On the cusp of the war decade of the 1860s, the revivified Irish community in Rutland developed new muscle. It aimed in several directions: a greater share of the benefits of industrialization, service in the Union army or protests against the Conscription Act (or both), and organizing to free Ireland. The first marble strike occurred in 1859, as did Irish strikes in other industrial centers in the region (Lowell, Massachusetts, and Troy, New York, for instance), and the quarry workers won a raise. Two strikes followed in the 1860s: in each case the owners brought in other ethnic groups as strikebreakers and, backed by American courts of law, evicted the Irish from their company homes and took their jobs away. But no records could be found that told exactly who led the strikes for workers or which workers' families, in addition to John Teelon's, were evicted and forced to move elsewhere. Teelon may have been the son of a tenant in Ballykilcline, as the evidence suggests. Other records from St. Bridget's Parish showed that 150 fewer Irish families lived in the parish in 1868 than had resided there a year earlier, before the third strike (Hannon 1986, p. 74). The record, unfortunately, holds a veil over how the experience of Ballykilcline's rent strike affected the marble strikes in Rutland—whether the workers from Ballykilcline instigated the strikes, advocated them, led them, or opposed them. Clearly, though, given their numbers and positions, at least some of the immigrants from the townland must have participated. By 1870 the Irish marble workforce living in Rutland had declined to 275 men from the 461 of ten years earlier. The newest quarry workers were French Canadians, Swedes, and Germans, and there were scores of them, some imported purposely to hold quarry labor costs down by pitting one ethnic group against another, as happened elsewhere and in other industrial sectors. American courts supported the marble quarry owners in these contests.

The evidence also showed that early on, the marble company owners had amassed fortunes of various sizes, and they were the wealthiest men in Rutland. A number of U.S. natives, especially the marble owners, by 1860 (and far more by 1870) had gained tens of thousands of dollars in personal wealth. Greater profit and control of labor and its costs rather than lack of means appeared to be the reasons that the owners denied workers the small raises for which they chose to strike three times during the decade after 1859. The owners paid low wages to help stabilize their workforces and create a dependency among quarry families. And the cause of the owners' success was the vast pool of immigrant labor available to them from Ireland, Canada, and Europe and their trust in the judiciary and government to side with them in labor contests. That trust was likely predicated on the government's role in putting down earlier canal and railroad strikes and also on class allegiances. The quarry wage generally was insufficient for the Irish to amass the funds necessary to buy Vermont farmland. The assets of those who went into farming locally and others who had moved west to farm in most cases exceeded the quarry man's for a comparable time period. Indeed, as they aged, some quarry workers, like Ballykilcline evictee William Neary, brother of two leaders of the Ballykilcline rent strike, went to the poor farm as paupers for lack of the ability to put savings by on quarry wages. As James Carney lamented, "It is a weary life to be . . . cutting the Marble Bawn" (*Violet-Book*, p. 17).

If working conditions were tough and remuneration was low, the quarry men nevertheless enjoyed the sense of camaraderie that Carney captured in the same poem. People take their joys where they find them. They felt pride in the manly marble operations as Rutland became a world center for the stone and, if the feelings of Civil War soldier Peter Welsh were typical, in their own contribution to the U.S. ability to compete with Britain in manufacturing strength and clout, viewing it as weakening Ireland's oppressor. Aiming a telescope into their future shows that by the middle 1880s the immigrants and their offspring took on the local power structure when they ratified separation of the western portion of town from Yankee-dominated Center Rutland, an association they viewed as disadvantaging their own community in West Rutland; thus, West Rutland and Proctor came into legal existence (Fink 1983). That was also when the Knights of Labor came to Rutland, and scores of quarry men signed up as union strength flexed its muscle across the U.S. landscape. Although the decade of the 1880s is beyond the scope of this study, it is helpful never-theless to see where this immigrant community was headed and to throw light on the development of workers' actions in their own interest.

CHALLENGING THE OLD FOE

The Fenians' initiatives against Canada may have come closest to mirror-ing the immigrants' earlier secret society actions in rural Ireland. The organization enrolled thousands of Irish, took in millions of dollars, drew attention at the highest levels of government, and greatly worried the Canadian and British governments. There were Fenians in Rutland, and evidence suggests that some of their leaders may have been from Kil-glass and had links to Ballykilcline. John Carlon, secretary of the Fenian circle in West Rutland, later became a businessman and an activist in Democratic politics in Indiana. It is not known whether he maintained a Fenian role in Indiana as well or whether he transferred his efforts there wholly into American politics and his business. (Additional research may explore this aspect, including plumbing the database of Fenian records that the Catholic University of America has assembled on the Internet.)

What the Ballykilcline people became in America belies the British au-thorities' characterizations of them in Ireland. In the American context they do not appear to have been criminals, to have shown pathological behavior, or—unless widowed, ill, or aged—to have become down-and-out charity cases, as Scally feared they might. Nor has evidence surfaced that they became part of the lumpenproletariat that Scally believed might engulf them. On the contrary, many became landowners and farmers, as well as wage workers. If they tangled with police authorities, it generally seemed to be for donnybrooks, often with each other, which reprised the faction fights back home. All of the large number of Kilglass Parish immigrants in Rutland would have shared to some extent much the same experience in Ireland, except that of actually perpetrating Ballykilcline's rent strike and being forced out because of it. Some, however, had faced eviction for other reasons, and unless they emigrated early, they had also shared the deeply disturbing famine experience. The Kilglass natives who arrived in America during the famine years had witnessed that long battle in Ballykilcline; some may have owed it their passage to America if, indeed, an underground market existed to "trade places in the line," as Scally suggested, Harris said happened elsewhere, and evidence showed occurred in the Peter Robinson emigration. The Crown passage of Ann McGann McGinty to the United States, where her family's first stop was in Rutland, suggested that indeed such an underground market had operated or that subterfuge had secured her passage.

It does not appear from the available Rutland record that the people from Ballykilcline were notably handicapped by their strike history in Ireland. Unfortunately, the dearth of strike and court records in Rutland and of immigrant journals and letters obscures individuals' roles in those actions. What is certain is that the arrival in Rutland in the 1830s of the Hanleys, the Colligans, and others from Ballykilcline, Kilglass, and Strokestown made important differences for the integration process of the family and neighbors who followed them years later. As O'Neill said, "Social memory was not a fixed attribute acquired in Ireland and carried abroad; rather it was, and is, an active search for meaning that seeks to integrate the received knowledge of past times and spaces with the realities of contemporary place and necessity" (2001, p. 122).

For the earliest immigrants, that process of integration undoubtedly was well under way before the evictees of 1847 and '48 arrived on the Rutland scene, and the evictees were its beneficiaries. The Colligans' church and marble work connections, the Hanleys' property acquisition and local contacts, Michael Hanley's loans, Kilglass men's early naturalization records, and others' placement in jobs with Rutland's elite substantiate as much. That work of integration and adjustment was the evictees' main task in their own early years in Rutland.

If the rural conflicts of Ireland expressed the Irish people's judgment of illegitimacy on the British Crown as ruler in Ireland, in accordance with Gurr's idea, then it is possible also to apply that notion to the immigrants' place in Vermont, where some former Kilglass people who were criminalized by the British at home appear as family men and active citizens. If Gurr's idea is a true one, then their American record and pursuit of citizenship accorded legitimacy to the U.S. government. Their U.S. activity that most closely corresponded to the agrarian violence of Ireland was Fenianism, and it was directed still at the *old* enemy. The Irish did not easily relinquish the cause of homeland freedom. They had not yet dealt with that enemy at home, but neither had they given up that fight in their new home. As was apparent in the aforementioned comments of the soldier Peter Welsh, they saw many ways in the United States to work for that cause. That and their war service may be all the more reason why they so embraced democratic American politics as the nineteenth century moved to its last quarter.

Though it is not clear whether the evictees from Ballykilcline—or which of them—saw themselves as winners or losers as a result of their rent strike, the experience apparently did not induce them to steer clear of situations that might lead to strikes in America, despite what their first protest cost them. The lack of other wage labor around Rutland meant that it was nearly impossible in any case to avoid a job with the potential of a strike action in that post-1850s industrializing and unionizing era unless a man farmed or was self-employed—work that was out of reach for many immigrants. Without more detail on the record about the three quarry strikes, though, it is hard to determine the specific roles of former Ballykilcline residents or the impact in Rutland of their memory of the strike in Ballykilcline.

Certainly, however, when the marble companies went to court in 1864 to evict approximately seventy workers and their families (probably some 350 people altogether) from company housing, remembrance of Ballykilcline came into play. The first case before the judge was that of Roscommoner John Teelon, who surely knew the history of Ballykilcline all too well. When he lost to the owners in court, the other workers capitulated, but many of them may have drawn on a long historical memory to recall the costs they and their neighbors had paid at home for opposing the "owner" or not meeting his expectations. To any man or woman who came out of western Ireland in famine time, the experience and memory of eviction were all too real and were overlaid with powerful recollections and bitter associations. And the Irish cultivated a faculty for memory. One wonders whether the eviction tactic employed against them in Rutland and their losses in the 1864 and 1868 strikes galvanized the Irish in later labor actions or local political activity. Perhaps it was that history of losses that moved them to embrace the Knights of Labor twenty years later, and to separate West Rutland from Rutland proper, as expressions of the transmission of their communal memory from one generation to another. If so, their history certainly impressed local labor and governmental structures.

A MEMORY OF THE BALLYKILCLINE BATTLE

Eric Hobsbawm has observed, "There is a twilight zone between history and memory; between the past as a generalized record which is open to relatively dispassionate inspection and the past as a remembered part of, or background to, one's own life" (qtd. in Dubofsky 1998, pp. 299–300). Without direct testimony from the immigrants, it is possible to reconstruct only that generalized record and to look for signs of the content and transmission of memory. The memory of Ballykilcline's strike was present in Rutland's quarrying community; the difficulty is to gauge its effect in action.

Tilly and Huggins showed how the forms of collective action evolved over time. "A remarkably coherent and rational consciousness" had guided the agrarian unrest across pre-famine Roscommon, Huggins found (2000, p. 6). It may be that the losses in Rutland's 1860s strikes, probably analyzed endlessly in the town's Irish homes, social centers, and fraternal organizations, coupled with the republicanism and American nationalism in the wake of the Civil War that were cited by O'Neill, steered the immigrants toward Democratic politics and trade unions as the best collective forces with the greatest promise of strength and results in the American setting. For many, those were the paths they took.

Scally alleged that the Irish lacked experience of citizenship. But the fact that they could not vote in Ireland and that the government was oppressive and not of their choosing had only engaged them more deeply and more fiercely in reaction to official policy. It nurtured their affiliations with one another, their identity of interests, and their capacity to act as one through group effort. The British grew to fear the will of the Irish when they gathered in huge numbers to hear Daniel O'Connell. There was their allegiance: to family, class, church, and their country in memory and in future. Their oath of allegiance was one they made to their own vision and to each other. Galen Broeker has said, "The public—in rural Ireland, the peasants—were turning increasingly from support of the ascendancy-made law of the magistrates to support of a law of their own, based upon the will of the peasant community. The duly constituted government was unwilling or unable to deal with the major concerns of the peasants—high rents, evictions, the tithe. Thus, not only did the peasant support his own body of law, but also over a considerable portion of Ireland he gave his assent to what was in effect his own government—government in the form of the agrarian secret societies whose political activity took the form of agrarian outrage" (1970, p. 229). It was no small matter to develop a structure of their own that worked underneath the suffocating British infrastructure. But they did.

Their lessons in citizenship recognized their common dilemma and priorities and identified their limited paths in pursuit of shared goals. The chase asked much of them: fierce commitment, a common vision, organization, and agency. Shifting to the United States, they persevered in what they knew worked. Against power, money, and status they brought the clout of numbers, activism, and their oaths of allegiance in pursuit of a future worth having, in memory of a past worth holding. If in Ireland they were compelled to cede their potato beds, in America they were seeding new ground.

Afterword

Just as *Ballykilcline Rising* headed to press, the independent Vermont researcher William Powers and the author found new data about some of the Colligans in Rutland, whose story is told in a family letter in Chapter 3, which identified them certainly as Ballykilcline evictees. The family is that of Patrick and Annie Colligan and their six children. While Patrick and sons Bernard and William do not appear in the known Vermont record, Annie Reynolds Colligan, her daughter, Eliza, and son, Michael, as has been noted, lived in Rutland's Poor Home in 1850. Daughters Mary and Anne worked in local homes then, the census showed. They were "hidden" evictees in Rutland, though, because only three of eight family members (all with common first names) were together in one place; the head-of-household, Patrick, was missing; information about them—for example, in the Poor Home list—was minimal; and two daughters married early and became camouflaged under their marriage names.

In 1851, daughter Mary Colligan married Samuel Butler, the man engaged in the lawsuits with John Hanley a decade later that are described in Chapter 3. The Butlers eventually had four children, and by the mid-1860s they lived in nearby Pittsford. Their granddaughter was Ruth Sigourney Butler, who wrote the family letters in the 1960s. Daughter Anne married William Capron by about 1855, and the couple joined his mother and brother on the Capron farm in Rutland. By 1868, they had two sons and two daughters. In 1881, their farm was 240 acres in size. Anne Colligan Capron was the only member of her family whose information available at the time of the study—her name and age and the names of her parents—warranted counting her as a Ballykilcline evictee. Eliza Colligan never married. The death records of the three sisters name their parents as Patrick and Anne Reynolds Colligan; Anne's also states that she was born in "Killglass" in County Roscommon. The son Michael seemed to drop out of sight after 1850.

Significantly, the new information adds more than a dozen Ballykilcline evictees (first and second generation) to the number found in and around Rutland and places on the record a family that knew some of its own story and passed it on, though the passage of time, the fickleness of memory, and losses due to aging may have clouded or altered some details—the name of the man whose family arrived in Rutland in 1847 was Patrick, not Bernard. Ruth Butler apparently mixed up some people in the family story. The story as she remembered it, however, also holds kernels of truth, though she likely did not know about the Ballykilcline rent strike, evictions, and Crown-paid passages to America.

Ruth Butler was eleven years old when her grandmother died in 1913. Her letters about her family may be the only known written documents in which a descendant describes the lives of Ballykilcline residents in Ireland from what may be personal knowledge learned directly from an evictee. The Ballykilcline story is a tapestry of many threads still in the weaving.

Appendix

Table 1. U.S. Census Searches for the Immigrants from Ballykilcline

Census Year	1850	1860	1870
RUTLAND COUNTY			
Rutland Town	x	x	x
Poultney	x	x	x
Fair Haven	x	x	x
Brandon	x		
Castleton	x		x
Chittendon	x		
Ira	x		x
Pittsford	x		
West Haven	x		
BENNINGTON COUNTY			
Dorset	x	x	x

Table 2A. Literacy of a Sample of Ballykilcline Immigrants per U.S. Censuses

Rutland Immigrant	Before 1850	1850	1860	1870	1880	Approximate Birth Year/Notes
Bridget Geelan Brennan			yes	yes		1831
Daniel Brennan				yes	yes	1823
Maria Kelly Brennan			yes	no	yes	1833
William Brennan			yes	yes		1821
Owen Carlon (Carolan)				yes		1840
Bernard Carlon (Carolan)				yes		1820
Susan Hanley Carrington			yes		read only	1822
Bernard Colligan				yes		1811
Michael Costello		yes	yes			1816
Jane Brennan Driscoll				yes	yes	1830
Eliza Foley		yes	yes			1810

Table 2A. (*continued*)

Rutland Immigrant	Before 1850	1850	1860	1870	1880	Approximate Birth Year/Notes
James Foley		yes	yes			1825
Margaret Hanley Hackett		yes			yes	1833
James Hanley		yes			dead	1817
John Hanley		yes			yes	1805
Michael Hanley*	yes (died 1848)					1821; (family knowledge, personal effects)
Owen Hanley			yes	dead		1825
Sabina Brennan Hanley	yes	yes			read only	1810
Catherine Geelan Igo				yes	dead	1829
Michael Igo				yes	no	1820
Eliza Cline Kelly	yes			no		1812
Patrick Kelly	yes		read only			1806
Thomas Kelly			yes			1836
William Kelly				yes		1840
Edward McCormick	yes	yes			yes	1808
Thomas McCormick					yes	1840
Ann McGann McGinty	yes	yes			yes	1815
John McGinty	yes	yes			dead	1800
Patrick McGinty			yes			1838
Ann Cox McGuire					no	1838
Ann Wynne McGuire					no	1827
Bartley McGuire					yes	1830
James McGuire					yes	1837
Terrance McGuire				yes	yes	1838
Bridget Mullera	yes	no	no			1797
Bridget Mullera (dau)				yes		1837
Denis Mullera				yes		1836
James Mullera	yes	dead				1797
Thomas Mullera	yes		read only			1827 (an "R" in census column headed "cannot read")
Bartholomew Neary	yes	prob dead				1802
William Neary	yes	no	yes			1811
Mary Ann Geelan Regan					yes	1826
Ann Stewart	yes	no				1797
John Stewart	yes	no				1825

Table 2A. (*continued*)

Rutland Immigrant	Before 1850	1850	1860	1870	1880	Approximate Birth Year/Notes
Honora Winters		yes		yes	dead	1787
Honora Winters (dau)		yes				1830
John Winters				yes	no	1825
Margaret Winters		yes				1823
Thomas Winters		yes	yes		yes	1818
Other Ballykilcline Immigrants						
John McGann			yes		yes	1823
Luke McGann			yes		yes	1827
Arthur Mullera					yes	1814
Patrick Mullera					yes	1820
Abby Carrington Neary			yes		yes	1824
Edward Neary					yes	1805
Luke Neary					yes	1824
Mary Padian			yes		dead	1817
Richard Padian			yes		yes	1815

*The source of information on Michael Hanley was unique and not a census but seemed sufficient to include here.

ANALYSIS

The initial plan was to take the literacy results that were reported in the 1850 census, since it was the first one after the immigrants left Ireland and thus seemed to promise the strongest data about their literacy in Ireland. In fact, though, a notable number of immigrants answered one way in 1850 and differently in a later census. In addition, in 1850 the immigrants appeared reluctant to disclose information about themselves, perhaps because of transference of their still-fresh hostility toward their former British government, the fear of intimidation they had known in Ireland, uncertainty about how the information would be used, or mere unfamiliarity with American ways. It also appeared that the year's census takers had not been rigorous in their inquiries. Therefore, a major effort was made to obtain information from a second census if the initial data was derived solely from the 1850 data. Doing so, however, risked the inclusion of immigrants who may have learned to read in their first decade or more in the U.S. which would then "cloud" the picture of literacy at the time of the strike. Nor was obtaining data from the following census always possible, since that decade was one of great mobility for the immigrants. In addition, a number of immigrants died during their early years in the United States. Such was the case, for instance, with Bartholomew and Patrick Neary and James Mullera, who all apparently passed away during the 1850s and thus are recorded in only one federal census.

Although my comprehensive study extended only to 1870, it was necessary to take information recorded in censuses up to 1880 on this issue so as to establish a good-sized cohort of subjects with more than one data point for each. Census searches for that year were conducted too when early data points produced contradictory information. Extension of the time period, however, both strengthened and somewhat weakened the results.

Data were found for fifty-eight individuals: thirty-seven men and twenty-one women. Evictees constituted about half of the group; the rest were linked to Ballykilcline by other records. Though efforts were made to obtain at least two responses for each individual, the number of replies for each individual is in fact one, two, or three over the four census years. The data showed that forty-four (or 76 percent) of them were literate, *and* the census never reported that they could not read or write.

In the outcome, the responses of 1850 were viewed as the least reliable; in fact, 21 percent changed their answers at least once between censuses. In a gender breakdown, 67 percent of the women professed literacy; 10 percent of the women said they could neither read nor write; and 10 percent acknowledged that they could read but not write. Of the men, 84 percent, or thirty-one of thirty-seven individuals, said they could read and write. Although none of the men consistently said they were not literate, three eventually changed their responses to not literate, and another two acknowledged that they could read only. One man and one woman said yes in an early census, no in the next one, and then yes in the final census record consulted. The oldest person in the study group, Honora Winters, who was born in 1787, twice reported that she could both read and write. The data source for one male was unique. Michael Hanley died of ship's fever in 1848; but family descendants have asserted that he was educated and that his personal effects included a number of books and papers. The Rutland newspaper reported that he had a letter waiting at the post office. The evidence seemed sufficient to include him in the literacy study, though his data were not derived from the census; indeed, he did not live until the time of the 1850 census.

Weaknesses are apparent, however, in the data: first, information was found at only one point in time for 47 percent of the group (51 percent of the men and 38 percent of the women). Second, for 7 percent of the cohort (but not including Michael Hanley) that single data point is from the 1850 census, deemed the least reliable one.

Table 2B. Analysis of the Census Literacy Data

How Subjects Answered	Males N= 37	% /Males	Females N= 21	% /Females	Total N= 58	%/Total
Subject answered *only* yes (i.e., could read, write) in 1–3 censuses*	31	84	13	62	44	76
Subject answered only no (i.e., could not read or write)	—	0	2	10	2	3
Subject's last answer in time was that he or she could read only	2	5	2	10	4	7
Subject gave a yes answer and in a later census answered no	3	8	3	14	6	10
Subject answered yes, in later census years no, but then yes again	1	3	1	5	2	3
Totals	37	100	21	101**	58	99**
Gauging Strength of Data						
Subject for whom only one data point on literacy was found	18	49	8	38	26	45
Subjects for whom the only data point on literacy was found in or before 1850	3	8	2	10	5	9

*Includes information on Michael Hanley, for whom the source was unique (and not the census).
**Numbers do not equal 100% because of rounding.

Table 3. Assets over Three U.S. Censuses of Quarry Men Either from Ballykilcline or Married to Women from Ballykilcline

Name	Approximate Birth Year	Occupation	Source/Notes	Assets[1] in 1860	1870
Patrick Carlon	1833	marble work	1860 U.S. census	$300	
Bernard Colligan	1811	quarry man	1870 U.S. census, Rutland	$0	$0
Patrick Colligan	1838	at Rutland Marble Co. in 1857	St. Bridget's census[2,3]/blacksmith after Civil War		
Michael Costello	1816	at Jackman's in 1857	St. Bridget's census	$0	
James Foley	1825	quarry blacksmith	1870 U.S. census; wife B. Hanley	$100	$2,500
Michael Foley	1807	at Rutland Marble Co. in 1857	father of James, per newspaper ad	$50	$0
Michael Hackett	1832	at Barnes in 1857	wife Margaret Hanley, dau John & Sabina	$125	$600
Gilbert Hanley	1838	marble sawyer in 1880	1870 U.S. census/family data 1880; Civil War vet	$0	$0
Owen Hanley	1825	at Jackman in 1857	St. Bridget's census	$0	
Michael Igo	1820	at Baxter in 1857	St. Bridget's census		$2,500
Thomas Kelly	1838	marble cutter	son of Pat & Eliza Cline Kelly; 1870 U.S. census	$0	$0

Table 3. (*continued*)

Name	Approximate Birth Year	Occupation	Source/Notes	Assets[1] in 1860	1870
William Kelly	1848	quarry man in 1857, Dorset farmer in 1860	son of Pat & Eliza Cline Kelly		$0
Edward McCormick	1808	at Baxter quarry man in 1857; quarrying still in 1870	St. Bridget's census; 1850, 1870 U.S. censuses	$100	$0
Michael McDermott	1831		1860 U.S. census		$0
Daniel McGuire	1804–		husband of Nancy Winters; St. Bridget's census; 1860 U.S. census		$0
James McGuire	1819–	at Barnes in 1857	St. Bridget's census	$100	$0
Patrick McLaughlin	1827–	at Rutland Marble Co. in 1857	husband of younger H. Winters		
Pat McLaughlin	1834	quarry man	husband of Bridget Wynne; children's birth records	$50	
Michael Neary	1826	quarry man	son of Bartley Neary; child's 1864 birth record says he's a quarry man		
William Neary	1816	at Barnes in 1857	St. Bridget's census/bro. of Bartley Neary	$0	$0
John Stewart	1825				

Table 3. (*continued*)

Name	Approximate Birth Year	Occupation	Source/Notes	Assets[1] in 1860	1870
John Teelon/ Toolan	1832	at Jackman in 1857	sketches of W. Rutland by Hannon evicted 1864 strike; TAB*		
John Winters	1824	quarry man	1870 U.S. Census/Civil War vet		$800
Thomas Winters	1819	Rutland Marble Co. boss in 1857	St. Bridget's census	$450	$2,100

*The Tithe Applotment Books (TAB) were Irish land records.

1. To give a sense of the modern equivalents of these assets, $50 in 1860 equaled approximately $1,212 in 2005. Thus, the $2,500 held by James Foley and Michael Igo in 1870 would have been about $38,597 in 2005.

2. While the notation in St. Bridget's parish census of 1857 says only "Co," it is my conclusion that the abbreviation refers to the Rutland Marble Co., the largest of the quarries there at the time.

3. There was no label for the first column of information in St. Bridget's parish census of 1857. The then pastor, Rev. Robert B. Whalen, who gave me access to the census record speculated that Barnes, Baxter, Jackman, and Parker referred to street names. But there were marble operations under each of those names as well, from which the street names likely were derived. Further, each household was grouped separately, and the number of people in the household was totaled. In some cases, two different names appeared in the first column next to individuals in the same household, which would not have been the case had the column merely identified the street location of the house. The evidence suggested that the column referred to employer. In addition, where John Hanley, a farmer in West Rutland, was listed, that there was no entry in the first column fits the employer hypothesis, since Hanley worked for himself. John Hanley did have a house on a particular street, nevertheless the first column was blank next to Hanley's name. The original record of the census and my transcription of it were in the possession of the pastor of St. Bridget's in November 2002. My thanks to the pastor for making it available and to Frances Dunn for helping to transcribe it.

Table 4. Assets of Immigrants from Ballykilcline Who Had Become Farmers in Vermont and Elsewhere by 1870

Name	Approximate Birth/Year (Male)	Assets			Notes
		1850[1] (Only Real Estate)	1860[2]	1870[3]	
Vermont					
John & Sabina Brennan Hanley	1805	$500	$3,000	$4,000	John, 65, a laborer in 1870; farmed earlier. emigrated ca. 1835
John & Mary Hanley	1838			$1,500	son of John & Sabina B. Hanley
William & Bridget Geelan Brennan	1821	$0	$3,500	$4,000	Poultney farmer; children: doctor, lawyer, teachers
Daniel & Maria Kelly Brennan	1823	$0	$1,500	$6,400	Poultney farmer; wife dau of Pat & Eliza Cline Kelly
John & Jane Brennan Driscoll				$3,200	one son a priest; other a newsman; in Poultney
Patrick & Eliza Cline Kelly	1806		$1,000	$3,900	Dorset farmer
Michael & Catherine Geelan Igo	1820			$2,500	Poultney farmer
Daniel & Nancy Winters Maguire	1804			$0	Dorset farmer
Thomas & Margaret Carroll Winters	1820		$450	$2,100	quarry worker, then small farmer in Rutland

Table 4. (*continued*)

Name	Approximate Birth Year (Male)	Assets			Notes
		1850[1] (Only Real Estate)	1860[2]	1870[3]	
Elsewhere					
Bernard Carlon (widower)	1820		$2,240	$12,900	stopped in Rutland; moved on to Illinois
James & Susan Carrington Hanley	1818		$2,165	$21,300	stopped in Rutland; moved on to Illinois
Patrick & Mary [?] Mullera	1820			$5,200	settled in Clayton Co., Iowa, 1857
John & Ellen [?] McGann	1823			$725	Farmer in Hennepin Co., Minn.; property adjoined McGintys'
John & Ann McGann McGinty	1800			$2,200	stopped in Rutland; moved on to Illinois, then to Minnetonka, Minn.
Richard & Mary Carlos Padian	1815			$5,620	Texas, Md.

1. For context, $500 in 1850 would be worth $12,900 in 2005 funds.
2. These are converted equivalents of 1860 money to 2005 value:
   $500 = $12,115; $1,000 = $24,231; $2,000 = $48,462; $3,000 = $72,692; $3,500 = $84,808.
3. Here are representative conversons of 1870 funds to 2005 value: $1,000 = $15,439; $2,000 = $30,877; $3,000 = $46,316; $4,000 = $61,755; $5,000 = $77,194; $6,000 = $92,632; $13,000 = $200,704; and $21,000 = $324,213.

Notes

INTRODUCTION AND METHODOLOGY

1. The AP story is posted at www.ballykilcline.com/blood.html.

2. Thanks to Ruth-Ann Harris, an editor of that series, who supplied me with a database of Kilglass people whose ads—more than seventy-five of them—are extracted there, a number of them placed by immigrants who lived in Rutland.

3. The manufacturing schedule supplements the population census; such information was first taken in 1810. In 1850, for instance, information was collected when a company's yearly gross product totaled at least $500. Manufacturing data is used in forecasting and tracking economic output.

4. There were, for instance, several John Hanleys in Rutland, several John Stewarts, and two pairs of Michael and James Foleys. In some instances, when the information was available, the individuals could be distinguished from each other in the records by approximate birth date or spouse's name.

5. The parish census presented information in columns without headings. It is my conclusion that the first column referred to employer: marble operations existed in West Rutland under each of the names listed there. Internal evidence pointed to that conclusion as well: different names were listed in column one for several people in the same household, eliminating the possibility therefore that it referred to the street where the household was located. Where the abbreviation "Co" was used, I believe it referred to the Rutland Marble Co., one of the largest in the town.

1. THE STORY OF BALLYKILCLINE

1. In Ireland, there were civil administrative units called parishes, as well as the religious units also known as parishes.

2. The society has a website at www.ballykilcline.com and a newsletter, *The Bonfire.*

3. Thanks to historian Kevin Whelan for directing my attention to Tyler Anbinder's Five Points work.

4. "The "Plantation" or "Irish" acre was approximately 1.6 times the area of the newer "Statute" acre." The Cromwellian and Williamite surveys were done in English Statute measure (i.e., acres, roods, perches), whereas the Irish acre dated to Tudor times (Scally 1995, pp. 239, 17).

5. Thanks to Elaine Swanson Forman, who posted the townland's Elphin (Synge) Census at www.ballykilcline.com.

6. Those who did not pay were Thomas Fitzmaurice, Thomas Magan, John Quinn, Patrick and Bartholomew Neary, Patrick McCormick, J. Wynne, and Denis Connor (Commissioners of Woods and Forests, pp. 10–13).

7. Scally named the Defendants as Bartholomew Narry, Patrick Narry, Patrick Croghan, Richard Padian, Terence Connor, Patrick Colligan, Michael Connor, John Connor, Patrick Stewart, James Stewart, James Reynolds, Joseph Reynolds, Hugh McDermott, and Bernard McDermott (1995, p. 244), evidently from their listing in a document from the Court of Exchequer. Elsewhere, however, Scally sometimes identified still another tenant, Mark Nary, as a Defendant (1995, pp. 244, 78). Two Patrick Colligans lived in Ballykilcline.

8. The Crown had booked passages from Liverpool for the evictees on these ships: the *Roscius, Metoka, Jane Classon, Creole, Channing, Laconic,* and *Progress.* The first one left in September 1847; the last sailed for New York City in late April 1848.

9. Two of Mahon's ships had the highest mortality of the more than four hundred ships arriving that summer with sizable passenger lists. Calculation of the overall number of deaths among Mahon's emigrants is based on figures about Mahon's ship passengers in Campbell 1994; information about deaths on each ship was collected at Grosse Ile and published in Charbonneau and Drolet-Dube 1997.

10. The Orange Order was founded in 1795 by Protestants as a counterweight to Irish Catholics' secret societies and to memorialize King William III and the Battle of the Boyne. It did much to exacerbate sectarian tensions. In 1825, the government had sought unsuccessfully to suppress it as a threat to social order.

11. Oliver Cromwell (1599–1658) led an English army to Ireland in 1649 and presided at the siege of Drogheda, where many Irish were slain. He became England's lord lieutenant in Ireland. His name is linked to the suppression of Irish Catholics—their capture, punishment, death, or transportation and the confiscation of their lands.

12. The known record does not identify this family.

2. SHIFTING GROUND IN ROSCOMMON

1. Many records were moved and hidden or lost in the eighteenth century as the clergy acted to protect the people, according to a personal communication with the parish priest at Carra church, County Kildare, 1993. Thus, even church documents recording a family's history are hard to find for any date before the early 1800s, and civil vital records about Catholics were not kept in Ireland until 1864.

2. See, for instance, Scally 1995, p. 76, and on pp. 224–25 his suggestion of a conspiracy by the tenants to trade their passages to New York.

3. Thanks to Lynne Sisk for locating the online database of IRLF records and sharing the information.

4. The calculation: The 1841 census showed Kilglass had 11,391 people. However, since no census figure is available for 1838, the Kilglass population that year was calculated using Orser's projected population growth rate of 2.1 percent per year, resulting in an estimate of 10,702 people in Kilglass in 1838. To determine the number of spalpeens in Kilglass in 1838, Orser's average family size of 5.6 people was used in estimating 1,911 households in Kilglass in 1838 and using O'Dowd's estimate of two spalpeens per nine Kilglass households. The calculation shows 425 spalpeens in Kilglass parish in 1838.

5. I estimated from internal evidence that this list was compiled about 1840. The comment concerning Michael Connor, however, appears to have been written in later, probably in 1847.

6. In 1830, England's canals had ten times the mileage of Ireland's system (Connolly 1998, p. 67).

3. RESETTLING IN RUTLAND

1. The 1847 list of Ballykilcline evictees shows an Edward McCormick, age 40, wife Margaret, 32, and children Thomas, 8, Edward, 4, and James, 1, along with relatives Annie, 24, Mary, 18, and Catherine, 6. Edward Sr., in this record, was born in 1807. Under a stone in St. Bridget's Cemetery in West Rutland lies Edward McCormick, a native of Roscommon, whose inscription says he was 88 when he died in August 1880. His wife was Margaret—a native of Canada according to the stone, but born in Vermont according to one census. With them are sons Edward and James and daughter Catherine. An 1856 naturalization record for Edward McCormick of Rutland says he was born in 1807 in County Roscommon. Further, St. Bridget's census of 1857 listed his age that year as 52 and showed his wife's maiden name as Mullens. Ballykilcline tenant logs suggested that Edward was born in 1800 or 1807. These various data raise the question whether this is the evicted Edward with a second wife, also named Margaret, who was born in Canada or the United States. Many reasons are possible for the discrepancy in Edward's reported age, but the ages recorded in the 1850s and on the tenant lists in Ireland likely were given by Edward himself and thus are more reliable than the gravestone information. I classify the McCormicks as Ballykilcline evictees.

2. Among the 1847 evictees were Michael McDermott, 44, wife Ellen, 40, and children Michael, 16, Betty, 14, Maria, 12, Ellen, 10, and Ann, 8. The Rutland Poor Farm was home in 1850 to a Michael and Ellen McDermott of approximately the right ages to be this couple; two of their children's names were the same as in the Ballykilcline family, but several children were missing, and the couple had a new baby. An orphan named Anne Colgan, 17, was listed in the McDermotts' household in Ballykilcline in 1840 (List of Tenants); interestingly,

there were Colligans—Ann, 36, Eliza, 8, and Michael, 6—at the Rutland Poor Farm at the same time. Were the McDermotts from Ballykilcline? They are judged so in this study.

3. Several unattached males appeared in Rutland's records who bear Ballykilcline names but for whom no records document a connection. There is, for instance, a William Donlon, 17, in the 1850 census; he may be the brother of Edward Donlan, whose Rutland naturalization record in 1843 declared that he was born in Ballykilcline. Both names appear on the list of evictees as part of a larger family; in fact, in 1840 there were two sets of brothers by those names in Ballykilcline. Edward Donlan disappeared from Rutland records; by 1880, though, an Edward Donlin was living in Hennepin County, Minnesota, where at least a couple of Ballykilcline evictees—the McGanns—farmed. A Patrick Connor, 35, living in Rutland in 1850, may be one of several Ballykilcline tenants of that name. His wife was Bridget Downey, whose surname was present in Ballykilcline in the 1830s (St. Bridget Parish Census); she may have been the sister of Ballykilcline's John Downey, who emigrated in 1842 and was in Boston in 1845 (Harris et al. 1989–, vol. 1); Bridget was not listed with the Downey family on the 1840 tenants' list, however. Of this group, I count only Edward Donlan a Ballykilcline evictee.

4. Ballykilcline Society members Ann Marie Bell and Maureen Hanley Cole initially established this cluster of immigrants from Kilglass by locating more than two dozen of their Rutland naturalization records in August 2000. I am grateful to them for sharing their research and for calling my attention to the Ballykilcline and sizable Kilglass communities there.

5. No evidence shows that the John Carrington in Rutland in 1830 (see first paragraph of this chapter) is the man from Ballykilcline; however, the fact that a young John Carrington, an evictee, went to Rutland before moving on to Illinois is suggestive.

6. Kilglass natives present in Rutland before 1847 include Michael and Dudley Costello; Michael, John, Patrick, James, Thomas, and Owen Hanley; William and Bryan Colligan; Michael, George, and Edward Duffy; Martin Sheridan; Peter Riley; James Maguire; Hubert Brannon; Michael Cain; Owen Clyne; Michael Carroll; John Stewart; Daniel Farrill; Patrick O. Harris; Owen Mulligan; Thomas Karagan; Peter Finn; Patrick Pheney (Feeny); Bernard Redican; and Patrick Winn (Rutland Courts). An Owen Milligan with three children under age 14 was recorded in Ballykilcline as early as the Synge Census of 1749. Several of these men may have lived in Ballykilcline.

7. Ruth-Ann Harris said this trade in tickets to leave was known to have happened elsewhere—for instance, in Donegal. As indicated earlier, it had also occurred when Peter Robinson organized his emigration scheme to Canada in the 1820s.

8. William Neary's naturalization record admits only that he had been a U.S. resident for "at least" five years.

9. Bernard Carolin was the son of Owen Carolan of Ballykilcline; he was recorded as Owen's eighteen-year-old son on the List of Tenants, dated about 1840.

10. Michael Hanley's naturalization papers stated that he was born in Lavaugh, which was adjacent to Ballykilcline. A Kilglass history, dated 1837, observed that "Tady Hanly of Clooncullaun, an honest upright man, says that the Hanlys of Lavagh were always a contentious people fond of law and wrangling and litigation" (O'Flanagan 1931, pp, 57, 58).

11. Their mother, Nancy McGuire Brennan, was named on the 1840 List of Tenants under the name Anne.

12. I am grateful to William Powers for sharing his extensive Colligan research, including this letter.

13. Nineteenth-century dollar amounts have been converted to modern equivalent values using the calculator at http://www.eh.net/hmit/ with the consumer price index in order to provide perspective and meaning for modern readers. All subsequent conversions to 2005 values (the most recent available at this writing) are shown in brackets after the nineteenth-century amount. Some figures have been rounded for the sake of readability.

14. Thanks to Gray FitzSimon, historian at Lowell National Historic Park, for directing me to Ferrie's study.

15. Thanks to Cathy Joynt Labath for this county history information and Mullera evidence.

16. Byrne wrote this letter in September 1848 when he was employed "in Section 35 rail road lines Middlebury post office state of Vermounth." Boughill was a Crown estate of 111 acres and 111 inhabitants in Galway, parish of Taghboy. Seventeen families held the property in common in 1846. Thirty-one people there emigrated to Quebec at Crown expense aboard the *Sea Bird*, arriving July 23, 1848 (though no contentious action preceded this emigration). The list of tenants from that estate included a "Michael Brien, Byrne or Bryne" who was twenty-two, single, and "very poor" (Ellis 1993).

17. A man might have holdings in more than one townland.

18. Thanks to Lynne Sisk for calling my attention to this advertisement.

19. Coleman identified John McGann "as a kind of country schoolmaster . . . supposed to be one of the party who was concerned in the murder of Mahon" (1999, p. 49). A police document reported that he lived in Ballykilcline (Fox memo, Nov. 26, 1847), but McGann never was arrested in the case and was emigrated at Crown expense in April 1848.

20. A cursory survey shows these marriage matches:
- Evictee William Brennan and former resident Bridget Geelan of Ballykilcline;
- Evictee Daniel Brennan and evictee Maria Kelly, both of Ballykilcline;
- Ballykilcline native Michael Igo and former resident Catherine Geelen of Ballykilcline;
- Ballykilcline native Bridget Wynne and Kilglass native Patrick McLoughlin;

- Evictee Thomas Winters and Kilglass emigrant Margaret Carroll;
- Nancy Jane Hanley, daughter of John and Sabina Hanley, and evictee Thomas Kelly, both of Ballykilcline;
- William Hanley, son of John and Sabina Brennan Hanley, and a woman named Connor, a legendary Roscommon name present in both Kilglass and Ballykilcline;
- Ellen Brennan, daughter of evictees Daniel and Maria Cline Brennan, and Bernard McLoughlin (a Kilglass name);
- Terrance Maguire, son of Kilglass native Daniel and Ballykilcline's Nancy Winters Maguire, and, first, Bridget Flanigan of Kiltrustan Parish (adjacent to Kilglass), then M. Connaught;
- James A. McGuire, great grandson of evictee Honora Winters, and Mary Josephine Considine, daughter of evictee Bridget Neary and John Considine;
- John McLoughlin, son of Patrick McLoughlin and evictee Honora Winters (the younger), and, first, Mary Welch, then Elizabeth Farrell, a Ballykilcline surname;
- Owen Carolan of Ballykilcline and Bridget Murray of Kilglass;
- Ballykilcline native Patrick Carlon and, first, Bridget Cunningham, a Kilglass native, then Sarah McGuire, undoubtedly of a Kilglass or Ballykilcline family as well;
- Ballykilcline evictee Thomas Mullera and Mary Kelly, a native of Strokestown.

21. Thanks to Roger Lamson for permission to recount this family history.

22. The reference is to the divorce of the younger Bridget Mullera and Terrance McGuire (a different man from the one of that name in Rutland); see chapter 5.

4. TO BATTLE WITH A "TWO-EDGED SWORD"

1. Several families of immigrants named Kelly had come to Rutland from Ballykilcline, but no Kilglass Parish connection has been established with this soldier.

2. The evidence is from an Associated Press story in which Maureen Mc-Dermott Humphreys talked about her family's immigration experience: www .Ballykilcline.com/blood.html.

3. Patrick Hanley's military records document that he was born in Roscommon. His descendants note that both of his parents' surnames (Gill, Hanley) were present in Ballykilcline and that Kilglass Parish is the ancient home of the Hanleys.

4. Thanks to Kathleen Healy, Carney descendant, for permission to quote from her ancestor's book of poetry and for providing a copy of it.

5. Kilnaghamore, also known as Culleenaghamore, was located in Kilglass Parish, next to Ballymoylin.

6. The older John Carlon in Rutland died at age 94 in 1874. Two Carolan/Carlon men in Dorset and possibly a third, and another who lived in Rutland before moving to LaSalle County, Illinois, appear to have been sons of the Owen Carolan of Ballykilcline.

7. The younger John Carlon, a Tuttle's print shop apprentice, left Rutland in the mid-1860s with his wife, Fannie Riley, to join the Indiana print shop of a friend named Downey (a Ballykilcline name). There, his business prospered, and he was seen as "a thorough, practical printer" who became an active Democrat (Nowland 1877, p. 547). Thanks to Julie Offutt, Carlon descendant, for information about the family). See chapter 5.

8. In his Fenian history, William D'Arcy identified Roche as Patrick Roche and cited LeCaron's book as his source (1947); the presumption is that D'Arcy, who was not directly involved and wrote years later, was mistaken in supplying Roche's first name.

9. The ad read, "Of James McCue and wife, whose maiden name was Honora Roch, from parish of Kilglass, Townland of Col (co. Roscommon)—was last heard from resided in Lockport, NY. Her sister Catherine, lies dangerously ill in Troy hospital. Any information respecting them will be thankfully received by Edward Sweeny, Cohoes, Albany County, NY."

Attempts to identify John Roche in Troy records were nonproductive. It is worth noting, though, that a John Roache, age nineteen, was reported with the Michael Moriarty household in the 1857 census of St. Bridget's Parish, West Rutland. Further, Murphy and Murphy (2000) list seven John Roches (under variant spellings) buried in Vermont cemeteries as famine immigrants. Efforts to obtain Troy or Philadelphia newspaper articles pertaining to the Fenian sessions in which Roche brought his charges also were unsuccessful.

5. Family Paths

1. Thanks to McGinty descendants Sister Joan McGinty of Minneapolis and Joseph McGinty of Buffalo, Minnesota, for much helpful information on their family. Though they knew nothing from their own research about Roscommon roots or a Rutland stopover, in 2006 Joe McGinty said they have come to believe the family's Ballykilcline/Kilglass connection.

2. Thanks to Bill Vinehout of Illinois for information about the several children of his ancestors Daniel and Nancy Winters McGuire and family photos, and to Rosemary Vandenburg of Rutland for much general information over several years about the Winters family, her ancestors, and others from Ballykilcline, and for photographs.

3. This Terrance McGuire is not the man of that name in Rutland who was the son of Daniel and Nancy Winters McGuire and a grandson of Honora Igo Winters.

4. Thanks to Margaret Alberts and her extended family for much of this Mullera information, especially about the events that took place in Illinois and James McGuire's court testimony, and for family photographs.

5. The gravestone of John Stuart of Ballykilcline and Dorset and his mother, Ann Murry Stuart, both evictees, reports the parish of Kilmore as their native place.

6. Thanks to Julie Offutt, descendant of the younger John Carlon, for family information about her ancestor's life in the Midwest and about Fran Carlon.

7. Thanks to Patty Pickett of the Rutland Rootsweb Listserv for providing this Neary information.

8. Thanks to Bill Vinehout of Illinois for information on his ancestors Patrick and Mary Haley Neary and her connection to the Brislins.

9. Thanks to John Patrick Gillooly for the information about his ancestors. We shared information for only a few weeks before he died in his sleep on an April 2006 family research trip to West Virginia; RIP.

10. Posting by Michael Lennon on the bulletin board at Leitrim-Roscommon website, June 1, 1998.

11. Thanks to Padian descendants who provided most of this family information to the Ballykilcline website and the society's newsletter, and to Cassie Kilroy Thompson for the text of the local church's anniversary booklet.

12. Thanks to Madeline Sisk for information about her McCormick ancestors in three countries, and for two family photographs.

13. John Riley and his siblings are my own famine-immigrant ancestors from Kilglass Parish. John arrived in New York City in April 1848; he had been in Kilglass throughout the Ballykilcline rent strike and evictions and arrived in New York City at the same time that the *Channing* brought some of the last evictees from Ballykilcline. He therefore shared much the same experience of famine-time Kilglass and must have witnessed the events in Ballykilcline.

6. QUARRY ACTIONS

1. The name Teelon in Rutland possibly evolved from the surname Toolan, which seemingly was indigenous to Roscommon. An elderly John Toolan was a tenant of record in Ballykilcline about 1840. Three other men of the surname Teelon appear in Rutland naturalization records, with the name variously spelled as Teilon, Telan, and Thalon (some witnesses to local naturalizations are listed as Teelon); the four men all named their home place as Roscommon. But that name is not found in a search of Roscommon surnames on the leitrim-roscommon website. Toolan, however, besides being a name present in Roscommon, appears in St. Bridget's Parish Census in 1857, which shows a Francis Toolan and a John Tooman (spelling unclear) working at the Jackman marble operations; however, one Teelan also appears in that census. The John Teelon in this court case may have been the son of the elderly John Toolan who

lived in Ballykilcline, but no naturalization record that might have clarified his home place has surfaced for a John Teelon.

2. A local newspaper alluded to a strike that took place in the nearby slate industry about the same time, Hancock reported (2001, p. 7), but he gave no details, and most of his study focuses on a later era in that industry.

Works Cited

ABBREVIATIONS

CUA   Catholic University of America
NAI   National Archives of Ireland
QRO   Quit Rent Office

PRIMARY SOURCES

Correspondence, Censuses, and Other Documents

Brassington and Gale Survey Map of Ballykilcline, 1836.

Brennan, Rev. Henry. Letter, April 12, 1848. Ballykilcline Papers, QRO, NAI.

———. Letter, August 18, 1848. Ballykilcline Papers, QRO, NAI.

Burke, John. Letter, February 17, 1848. QRO File 67-06-07, NAI.

Butler, Ruth Sigourney (Colligan descendant). Letter to William Powers, March 12, 1969. (Thanks to William Powers for sharing this document.)

Carney, James. *The Violet-Book of Neshobe: Being a Complete Collection of the Songs of Jimmy Carney*. Rutland, Vt.: Privately published with assistance of the Owls of Neshobe Island and Eagles of Cedar Mountain, 1883. (Thanks to Kathleen Healy for sharing her ancestor's work.)

Commissioners of Woods and Forests. Official Correspondence on Ballykilcline. Ballykilcline Papers, QRO, NAI.

Convict Reference File. 1847 M 11, NAI. Thanks to Susie Zada for this source and a transcript of John Ross Mahon's testament.

Dickson, Maxine. Legacy of the McGinty Family in Minnetonka. *West Minnetonka/Deephave Sun*Sailor*, Nov. 29, 2000, p. 4A.

Dillon, Thomas. Letter on firearms in Roscommon, with enclosure, March 25, 1842. Ballykilcline Papers, QRO, Chief Secretary's Office 25/5225, 25/9027, NAI.

Fenian Brotherhood Collection. CUA. Archive. online at www.aladin.wrlc .org/gsdl/collect/fenian/fenian.shtml. Thanks to Timothy Meagher and Patrick Cullom for providing access to this site.

Forristal, John. Letter to John O'Mahony, June 28, 1864. Fenian Brotherhood Collection, CUA website.

Fox, Michael. Confidential memo, November 26, 1847. Outrage Papers, 1848, Roscommon, 25/, NAI. Thanks to Helen and Michael Brennan for finding and sharing this record.

Freemasons Lodge, Strokestown Membership List, 1760–1854. Freemasons' Archive, Dublin.

Griffith's Valuation. Online at http://www.leitrim-roscommon.com.

Hogg, Godfrey. Letter, September 24, 1836. Ballykilcline Papers, QRO, NAI.

———. Letter, August 16, 1842. Ballykilcline Papers, QRO. NAI.

———. Deposition, October 17, 1843. Document 30-500/A, Outrage Papers for Roscommon, 1843, NAI.

———. Letter to Lucas, July 23, 1844, 20843/22799 25/13017, Outrage Papers for Roscommon, 25, NAI.

Johnson, Betty. Letter to Esther McGinty of Hopkins, February 17, 1977. Based on interviews with family by Dana Frear. Courtesy of descendant Sr. Joan McGinty.

Kelly, John T. The 1864 Diary of Private John T. Kelly Second Vermont Regiment. 1994. *Rutland Historical Society Quarterly* 24, no. 2.

Kelly, Patrick. Letter, March 18, 1848. Ballykilcline Papers, QRO, NAI.

Kilglass Gravestone Inscriptions, Friends of Ballykilcline.

Kilglass Parish Freeholders List. 1796. Roscommon Public Library.

Kincaid, Joseph. Testimony, June 21, 1847, before the Select Committee of the British House of Lords on Colonisation from Ireland. In *British Parliamentary Papers*, vol. 6. Shannon, Ire.: Irish University Press, 1847.

Lands of Ballykilcline, County Roscommon. Returns to Orders of the House of Lords, February 16 and 19, 1847. QRO, NAI.

List of Tenants on the Crown lands of Ballykilcline, County of Roscommon. Undated, ca. 1840. QRO, NAI.

Middlesex Records Center. Vital and military records. Montpelier, Vt.

Minnesota vital records, Minnesota Department of Health.

Nicholson, William J. Letter to James Stephens, September 20, 1866. Fenian Brotherhood Collection, CUA website.

O'Ferrall, Hugh. Letter concerning an attack on Donnellan, September 28, 1842. Ballykilcline Papers 25/18745, 25.899, QRO. NAI.

Outrage Papers, August 10, 1842, and x 25/16609, Roscommon, NAI.

Rutland Courts. Naturalization records, court offices, and National Archives and Records Administration, Waltham, Mass.

Rutland Poor Farm. Reports 1857–1904. Online at Rootsweb Rutland Listserv.

Samuel Butler v. John Hanley et al., No. 74, January 2, 1862; *John Hanley v. Samuel Butler*, No. 82, February 10, 1862. Rutland County Court records, court offices.

Seventeenth Registration Report. Vermont, 1873. Prepared under the direction of George Nichols, Secretary of State. Rutland: Tuttle & Company, Printers, 1875.

Shanley, Dr. Letter to Central Board of Health, December 8, 1847. British Parliamentary Papers Relating to Proceedings for the Relief of the Distress and the State of the Unions and Workhouses in Ireland, 4th and 5th Series—1847–1848; Famine Relief in Ireland, #2, p. 204. Roscommon Union.

St. Bridget's Parish. Census. Transcript made by Mary Lee Dunn and Frances Dunn, October 2002, from the 1857 original at the parish office in West Rutland. Thanks to Rev. Robert B. Whalen, pastor, for allowing me to transcribe this record.

———. St. Bridget's Parish. Centennial Pamphlet, 1860–1960. Thanks to Cathy Habes of the Rutland Rootsweb Listserv for a copy of this pamphlet.

Synge Census, 1749. Diocese of Elphin, Church of Ireland. Online at Ballykilcline website.

Tithe Applotment Books (TAB), Ireland.

U.S. Census. Various LaSalle County, Illinois townships, 1850, 1860, 1870, and 1880.

———, Highland, Clayton County, Iowa, 1870 and 1880.

———, Baltimore (Texas), Maryland, 1850, 1860, 1870, and 1880.

———, Minnetonka, Minnesota, 1860, 1870, and 1880.

———, Various towns, Vermont, 1830, 1840, 1850, 1860, 1870, and 1880.

———, Manufacturing Census of U.S., Rutland, Vermont, 1850, and 1860.

Vice Guardians to the Commissioners, January 12, 1848. British Parliamentary Papers Relating to Proceedings for the Relief of the Distress and the State of the Unions and Workhouses in Ireland, 4th and 5th Series—1847–1848; Famine Relief in Ireland, #2, p. 532. Roscommon Union.

Wheeler, Edward. Letter from Port Robinson, August 10, 1849. Outrage Papers for County Roscommon, 1849, NAI.

Newspapers, Newsletters, Reports

Armagh Guardian. 1845. Online at www.newspaperabstracts.com/link.php?id=50.

Freeman's Journal. 1848.

Illustrated London News. 1849. Online at http://vassun-vassar.edu/~sttaylor/FAMINE/ILN/.

Jubilee Book. St. Joseph's Parish, Texas, Md.

Providence Journal. 1943.

Roscommon Journal and Western Reporter. 1844.

Roscommon and Leitrim Gazette. 1845–1847.

Rutland Courier. 1848–1868.

Rutland Globe. 1877.

Rutland Herald. 1848–1868.

Rutland Weekly Herald. 1871.

The Bonfire (newsletter of the Ballykilcline Society). 2006.

SECONDARY SOURCES
Books, Articles, Film

Anbinder, Tyler. 2002. From Famine to Five Points: Lord Lansdowne's Irish Tenants Encounter North America's Most Notorious Slum. *American Historical Review* 107, no. 2. The History Cooperative. Online at http://www.historycooperative.org/cgibin/justtop.cgi?act=just-top&url=http://www.historycoop.org/journals/ahr/107.2/iti.html.

Andrews, Hillary. 2001. *The Lion of the West.* Dublin: Veritas.

Austin, Michael. 2002. Carving Out a Sense of Place: The Making of the Marble Valley and the Marble City of Vermont. Ph.D. dissertation, University of New Hampshire.

Benedict, George Grenville. *Vermont in the Civil War,* chap. 2. Burlington, Vt.: Free Press Association, 1888. Online at www.vermontcivilwar.org.

Bernard, Bailyn. 1982. American Historical Association Presidential Address, 1981. *American Historical Review* 87, no. 1:1–24. Online at www.historians.org/info/AHA_History/bbailyn.htm.

Blewett, Mary H. 2000. *Constant Turmoil: The Politics of Industrial Life in Nineteenth-Century New England.* Amherst: University of Massachusetts Press.

Boyle, John W. 1988. *The Irish Labor Movement in the Nineteenth Century.* Washington, D.C.: Catholic University of America Press.

Brighton, Stephen A., and Jessica M. Levon White. 2005. Teacups, Saucers, and Dinner Plates: English Ceramic Exports to Ballykilcline. In *Unearthing Hidden Ireland: Historical Archaeology in County Roscommon,* ed. Charles B. Orser. Bray, Ire.: Wordwell.

Broeker, Galen. 1970. *Rural Disorder and Police Reform in Ireland 1812–1836.* Ed. T. W. Moody, J. C. Beckett, and T. D. Williams. London: Routledge and Kegan Paul.

Browne, Sandra. N.d. History of the Right to Vote in the U.S. Online at www.lwvabc.org/services/history.html.

Campbell, Stephen J. 1990. The Strokestown Famine Papers. Manuscript, Famine Museum. Cited with Museum permission.

———. 1994. *The Great Irish Famine.* Strokestown: Famine Museum.

Carroll, James. 2007. A Time to Ponder Time. *Boston Globe,* January 1, p. A13.

Charbonneau, Andre, and Doris Drolet-Dube. 1997. *A Register of Deceased Persons at Sea and on Grosse Ile in 1847.* Ottawa: Parks Canada.

Clark, Samuel, and James S. Donnelly Jr. 1983. *Irish Peasants: Violence and Political Unrest, 1780–1914.* Dublin: Gill and Macmillan.

Coffin, Howard. 1995. *Full Duty: Vermonters in the Civil War.* Woodstock, Vt.: Countryman Press.

Coleman, Anne. 1999. *Riotous Roscommon: Social Unrest in the 1840s.* Dublin: Irish Academic Press.

Connolly, S. J., ed. 1998. *The Oxford Companion to Irish History*. Oxford: Oxford University Press.

Coyle, Liam. 1994. *A Parish History of Kilglass Slatta Ruskey*. Boyle, Ire.: Kilglass Gaels.

Crossman, Virginia. 1996. The Army and Law and Order in the Nineteenth Century. In *A Military History of Ireland*, ed. Thomas Bartlett and Keith Jeffery. Cambridge: Cambridge University Press.

D'Arcy, William. 1947. *The Fenian Movement in the United States, 1858–1886*. Washington D.C.: Catholic University of America Press.

DeGrazia, Laura Murphy, and Diane Fitzpatrick Haberstroh. 2001. *Irish Relatives and Friends: From "Information Wanted" Ads in the "Irish-American," 1850–1871*. Baltimore: Genealogical Publishing.

Diner, Hasia. 1983. *Erin's Daughters in America: Irish Immigrant Women in the Nineteenth Century*. Baltimore: Johns Hopkins University Press.

Donnelly, James S. Jr. 1996. The Construction of the Memory of the Famine in Ireland and the Irish Diaspora, 1850–1900. *Éire-Ireland* 31, nos. 1–2: 55, 56.

———. 1997. Mass Eviction and the Great Famine: The Clearances Revisited. In *The Great Irish Famine*, ed. Cathal Poirteir. Chester Springs: Dufour.

———. 2001. *The Great Irish Potato Famine*. Phoenix Mill, Eng.: Sutton.

Dubofsky, Melvin. 1993. In Tamiment Institute "Symposium." In *Steelworkers in America: The Nonunion Era* by David Brody. 1998. Urbana: University of Illinois Press. Hobsbawm quote is from *The Age of Empire, 1875–1914*.

Duffy, Peter. 2007. *The Killing of Major Denis Mahon*. New York: HarperCollins.

Duffy, Sean, Gabriel Doherty, Raymond Gillespie, James Kelly, Colm Lennon, and Brendan Smith. 1997. *The Macmillan Atlas of Irish History*. New York: Macmillan.

Dunn, Mary Lee. 2000. The Strike of 1859 by Irish Women Workers in Lowell's Mills. Unpublished paper, University of Massachusetts Lowell.

———. 2001. The Worst Coffin Ships Carried Roscommon People to Grosse Ile. *The O'Beirne Family Journal*. Online at www.obeirnefamily.mcmail.com/issue6/worst_coffin_ships.htm.

———. 2002. An Agenda for Researching the Famine Experience of Kilglass Parish, County Roscommon. In *Ireland's Great Hunger: Silence, Memory, and Commemoration*, ed. David A. Valone and Christine Kinealy. Lanham, Md.: University Press of America.

Eisenschiml, Otto, ed. 1960. *Vermont General: The Unusual War Experiences of Edward Hastings Ripley, 1862–1865*. New York: Devin-Adair. Thanks to Cathy Habes for pointing out this source.

Ellis, Eilish. 1993. *State-Aided Emigration Schemes from Crown Estates in Ireland c. 1850*. Reprint. Baltimore: Genealogical Publishing.

Ellis, Peter Berresford. 1972. *A History of the Irish Working Class*. London: Pluto Press.

Famine to Freedom: The Great Irish Journey. 2003. Documentary produced by TerraNova Television for Moments in Time, Discovery Channel, September.

Fentress, James, and Chris Wickham. 1992. *Social Memory.* Oxford: Blackwell.

Ferrie, Joseph P. 1999. *Yankeys Now: Immigrants in the Antebellum U.S., 1840–
1860.* New York: Oxford University Press.

Fink, Leon. 1987. Politics as Social History: A Case Study of Class Conflict and
Political Development in Nineteenth-Century New England. In *The New En-
gland Working Class and the New Labor History,* ed. Herbert G. Gutman and
Donald H. Bell. Urbana: University of Illinois Press. Reprinted from *Social
History* 7 (January 1982): 43–58.

Gacquin, William. 1996. *Roscommon before the Famine.* Dublin: Irish Academic
Press.

Gray, Peter. 1998. Review of *The End of Hidden Ireland* by Robert James Scully.
Bullan: An Irish Studies Journal 4, no. 1:146.

———. 1999. *Famine, Land, and Politics: British Government and Irish Society,
1843–50.* Dublin: Irish Academic Press.

Gross, Lawrence F. 1993. *The Course of Industrial Decline: The Boott Cotton Mills of
Lowell, Massachusetts, 1835–1955.* Baltimore: Johns Hopkins University Press.

Gurr, Ted Robert. 1970. *Why Men Rebel.* Princeton, N.J.: Princeton University
Press.

Hachey, Thomas E., Joseph M. Hernon Jr., and Lawrence J. McCaffrey. 1989.
The Irish Experience. Englewood Cliffs, N.J.: Prentice-Hall.

Hamill, Pete. 2003. *Forever.* Boston: Little, Brown.

Hance, Dawn D. 1991. *The History of Rutland, Vermont, 1761–1861.* Rutland, Vt.:
Rutland Historical Society, Academy Books.

Hancock, Paul R. 2001. The Labor Movement in the Vermont–New York Slate
Industry. In *North American Journal of Welsh Studies* 1, no. 2. Online at http://
spruce.flint.umich.edu/~ellisjs/Hancock.PDF.

Handlin, Oscar. 1941. *Boston's Immigrants, 1790–1880.* Cambridge: Harvard
University Press.

Hannon, Patrick T. 1986. *Historical Sketches on West Rutland, Vermont.* Rutland,
Vt.: Academy Books.

Harris, Ruth-Ann M. 1994. *The Nearest Place That Wasn't Ireland: Early Nineteenth-Century Irish Labor Migration.* Ames: Iowa State University Press.

———. 1996. Review of *The End of Hidden Ireland* by Robert James Scally. *Irish
Studies Review.* Bath, Eng.: Bath Spa University. Computer text file supplied
by Harris.

Harris, Ruth-Ann M., Emer O'Keeffe, and Donald M. Jacobs, eds. 1989– .
8 vols. *The Search for Missing Friends.* Boston: New England Historic Genealogical Society.

Hawthorne, Nathaniel. 1835. The Inland Port. Published anonymously in
New-England Magazine, No. 9 (December). Online at www.history.rochester
.edu/canal.bib/hawthorne/inland.htm.

Heslin, Brid. 2004. Cloone, County Leitrim: A Monastery Village, 1798–1801. In *Irish Villages: Studies in Local History*, ed. Karina Holton, Liam Clare, and Brian O Dalaigh. Dublin: Four Courts Press.

History of Clayton County, Iowa. Chicago: Inter-State Publishing, 1882.

Hood, Susan E. 1994. The Landlord Planned Nexus at Strokestown, County Roscommon: A Case Study of an Irish Estate Town, 1660–c1925. Dissertation, University of Ulster.

Huggins, Michael. 2000. A Secret Ireland: Agrarian Conflict in Pre-Famine Roscommon. Winner of the Four Courts Press J. C. Beckett Prize in Modern History, 2000; In *Social Conflict in Pre-Famine Roscommon* (2007. Dublin: Four Courts Press). I am grateful to the author for sharing his essay before publication.

Huston, Reeve. 2000. *Land and Freedom: Rural Society, Popular Protest, and Party Politics in Antebellum New York*. Oxford: Oxford University Press.

Ignatiev, Noel. 1995. *How the Irish Became White*. New York: Routledge.

Inglis, Brian. 1956. *The Story of Ireland*. London: Faber.

Irby Jr., Richard E. New York City Draft Riots. Online at www.geocities.com/ irby.geo/nycdr.html.

Isle of Man Family History Society Journal. 1986. Extracts from History of Rutland County, Vermont, by H. P. Smith and W. S. Raun (published 1886). Vol. 8, no. 3. Online at www.isle-of-man.com/manxnotebook/famhist/ 08n3.htm.

Jacobson, Matthew Frye. 2002. *Special Sorrows: The Diasporic Imagination of Irish, Polish, and Jewish Immigrants in the United States*. Berkeley: University of California Press.

Jones, Walter A. 2003. Kilmore and the O'Beirnes. *The O'Beirne Family Journal*, no. 8. Online at www.obeirnefamily.mcmail.com.

Katznelson, Ira. 1986. Working-Class Formation: Constructing Cases and Comparisons. In *Working-Class Formation: Nineteenth-Century Patterns in Western Europe and the United States*, ed. Ira Katznelson and Aristide R. Zolberg. Princeton, N.J.: Princeton University Press.

Kee, Robert. 1972. *The Most Distressful Country*. New York: Penguin Books.

Kenny, Kevin. 1998. *Making Sense of the Molly Maguires*. New York: Oxford University Press.

———. 2000. *The American Irish: A History*. Harlow, UK: Pearson Education.

Kerr, Donal. 1994. *"A Nation of Beggars"? Priests, People, and Politics in Famine Ireland, 1846–1852*. Oxford: Clarendon Press.

Killen, John. 1995. *The Famine Decade: Contemporary Accounts, 1841–1851*. Belfast: Blackstaff Press.

Kinealy, Christine. 1997. *A Death-Dealing Famine*. London: Pluto Press.

Knight, Kevin. 1910. *Catholic Encyclopedia*, vol. 8. Online ed., 1999, at http:// www.newadvent.org/cathen/08132b.htm.

Kundera, Milan. 1980. *The Book of Laughter and Forgetting*. New York: Knopf.

Lalor, Brian, ed. 2003. *The Encyclopedia of Ireland.* New Haven: Yale University Press.

Lavin, Patrick. 2003. *Celtic Ireland West of the River Shannon: A Look Back at the Rich Heritage and Dynastic Structure of the Gaelic Clans.* Lincoln, Neb.: IUniverse.

Laxton, Edward. 1996. *The Famine Ships.* New York: Henry Holt.

Le Caron, Henri. 1974. *25 Years in the Secret Service,* 10th ed. Yorkshire, Eng.: EP Publishing.

Lewis, Samuel. 1837. *A Topographical Dictionary of Ireland . . .* 2 vols. London: S. Lewis. Online at www.booksulster.com/library/topog/index.php.

Libby, Gary W. 2004. Maine and the Fenian Invasion of Canada, 1866. In *They Change Their Sky,* ed. Michael C. Connolly. Orono: University of Maine Press.

Lombard, Pat, and Thomas Mullaney. 1999. *The Roscommon and Leitrim Gazette, 1822–1887: A Chronicle of the 19th Century.* Boyle, Ire.: Roscommon and Leitrim Gazette.

Lord, Robert H., John E. Sexton, and Edward T. Harrington. 1945. *History of the Archdiocese of Boston in the Various Stages of Its Development, 1604 to 1943.* 3 vols. Boston: Pilot.

Mackay, Charles. 1849. In Forty Years Recollections of Life, Literature, and Public Affairs. In *Through Liverpool to North America 1830–1907: A Selection of Emigrant Narratives,* ed. J. Gordon Read. Liverpool: Merseyside Maritime Museum, n.d.

Mackay, Donald. 2002. *Flight from Famine: The Coming of the Irish to Canada.* Plattsburgh, N.Y.: McClelland and Stewart.

McDonnell-Garvey, Maire. 1995. *Mid-Connacht: The Ancient Territory of Sliabh Lugha.* Manorhamilton, Ire.: Drumlin.

Miller, Kerby A. 1999. Revenge for Skibbereen. In *The Great Famine and the Irish Diaspora in America,* ed. Arthur Gribben. Amherst: University of Massachusetts Press.

Miller, Kerby, and Paul Wagner. 1994. *Out of Ireland: The Story of Irish Emigration to America.* Washington, D.C.: Elliott and Clark.

Mitchell, Brian C. 1988. *The Paddy Camps: The Irish of Lowell, 1821–61.* Urbana: University of Illinois Press.

Mokyr, Joel. 1983. *Why Ireland Starved: A Quantitative and Analytical History of the Irish Economy, 1800–1850.* London: George Allen and Unwin.

Montgomery, David. 1993. *Citizen Worker: The Experience of Workers in the United States with Democracy and the Free Market during the Nineteenth Century.* Cambridge: Cambridge University Press.

Moran, Gerard. 2004. *Sending Out Ireland's Poor: Assisted Emigration to North America in the Nineteenth Century.* Dublin: Four Courts Press.

Murphy, Ronald Chase, and Janice Church Murphy. 2000. *Irish Famine Immigrants in the State of Vermont: Gravestone Inscriptions.* Baltimore: Genealogical Publishing.

Neeson, J. M. 1993. *Commoners: Common Right, Enclosure, and Social Change in England, 1700–1820.* Cambridge: Cambridge University Press.

Newsinger, John. 1994. *Fenianism in Mid-Victorian Britain.* London: Pluto Press.

Norton, Desmond. 2002. Stewart and Kincaid, Irish Land Agents in the 1840s. Online at Centre for Economic Research, University College Dublin, www.ucd.ie/economic/workingpapers/WP02.08.pdf.

Nowland, John H. B. 1877. Sketches of Prominent Citizens of 1876. Indianapolis: Tilford-Carlon. Thanks to Julie Offitt for a copy of this short biography of her ancestor John Carlon.

O'Connor, John. 1995. *The Workhouses of Ireland: The Fate of Ireland's Poor.* Dublin: Anvil Books.

O'Connor, Thomas H. 1995. *The Boston Irish: A Political History.* Boston: Little, Brown.

O'Dowd, Anne. 1991. *Spalpeens and Tattie Hokers: History and Folklore of the Irish Migratory Agricultural Worker in Ireland and Britain.* Dublin: Irish Academic Press.

O'Ferrall, Fergus. 1981. *Daniel O'Connell.* Dublin: Gill and Macmillan.

O'Flanagan, Michael, ed. 1931. *Letters Containing Information Relative to the Antiquities of the County of Roscommon Collected during the Progress of the Ordnance Survey in 1837,* vol. 1. Bray, Ire.

O'Grada, Cormac. 2002a. Savings Banks as an Institutional Import: The Case of Nineteenth-Century Ireland. Online at Centre for Economic Research, University College Dublin, www.ucd.ie/economics/research/papers/2002/WP02.03.pdf.

———. 2002b. Who Panics during Panics? Evidence from a Nineteenth Century Bank. Online at Centre for Economic Research, University College Dublin, http://www.ucd.ie/economics/research/papers/2002/WP02.12.pdf (March).

———. 2005. The New York Irish in the 1850s: Locked in by Poverty? Online at Centre for Economic Research, University College Dublin, www.ucd.ie/economics/research/papers/2005/WP05.17.pdf (November).

O'Neill, Kevin. 2001. The Star-Spangled Shamrock. In *History and Memory in Modern Ireland,* ed. Ian McBride. Cambridge: Cambridge University Press.

Orser, Charles E., Jr. N.d. How Many Perished? Online at http://www.webcom.com/famine/orser.htm (but no longer seems to be posted).

Ó Tuathaigh, Gearóid. 1972. *Ireland before the Famine, 1798–1848.* Dublin: Gill and Macmillan.

Peck, Deborah. 2002. Silent Hunger: The Psychological Impact of The Great Hunger. In *Ireland's Great Hunger: Silence, Memory and Commemoration,* ed. David A. Valone and Christine Kinealy. Lanham, Md.: University Press of America.

Porteir, Cathal. 1995. *Famine Echoes.* Dublin: Gill and Macmillan.

Potter, David M. 1976. *The Impending Crisis, 1848–1861.* Completed and edited by Don E. Fehrenbacher. New York: Harper and Row.

Potter, George. 1960. *To the Golden Door: The Story of the Irish in Ireland and America*. Boston: Little, Brown.

Powers, William. 2002. Biography of Patrick Colligan. Online at http://www .vermontcivilwar.org/1cav/callaghan.shtml.

Quinn, Peter. *Looking for Jimmy: A Search for Irish America*. Quoted in How the Irish Claimed their Place in the New World, review by Jonathan Yardley. *Washington Post*, February 25, 2007.

Ranelagh, John O'Beirne. 1983. *A Short History of Ireland*. Cambridge: Cambridge University Press.

Rees, Jim. 2000. *Surplus People: The Fitzwilliam Clearances, 1847–1856*. Wilton, Cork, Ire.: Collins Press.

Resch, Tyler. 1989. *Dorset: In the Shadow of the Marble Mountain*. West Kennebunk, Maine: Dorset Historical Society by Phoenix Publishing.

Revised Roster of Vermont Volunteers and Lists of Vermonters Who Served in the Army and Navy of the United States during the War of the Rebellion, 1861–66. 1892. Compiled by authority of the Vermont General Assembly under the direction of Theodore A. Peck, Adj. Gen. Montpelier, Vt.: Watchman Publication.

Robinson, Rowland E. 1890. *Century Magazine*. Online at pbperazzzo@attbi.com.

Rude, George. 1995. *The Ideology of Popular Protest*. Chapel Hill: University of North Carolina Press.

Salvatore, Nick. 2004. Biography and Social History: An Intimate Relationship. *Labour History*, no. 87 (November). Online at www.history cooperative. org/journals/lab/87/Salvatore.html.

Scally, Robert James. 1995. *The End of Hidden Ireland: Rebellion, Famine, and Emigration*. New York: Oxford University Press.

Sessions, Gene. 1992. Vermont's Nineteenth Century Railroad Workers. In *We Vermonters: Perspectives on the Past*, ed. Michael Sherman and Jennie Versteeg. Vermont Historical Society.

Sharkey, P. A. 1927. *The Heart of Ireland*. Boyle, Ire.: M. J. Ward, Princess Hotel, Publisher.

Short, Hugh. 1984. A Heritage Recalled: The Middle Years—The Irish in Rutland in 1880. *Rutland Historical Society Quarterly* 14, no. 1.

Somerville, Alexander. 1994. *Letters from Ireland during the Famine*. Ed. K. D. M. Snell. Dublin: Irish Academic Press.

Spiers, E. N. 1996. Army Organisation and Society in the Nineteenth Century. In *A Military History of Ireland*, ed. Thomas Bartlett and Keith Jeffery. Cambridge: Cambridge University Press.

Steckel, Richard H. 1999. Review of *Yankeys Now: Immigrants in the Antebellum U.S., 1840–1860* by Joseph P. Ferrie. Economic History Services Book Reviews. Online at www.eh.net/bookreviews/library/0177.shtml.

Stern, Gerald J. 1976. *The Buffalo Creek Disaster*. New York: Random House.

Stern, William J. 1997. How Dagger John Saved New York's Irish. *City Journal* 7, no. 2. Online at www.city-journal.org/html/7_2_a2.html.

Takaki, Ronald. 1990. *Iron Cages: Race and Culture in 19th-Century America*. New York: Oxford University Press.

Tanner, Marcus. 2001. *Ireland's Holy Wars*. New Haven: Yale University Press.

Thernstrom, Stephan. 1964. *Poverty and Progress: Social Mobility in a Nineteenth Century City*. Cambridge: Harvard University Press.

Thompson, E. P. 1966. *The Making of the English Working Class*. New York: Vintage Books.

Tilly, Charles. 1995. *Popular Contention in Great Britain, 1758–1834*. Cambridge: Harvard University Press. Thanks to Chris Tilly for lending this book to me.

Trecker, Janice. 2000. *Discovering Hampton: A Connecticut Town*. Willimantic, Conn.: Hampton Antiquarian & Historical Society, Hall and Bill Printing.

Trench, Charles Chenevix. 1984. *The Great Dan: A Biography of Daniel O'Connell*. London: Jonathan Cape.

Vesey, Patrick. 2002. The Murder of Major Mahon. M.A. thesis, National University of Ireland, Maynooth.

Wakefield. 1999. Wakefield's View. *Moylfinne Journal* 6, no. 4 (quoting Arthur Young, *Travels in France*, 1:484).

Washington, Ida H. 1992. Dorothy Canfield Fisher's Vermont Tradition. In *We Vermonters: Perspectives on the Past*, ed. Michael Sherman and Jennie Versteeg. Vermont Historical Society.

Way, Peter. 1993. *Common Labor*. Baltimore: Johns Hopkins University Press Paperbacks.

Whelan, Kevin. 1996. *The Tree of Liberty: Radicalism, Catholicism, and the Construction of Irish Identity, 1760–1830*. Notre Dame, Ind.: University of Notre Dame Press.

Williamson, Samuel H. "What Is the Relative Value?" Economic History Services, January 2006. Online at http://www.eh.net/hmit/compare/.

Websites

Albany History: www.Albany.edu/history/riverspark.html.

Answers: www.answers.com/topic/crown-estate; and www.answers.com/topic/British-monarchy.

Ballykilcline: www.ballykilcline.com.

Bolton, England: www.bolton.org.uk/industry.html.

Center for Lowell History, University of Massachusetts, Lowell: http://library.uml.edu/clh/ApA.html.

Fox Family: http://www.sevierlibrary.org/genealogy/Rayshouse/fox/tdfox.htm.

Gilder Lehrman Center for the Study of Slavery, Resistance, and Abolition: www.yale.edu/glc/archive/896.htm.

Irish Ancestors RootsWeb: http://freepages.genealogy.rootsweb.com/~irishancestors/Add18.html.

Irish Excavations Reports database: www.excavations.ie. See 1999 Ballykilcline report by Charles Orser at www.excavations.ie/Pages/Details.php?Year=

1999&County=Roscommon&id=761. (Other Roscommon reports cover 1996–2000.)

Leitrim-Roscommon: www.leitrim-roscommon.com.

Marble History: pbperazzzo@attbi.com.

Maynooth College: http://mamaynooth.freeservers.com/scally.htm.

Michael McTiernan: Defenderism in Co. Leitrim in the 1790s (second half) by Rev. Liam Kelly, http://mctiernan.com/defend2.htm.

Newport Historical Society: www.geocities.com/Heartland/Park/7461/head stones.htm.

Railroad History: www.lsc.vsc.edu/faculty/yalea/Railroads.htm.

This Week in the Civil War at http://civilweek.com/1863/jun1463.htm.

28th Wisconsin: www.28thwisconsin.com/veterans/p_hanley.html.

UK Moving Here for Irish Reproductive Loan Fund (IRLF): www.movinghere .org.uk/galleries/roots/irish/irishrecordsuk/reproductiveloans.htm.

University College Dublin: www.ucd.ie/~library/e-lib/web/papers.html.

Vermont Business Magazine: www.vtbusinessmagazine.com/millennium.htm.

Vermont Civil War: http://www.vermontcivilwar.org.

Vermont History: http://www.majbill.vt.edu/history/barrow/oldclasses/Hist 3144S99/readings/mckibben1.html.

Wikipedia online at http://en.wikipedia.org.

Personal Communications with Author

Alberts, Margaret, Mullera descendant, 2004, 2005.

Bell, Anne Marie. Hanley-Brennan descendant. Spring 1999, August 2001.

Bunzel, David. Patrick Hanley descendant. January 2007.

Geelan, Moira, and Pat Geelan. June 2005.

Harris, Ruth-Ann M. Spring 2000, 2003.

Healy, Kathleen. July 2002.

Kelly, Francis. Brislin relation. October 2002.

Lamson, Roger. Kelly descendant. Spring 2002, Summer 2006.

Madden, Kathleen. Colligan-Carroll-Madden descendant. Winter, Spring 2002.

Offutt, Julie. Carolan descendant. 2002, 2003.

Padian, P. Padian relation. September 2006.

Parish priest, Carra church, County Kildare, Ireland. 1993.

Sisk, Madeline. 2002–2006.

Thompson, Cassie Kilroy. 2002–2006.

Vandenburg, Rosemary. Winters descendant. Spring and November 2002, 2005, 2006.

Vinehout, William. McGuire and Neary descendant. November 2005.

Ward, Andrew, 2002.

Zada, Susie. Murray descendant. October 2006.

Index

women: in domestic service, 81, 162; literacy among, 85–86; as migrant workers, 63; remittances to Ireland from, 88; as savings bank depositors, 66–67
Wynne, Bridget, 62, 63, 74, 117, 185n.20
Wynne, Bridget Winters, 117–18
Wynne, J., 182n.6

Wynne (Winn), Patrick, 73, 184n.6
Wynne, Terrence, 117–18

Young Ireland: on O'Connell, 49; priests oppose revolt of, 2; priests prohibited from involvement in, 31; rent strike called by, 16; *Rutland Courier* covers, 96, 162